Canadian Broadcasting:
Market Structure and Economic Performance

Stuart McFadyen
Colin Hoskins
David Gillen

The Institute for Research on Public Policy
L'Institut de Recherches Politiques
Montreal
1980

BRESCIA COLLEGE
LIBRARY

45894

© The Institute for Research on Public Policy 1980
All rights reserved

ISBN 0 92038 68 9

Legal Deposit Third Quarter
Bibliothèque nationale du Québec

The Institute for Research on Public Policy/L'Institut de Recherches Politiques
2149 Mackay Street
Montreal, Quebec
H3G 2J2

typesetting by Judy Bradley assisted by Susan Fraser
printing by Tri-Graphic Printing (Ottawa) Ltd.

BRESCIA COLLEGE
LIBRARY

Founded in 1972, THE INSTITUTE FOR RESEARCH ON PUBLIC POLICY is a national organization whose independence and autonomy are ensured by the revenues of an endowment fund, which is supported by the federal and provincial governments and by the private sector. In addition, The Institute receives grants and contracts from governments, corporations, and foundations to carry out specific research projects.

The *raison d'être* of The Institute is threefold:

— To act as a catalyst within the national community by helping to facilitate informed public debate on issues of major public interest

— To stimulate participation by all segments of the national community in the process that leads to public policy making

— To find practical solutions to important public policy problems, thus aiding in the development of sound public policies

The Institute is governed by a Board of Directors, which is the decision-making body, and a Council of Trustees, which advises the board on matters related to the research direction of The Institute. Day to day administration of The Institute's policies, programmes, and staff is the responsibility of the president.

The Institute operates in a decentralized way, employing researchers located across Canada. This ensures that research undertaken will include contributions from all regions of the country.

Wherever possible, The Institute will try to promote public understanding of, and discussion on, issues of national importance, whether they be controversial or not. It will publish its research findings with clarity and impartiality. Conclusions or recommendations in The Institute's publications are solely those of the author, and should not be attributed to the Board of Directors, Council of Trustees, or contributors to The Institute.

The president bears final responsibility for the decision to publish a manuscript under The Institute's imprint. In reaching this decision, he is advised on the accuracy and objectivity of a manuscript by both Institute staff and outside reviewers. Publication of a manuscript signifies that it is deemed to be a competent treatment of a subject worthy of public consideration.

Publications of The Institute are published in the language of the author, along with an executive summary in both of Canada's official languages.

THE MEMBERS OF THE INSTITUTE

Board of Directors

The Honourable John B. Aird, Q.C.
(Chairman)
  Aird & Berlis, Toronto
James Black
  President, The Molson Companies
  Limited, Toronto
Claude Castonguay
  President, The Laurentian Fund Inc.,
  Quebec
Guy Chabot
  Raymond, Chabot, Martin & Paré,
  Montreal
James S. Cowan
  Stewart, MacKeen & Covert, Halifax
Louis Desrochers, Q.C.
  McCuaig Desrochers, Edmonton
Dr. H.E. Duckworth
  President, University of Winnipeg
Dr. James Fleck
  Faculty of Management Studies, University
  of Toronto
Dr. Reva Gerstein
  Consultant, Toronto
The Honourable William Hamilton, P.C.
  President & Chief Executive Officer,
  Employers' Council of British
  Columbia, Vancouver
Tom Kent
  Dean of Administrative Studies,
  Dalhousie University, Halifax
The Honourable Donald Macdonald, P.C.
  McCarthy & McCarthy, Toronto
Gerald A.B. McGavin
  President, Yorkshire Trust, Vancouver
E.M. Mills
  Associate Director, Banff Centre, Banff
Pierre O'Neil
  Director, Television News, Radio-Canada,
  Montreal
James F. O'Sullivan
  Vice-President, Finance & Administration,
  University of New Brunswick,
  Fredericton
Gordon Robertson
  President, The Institute for
  Research on Public Policy
The Honourable Robert Stanfield, P.C., Q.C.
  Former Leader, Progressive Conservative
  Party of Canada
Eldon D. Thompson
  President, Telesat Canada, Ottawa
Bryan Vaughan
  Honorary Chairman, Vickers & Benson,
  Toronto

Secretary
Peter C. Dobell
  Parliamentary Centre, Ottawa

Treasurer
Dr. Louis G. Vagianos
  Executive Director, The Institute for
  Research on Public Policy

Executive Committee
The Honourable John B. Aird (Chairman)
Eldon D. Thompson (Vidce-Chairman)
E.M. Mills
Pierre O'Neil
Gordon Robertson

Investment Committee
The Honourable Donald Macdonald
  (Chairman)
Tom Kierans (Vice-Chairman)
Peter C. Dobell
Paul Little

Council of Trustees

Government Representatives
Fred Dickson, Nova Scotia
Harry Hobbs, Alberta
Darwin Kealey, Ontario
Don Leitch, Manitoba
Douglas T. Monroe, Yukon
Robert Normand, Quebec
John H. Parker, Northwest Territories
Gordon Smith, Canada
Barry Toole, New Brunswick
David Vardy, Newfoundland
Murray Wallace, Saskatchewan
Andrew Wells, Prince Edward Island

Members at Large
Dr. Stefan Dupré (Chairman)
  Department of Political Economy,
  University of Toronto
Doris Anderson
  Chairman, Advisory Council on the Status
  of Women, Toronto
Dr. Frances Bairstow
  Director, Industrial Relations Centre,
  McGill University, Montreal
Dr. Roger Blais, P.Eng.
  Dean of Research, Ecole Polytechnique,
  Montreal
Robert W. Bonner, Q.C.
  Bonner & Fouks, Vancouver
Professor John L. Brown
  Faculty of Business Administration &
  Commerce, University of Alberta,
  Edmonton

Dr. Mark Eliesen
  Director, Federal NDP Caucus Research
  Bureau, Ottawa
W.A. Friley
  President, Skyland Oil, Calgary
Judge Nathan Green
  The Law Courts, Halifax
Donald S. Harvie
  Chairman, Devonian Foundation, Calgary
Dr. Leon Katz
  Department of Physics, University of
  Saskatchewan, Saskatoon
Tom Kierans
  Vice-Chairman, McLeod, Young, Weir,
  Toronto
Dr. Leo Kristjanson
  Vice-President, Planning
  University of Saskatchewan, Saskatoon
Andrée Lajoie
  Director, Centre for Research on Public
  Law, University of Montreal
Allen T. Lambert
  Chairman, Toronto-Dominion Bank,
  Toronto
Terry Mactaggart
  Executive Director, Niagara Institute,
  Niagara-on-the-Lake
Professor William A.W. Neilson
  Faculty of Law, University of Victoria
Marilyn L. Pilkington
  Tory, Tory, DesLauriers, Binnington,
  Toronto
Adélard Savoie, Q.C.
  Yeoman, Savoie, LeBlanc & DeWitt,
  Moncton
Philip Vineberg, Q.C.
  Phillips, Vineberg, Goodman, Phillips &
  Rothman, Montreal
Dr. Norman Wagner
  President, University of Calgary
Ida Wasacase
  Director, Saskatchewan Indian Federated
  College, University of Regina
Professor Paul Weiler
  Mackenzie King Professor,
  Harvard University
Dr. John Tuzo Wilson
  Director General, Ontario Science Centre,
  Toronto
Rev. Lois Wilson
  Rector, Chalmers United Church, Kingston
Ray Wolfe
  President, The Oshawa Group, Toronto

Ex Officio Members
Dr. Owen Carrigan
  Representing the Canada Council
Denis Cole
  President, Institute of Public
  Administration of Canada
A.J. Earp
  President, Association of Universities &
  Colleges of Canada
Dr. Claude Fortier
  President, Science Council of Canada
Larkin Kerwin
  President, Royal Society of Canada
Dr. William G. Schneider
  President, National Research Council
Dr. René Simard
  President, Medical Research Council
Dr. David Slater
  Acting Chairman, Economic Council of
  Canada
Professor André Vachet
  Representing the Social Science Federation
  of Canada

Foreword

The objectives set by Parliament for the Canadian system of broadcasting and its regulators are daunting. The system should be owned and controlled by Canadians "so as to safeguard, enrich and strengthen the cultural, political, social and economic fabric of Canada." At the same time, it must be recognized that for private owners broadcasting is a business. In the words of the authors, "the economic product ... is the audiences [private broadcasters] supplies to advertisers. The product is not ... the programs offered." The economic characteristics of the industry, therefore, inevitably come into conflict with the broader social and political objectives of broadcasting regulation.

This study examines the structure of radio, television and cable television markets and its impact on such measures of economic performance as the pricing of advertising and profitability. Of particular interest is the assessment of the impact of multiple and cross-media ownership on the economic performance of broadcasting enterprises. The authors also explore the relationship between programming format and financial performance. This is a matter of considerable concern because of the high cost of producing quality Canadian programs and the low cost of importing programs from the United States.

At a time when both regulatory institutions and constitutional powers are under review, this volume provides some empirical evidence with which to make better decisions concerning Canadian broadcasting.

R. Gordon Robertson
President
August 1980

Avant-propos

Le Parlement a fixé des objectifs rigoureux à la radiodiffusion canadienne et à l'organisme qui la réglemente. En effet,
les sociétés de ce secteur doivent être de propriété canadienne,
c'est-à-dire que des Canadiens doivent en avoir la maîtrise, de
manière "à sauvegarder, enrichir et raffermir la structure culturelle, politique, sociale et économique" du pays. D'un autre
côté, force est bien de reconnaître que, pour les propriétaires du
secteur privé, la radiodiffusion est une entreprise commerciale.
Dans les mots de l'auteur, "le produit économique des entreprises
de radio et de télévision, ce sont les publics-cibles qu'elles
assurent aux annonceurs: (...) ce n'est pas le programme mis en
ondes." Il s'ensuit qu'il y a nécessairement conflit entre l'orientation économique de l'industrie et, d'autre part, les objectifs
socio-politiques plus larges de la réglementation.

L'étude qu'on va lire examine la structure des marchés de la
radio, de la télévision traditionnelle et de la télévision par
câble et la façon dont cette structure détermine certaines mesures
de performance économique telles que les tarifs publicitaires et
la rentabilité des entreprises. L'évaluation des effets de la
multipropriété (propriété de plusieurs media de même nature ou de
nature différente) sur la performance économique des entreprises
de radiodiffusion est d'un intérêt tout particulier. Les auteurs
analysent aussi la corrélation entre le rendement de ces entreprises et la nature de leur programmation. C'est là une question
d'importance capitale étant donné le coût de production élevé des
programmes canadiens de qualité et le coût modique des programmes
importés des États-Unis.

A l'heure où l'on réexamine le rôle des organismes de réglementation et la question des pouvoirs constitutionnels, les données empiriques que présente cet ouvrage sont de nature à éclairer
la prise des décisions dans le domaine de la radiodiffusion canadienne.

Le président,
Gordon Robertson
Août 1980

Table of Contents

iii

Acknowledgements

We wish to note the excellent support and "feedback" provided by Gilles Desjardin of the Social Policy and Program Branch of the Department of Communications.

The co-operation extended by Mr. Everett King, and the staff in Statistical Information Services, Department of Communications, has contributed materially to the success of the project. We are particularly grateful for the statistical and econometric help provided by Mrs. Gina Smith.

The Canadian Radio-Television and Telecommunications Commission provided invaluable unpublished program data.

We would like to thank our research assistants, Barry Myrvold, Bernard Lee, Neil Lemke, Mitchell Tarr, Ann Church, and Dick Haney for their valuable contribution.

Dean Gordon Tyndall and Department Chairmen, Glenn Mumey and Ron Savitt, of the Faculty of Business Administration and Commerce, University of Alberta, provided personal support as well as supplementary resources in the form of typing, copying and funds for research assistants.

Jeanette Shah, Ann Stark, Marlys Rudiak, Lillan Buckler, Beth Kenyon, and Sandy Dorian provided invaluable typing help.

Of the many people who donated their time to us, we particularly wish to thank Sundar Magun, now with the Economic Council, and Bill Ross of the CBC, for their excellent advice and their patience.

Views expressed are those of the authors alone and they remain responsible for all errors of omission and commission.

The Authors

Stuart McFadyen is Professor and Chairman of the Department of
Marketing and Economic Analysis in the Faculty of Business Admin-
istration at the University of Alberta. He obtained his Ph.D. in
Economics at the University of California, Berkeley and is also a
Chartered Accountant. Prof. McFadyen has published articles on
housing, and local government finance.

Colin Hoskins is Professor of Finance in the Faculty of Business
Administration at the University of Alberta. He obtained his
Ph.D. in Economics from the University of Manchester. Prof. Hoskins has published several articles on the investment decision
making process in firms.

David Gillen is Associate Professor in the Department of Economics
at the University of Alberta. He obtained his Ph.D. in Economics
at the University of Toronto. Prof. Gillen has published articles
on transportation economics and regulation. Currently, with Prof.
Tae Oum, he is completing a study of the efficiency of Canadian
airlines for The Institute for Research on Public Policy.

Executive Summary

The Canadian broadcasting system should be effectively owned and controlled by Canadians so as to safeguard, enrich and strengthen the cultural, political, social and economic fabric of Canada.

The programming provided by the Canadian broadcasting system should be varied and comprehensive and should provide reasonable, balanced opportunity for the expression of differing views on matters of pubic concern, and the programming provided by each broadcaster should be of high standard, using predominantly Canadian creative and other resources. (Section 3(b) and (d) of the Broadcasting Act.)

There is ample evidence, such as that provided by the CRTC in its Special Report on Broadcasting 1968-1978, that private broadcasters are not fulfilling the role intended by the Act. The CRTC reveals that CTV, the network comprising the major component of the private television system and whose programming was available to 92 percent of the population by 1977, although meeting the letter of its Canadian content quota requirements, nevertheless showed less than 6 percent Canadian content during the peak viewing period (8 p.m. to 10.30 p.m.) in 1978-79. The vast majority of its peak period offerings were American. Such a performance can scarcely be said to "safeguard, enrich and strengthen the cultural, political, social and economic fabric of Canada." The American influence is accentuated by the widespread availabililty, either over-the-air or by cable, of the signals of U.S. stations. If we examine what Canadians actually choose to watch, we find that the audience share in English-speaking Canada of U.S. stations was 29 percent in 1977, that less than 20 percent of the total viewing time for CTV network programming was allocated to Canadian programs in 1976, and that the corresponding figure for all English language stations was less than 30 percent. When we consider that the Bureau of Broadcast Measurement has estimated that the average Canadian spends approximately 24 hours a week watching television, by far the most time consuming leisure activity, the significance of these figures is obvious.

The question arises why the private sector of the Canadian broadcasting system is failing to perform in the manner envisaged by the Broadcasting Act. The debate on this and related questions has largely taken place without a thorough examination and understanding of the economics of the television, radio, and cable industries. This study attempts to fill this void. Using the structure-conduct-performance approach of industrial organization, we examine and attempt to answer the following questions using data for 1975:

(a) What are the ownership patterns (both at the local market and national levels) in the television, radio, and cable-television industries?

(b) What are the effects of ownership and cross-ownership on the conduct of firms in areas such as pricing and programming?

(c) What effects do the ownership patterns have on various performance measures such as profitability, audience size, and program choice and diversity?

The answers to these questions can be expected to have important implications for public policy.

Economics of Broadcasting

In economics it is usual to assume that the objective of the firm is profit maximization. As there is no reason to believe that this assumption is less valid for private companies in the television radio, and cable industries, than it is for firms in other industries, we adopt the profit maximization assumption in this study.

Profits depend on the revenues and costs associated with producing the product of the firm. Cable is a delivery system for television signals and the product it sells is the provision of signals unavailable over-the-air and improved reception of signals that can be obtained over-the-air. The economic product of private television and radio companies is the audiences they supply to advertisers. The product is not, as is often erroneously believed, the programs offered. The role of programs is to attract an audience for exposure to commercial messages.

Industry Structure

Other studies, particularly in the U.S., have treated the market as a national one. This is incorrect because distant stations are not in competition to supply the same audience to advertisers. The relevant market is the "signal shed," that area about urban areas in which viewers/listeners may substitute one signal for another, and we measure concentration accordingly. Cable companies are monopolists in their franchise area.

For 14 major Canadian television markets and 16 major radio markets, we measure the Herfindahl index of concentration. This index (given by the sum of the squared market revenue share of each firm) takes on a value of 1.00 for a monopoly and approaches zero for a perfectly competitive market. For television, the Herfindahl index varies from 1.00 in Kitchener and London to .27 in Toronto. Radio markets are generally more competitive with the Herfindahl varying from .52 in St. John's (except for the unusual Windsor market) to .13 in Montreal.

Supply side considerations include the nature of the product and the technology of production and distribution. The technology differs between television and radio, which utilize the airwaves, and cable-television which distributes its product through cable. At the station level there are substantial economies of scale because the cost of supplying increments in audience to advertisers is very small. Operation and managerial economies may also occur when one firm owns more than one television (or radio) station or when firms owning television stations also own radio stations or newspapers - this is referred to as cross-media ownership. A trend to group ownership has been identified in the 1978 CRTC study, The Contempory Status of Ownership and the Level of Concentration in the Canadian Broadcasting Industry. In 1968, 38 percent of television stations were group-owned, whereas by 1975 56 percent were group-owned and the Baton and Telemetropole groups accounted for 24 percent of the revenue of the industry. In 1968, 64 percent of radio stations were group-owned, whereas by 1975 81 percent were group-owned and the Standard and CHUM groups acounted for 14 percent of industry revenue. Similarly, in 1975, the largest cable groups (Premier, Cablesystems, Nationale, and Maclean-Hunter) accounted for 41 percent of industry revenue.

Where group ownership involves cross-media ownership in the same market this has demand as well as supply implications. Since television, radio, and newspapers in the same market are, to a greater or lesser degree, competitors for advertising revenue, cross-ownership will reduce competion. Markets where such a reduction in competion is likely to be significant include Regina, where the Armdale group owns CKCK-TV, CKOK-AM, and the Leader Post newspaper, and London where the W.J. Blackburn group owns CFPL-TV, CFPL-AM, CFPL-FM, and the London Free Press newspaper.

Competition for Canadian Television Viewers

Since television stations are selling audience exposures to commercial messages, audience size is obviously an important influence on the price of commercial time and on station profitability. As one would expect, stations in major population centres had a better chance of attracting large numbers of viewers.

However, adding a new station (whether over-the-air or cable-only) tends to reduce the audience of all other station in a market. Network affiliation is also an important influence on a station's audience size with CTV affiliation drawing more viewers than CBC affiliation, and CBC in turn drawing more than independents (defined to include Global and TVA).

Canadian broadcasters have long expressed concern over viewers lost to American stations. American stations available over-the-air in Canadian markets are found to be attractive to Canadian viewers, in fact, outdrawing Canadian independants. On the other hand, American stations available only on cable were able to attract relatively few viewers.

The Influence of Market Structure on Television Pricing and Profitability

Previous broadcasting research (on both television and radio) has analyzed these industries on a national basis, i.e., implicitly considering stations to compete with one another regardless of their geographic location. While this approach may be useful for certain purposes it does not provide a proper basis for economic analysis. Stations, whether they be television or radio, compete with one another only if they are available to a common group of viewers (or listeners).

While we have not totally abandoned the national basis analysis (ownership structure, for example is treated on both a national and a local market basis), shifting the focus of the analysis to the local market has permitted a much better understanding of how the basic structure of the television (and radio) industries affects pricing and profitability in these industries.

Probably the most significant single result of our work has been the indentification of the crucial influence of market concentration on pricing and profitability in broadcasting. In television an increment of .1 in the Herfindahl index for a station's market was associated with an increase of more than $25 in the price of a 30 second commercial on the station. With the Herfindahl indices for television markets varying from .27 to 1.00 and the average price of a thirty second commercial only $271.50, it is clear that the market power of stations located in concentrated local markets permits them to exact large increases in the price of commercial television time. In addition, such stations are found to have much higher levels of profit than stations in more competitive markets.

The average income level in a station's prime market (i.e., the Census Metropolitan Area) proves to be an extremely important factor in station profitability. Stations in higher income markets are much more profitable. Those which attempted to serve large numbers of viewers outside their prime market are less profitable. Service to such viewers entails considerable additional expenditure with little offsetting revenue.

From an economic point of view, television appears to be basically an entertainment medium. Increased budgets for entertainment programming adds to profits; increased budgets for news programming reduces profits. More (relatively expensive) Canadian programming decreases profits while more (relatively cheap) local programming cuts expenses and increases profits. An extra hour a day of prime time Canadian programming would roughly double the expenses of an average station.

The Influence of Ownership Structure on Television Pricing and Profitability

Cross-ownership was analyzed at both the local market and national levels but regardless of which approach is used, the story on advertising rates is the same. Membership in a group holding both television and radio stations increases rates while membership in a group holding both television stations and newspapers decreases rates. Those stations that are lucky enough to compete against others belonging to national television/radio groups are also able to raise their prices. On the other hand, there is evidence that on a cost per viewer basis CBC owned stations, and those forced to compete with them, offer lower rates.

The overall average rate of return in 1975 for all 59 corporations owning television stations in major markets is 32 percent. The largest corporations earn almost 40 percent; those owning more than one television station average 45 percent; those owning both television and radio stations 20 percent. Detailed investigation produces no evidence that broadcasting is an inherently risky industry, therefore higher profits (than say a 13 percent bench mark) cannot be explained in terms of compensation for above average risk. It would appear that Lord Thomson was on to something.

One problem encountered in attempting to unravel the factors responsible for these high profits is that profits are measured at the corporate level but influences on profit rates must be examined at the individual station level. Our approach to this problem was to adopt price-cost margin (revenues net of costs divided by revenues) as a proxy for profits at the station level. This approach leads to certain anomalous results. Whereas corporations owning more than one television station earned the highest rate of return, the individual stations of this type have price-cost margins no higher than the typical station. Similarly, although corporations owning both radio and television stations earn below average profit rates, the individual stations experience higher revenues, reduced expenses, and accordingly increased price-cost margins.

It would appear that new entrants should beware of competing against stations belonging to radio/television groups or CBC stations. Competitors of such stations experience greatly reduced price-cost margins. Much better to seek out a market with a station belonging to a television/newspaper group. Competition of this type typically enhances price-cost margins.

Competition for Canadian Radio Listeners

Although radio stations sell audience-exposures to commercial messages in the same way as television stations, the nature of audience competition is quite different. Stations (aside from CBC stations) do not belong to networks, American stations are less of a factor, and cable-television is less important. Audience competition in radio seems to hinge primarily on station location, broadcast band, and programming format. Stations not located in the Census Metropolitan Area are handicapped as are those broadcasting on the FM band. (The latter is gradually changing.)

Programming format is not as crucial as one might expect, perhaps in part because of competitive and regulatory balancing of the number of offerings of popular formats. Those formats conferring an advantage are minority language and classical music in the case of FM stations and middle of the road in the case of AM stations. On the other hand, middle of the road, progressive, and jazz handicapped FM stations while minority language and country and western handicapped AM stations.

Influence of Market Structure on Radio Pricing and Profitability

Our results indicate that commercial radio time is priced primarily on the basis of audience delivered in a station's home city. Generally, these higher prices cannot be translated into higher profits. In fact, the expenditure increases required to generate large audiences are so substantial that they more than offset the revenue increases leaving the bigger stations with lower price-cost margins.

As in the case of television, analysis at the local market level reveals that market concentration has a strong influence on radio advertising rates. When the price of a 30 second spot commercial is considered, a .10 increase in the Herfindahl index of market concentration is estimated to result in rate increases of approximately $4.00 for AM stations (average rate $41.43) and approximately $5.00 for FM stations (average rate $18.77).

Contrary to the case of television, radio appears to be basically a news medium. News programming expenditures were found to be just as important as, if not more important, than entertainment programming expenditures in increasing radio station revenues and profitability.

The Influence of Ownership Structure on Radio Pricing and Profitability

Both AM and FM radio stations owned by corporations which also own newspapers charge significantly higher prices for commerical air time. Similarly, companies with more than one radio station in a particular local market, typically an AM/FM pair, are able to impose higher advertising rates for such stations. Ownership by a company of a number of radio stations located in different markets, on the other hand, confers no ability to elevate prices. There is, as well, no evidnece that radio/television cross-ownership has any effect on AM station advertising rates.

The overall rate of return for all 216 radio corporations in 1975 is 18 percent. Corporations owning more than one radio stations average 20 percent; those owning both radio stations and television stations average 20 percent; those with radio stations and newspaper averaged 28 percent.

There is no evidence that any type of national group or cross-ownership arrangements has any effect on radio station price-cost margins. On the other hand, corporations owning both a radio station and a television station in the same market or a radio station and newspaper in the same market, experience reduced price-cost margins in the radio station involved.

Programming Performance and the Effect of Industry Structure

As we have already indicated, the role of programming is to attract an audience for exposure to commercial messages. If the costs of programs are equal, and if each viewer/listener is worth the same to the advertiser, a broadcaster will maximize advertising revenue and profits by choosing the program mix that maximizes audience size. In television, there is ample evidence that the programs that attract the most viewers are the entertainment programs of a crime drama or situation comedy variety imported from the United States. In addition, such programs can be procured from the U.S. at substantially less cost than similar programs can be produced in Canada. The economics of program purchase from the U.S. versus production in Canada thus accentuate the attraction of such programs to Canadian stations. It is obviously in the interests of the television broadcasters to offer a large proportion of these popular U.S. programs. Even if this is considered undesirable from a national social welfare viewpoint, it is unreasonable to expect private broadcasters to voluntarily act against the interests of their shareholders.

CRTC policy has been to attempt to force or entice private broadcasters to offer programming they would not otherwise undertake. An example of compulsion is the Canadian content regulations. As expected, however, we find broadcasters try and maximize profits subject to this constraint by offering Canadian programs at the less popular times and by producing the least costly types of programs. An example of enticement is provided by the reluctance of the CRTC to make licensing or cable decisions that would adversely affect the profits of private broadcasters. The CRTC view appears to be that such profits are necessary to provide the means for production of quality Canadian programming. Whether the level of expenditure on Canadian programming is actually determined by profitability, however, is open to question.

One structural element that does provide inducement for different programming is the presence of a public corporation, the CBC. CBC television relies on advertising for only about 20 percent of its revenue with its major source of finance being the annual parliamentary appropriations. Even this 20 percent, however, can be expected to exert some influence on programming. CBC radio, on the other hand, does not carry commercial messages.

Using 1974-75 data, we find that CBC-owned French stations and CBC-owned English stations provide a better overall balance of programming and more diversity than the other Canadian networks or groupings. This suggests that the CBC is fulfilling its mandate in this regard. In addition, our examination suggests reception of a CBC station or a PBS station adds more to viewer choice than the availability of a private Canadian station. It appears that private stations, dependent on advertising revenue and acting on behalf of their shareholders, cannot be expected to provide the balance, diversity, and choice deemed desirable by the Broadcasting Act.

Cable Television

Cable television exerts a significant influence on the types of television programming that Canadians watch as a result of its importation, at zero cost, of American signals. In economic terms it expands the market area of Canadian stations but fragments their audiences. This fragmentation reduces the market power and potential profits of television broadcasters.

Examination of the costs of cable television firms reveal substantial economies of density, i.e., as cable firms get more subscribers per mile of cable, their cost per subscriber falls. Neither the size of cable firms nor their profitability appear to have any influence on their local programming expenditures.

Abrégé

que le système de la radiodiffusion canadienne devrait
être possédé et contrôlé effectivement par des Canadiens
de façon à sauvegarder, enrichir et raffermir la structure culturelle, politique, sociale et économique du
Canada;

que la programmation offerte par le système de la radiodiffusion canadienne devrait être variée et compréhen-
sive et qu'elle devrait fournir la possibilité raison-
able et équilibrée d'exprimer des vues différentes sur
des sujets qui préoccupent le public et que la programmation de chaque radiodiffuseur devrait être de haute
qualité et utiliser principalement des ressources canadiennes créatrices et autres. (Article 3, paragraphes
(b) et (d), de la Loi sur la radiodiffusion.)

Les faits, tels que ceux qu'a présentés le Conseil de la
radiodiffusion et des télécommunications canadiennes dans son Rapport spécial sur la radiodiffusion au Canada 1968-1978, démontrent
clairement que les radiodiffuseurs du secteur privé ne s'acquit-
tent pas comme il se doit des responsabilités que la Loi leur as-
signe. On sait que CTV est le réseau le plus important du système
de télévision privé et que, dès 1977, ses émissions étaient accessibles à 92 % de la population. Selon le CRTC, le réseau se
conforme à la lettre des règlements relatifs au contenu canadien;
mais le contenu canadien des programmes qu'il a diffusés aux
heures "de très grande écoute" (de 20 h à 22 h 30) en 1978-1979
était inférieur à 6 % de leur contenu global, la majorité des
émissions durant cette période de pointe étant d'origine américaine. Cela n'est guère de nature "à sauvegarder, enrichir et
raffermir la structure culturelle, politique, sociale et économique du Canada".

L'influence américaine sur la programmation est renforcée par
la grande accessibilité, soit sur les ondes, soit par câble, des
signaux qui émanent des stations outre-frontière. Si l'on examine
les préférences des téléspectateurs, on constate que, dans le Canada anglais, les stations des États-Unis se sont assuré 29 % de
l'auditoire en 1977 et que moins de 20 % du temps d'écoute con-
sacré aux programmes du réseau CTV en 1976 était alloué à des
programmes canadiens. Pour l'ensemble de toutes les stations de
langue anglaise, la proportion s'établissait à 30 %. Si l'on
songe que, d'après le Bureau of Broadcast Measurement, le Canadien
passe en moyenne 24 heures par semaine devant son petit écran,
soit plus de temps qu'il n'en consacre à toute autre activité de
loisir, on comprendra d'emblée l'importance de ces chiffres.

La question se pose de savoir pourquoi le secteur privé de la
télévision canadienne se fait faute de respecter l'esprit de la
Loi sur la radiodiffusion. Dans une large mesure, on a engagé le
débat sur cette question et sur les questions connexes sans un
examen approfondi et une claire intelligence de la situation économique des industries de la télévision, de la radio et du câble.
Notre étude se propose de combler cette lacune. En nous reportant
aux données de l'année 1975 et en nous situant dans l'optique
structure-comportement-performance propre à l'organisation indus-
trielle, nous tentons de répondre aux questions suivantes:

a) Quelles sont (tant sur le plan local que sur le plan national) les structures de la propriété des industries de la télévision, de la radio et du télécâble?

b) Quels sont les effets des structures de la propriété (y
compris la propriété multiple) sur les décisions des entreprises
en matière de prix et de programmation?

c) Quels sont les effets des structures de la propriété sur
diverses mesures de performance telles que la rentabilité, les indices d'écoute, ainsi que le choix et la diversité des programmes?

Il est à prévoir que les réponses à ces questions auront
d'importantes répercussions sur les politiques publiques.

La situation économique de la radio-télévision

En économie, il est normal de présumer que l'objectif d'une
entreprise est de maximiser ses bénéfices. Nous adoptons ici
cette hypothèse de travail, car il n'y a aucune raison de croire
qu'elle soit moins valide dans le cas des sociétés privées de
radio, de télévision et de télécâble qu'elle ne l'est dans le cas
de toute autre industrie. Les bénéfices d'une entreprise sont
évidemment reliés à ses revenus eu égard à ses coûts de production. Le câble est un véhicule pour la transmission des signaux
de télévision. Le "produit" que vend l'industrie du câble, ce
sont les signaux impossibles à capter directement sur les ondes,
mais aussi l'assurance que les signaux captés de cette manière
seront de meilleure qualité. Le produit économique des entreprises de radio et de télévision, ce sont les publics-cibles
qu'elles assurent aux annonceurs: contrairement à ce qu'on croit
généralement, ce n'est pas le programme mis en ondes, la fonction
du programme étant de rassembler des téléspectateurs ou des auditeurs pour leur communiquer des messages commerciaux.

La structure de l'industrie

D'autres études, particulièrement aux États-Unis, ont traité
le marché comme une institution à l'échelle du pays. C'est une
erreur, car les stations qui desservent des régions différentes
n'entrent pas en concurrence pour offrir les mêmes publics aux
annonceurs. Le marché effectif, c'est ce qu'on pourrait appeler

l'"arsenal" des signaux, à l'orée des agglomérations urbaines, où téléspectateurs et auditeurs choisissent à leur gré tel ou tel signal plutôt que tel ou tel autre: c'est ce qui sert de base aux mesures de la concentration. En deçà de leur rayonnement-limite, les sociétés de télévision par câble jouissent d'un monopole.

Nous mesurons la concentration dans les quatorze principaux marchés de la télévision canadienne et les seize principaux marchés de la radio au moyen de l'indice Herfindahl. Cet indice (qui représente la somme, élevée au carré, des revenus respectifs des entreprises) enregistre une valeur de 1 dans le cas d'un monopole et une valeur qui tend vers zéro dans le cas d'un marché de parfaite concurrence. Pour la télévision, l'indice varie de 1 (Kitchener et London) à 0,27 (Toronto). Les marchés de la radio sont généralement plus concurrentiels: l'indice oscille entre 0,52 pour Saint-Jean de Terre-Neuve (à l'exception du marché bien particulier de Windsor) à 0,13 pour Montréal.

Sur le plan de la transmission proprement dite, il faut prendre en considération la nature du produit, ainsi que les techniques de production et de distribution. La technologie de la télévision et de la radio, qui utilise les ondes, diffère évidemment de la technologie du câble. La station de radio ou de télévision peut réaliser d'importantes économies d'échelle parce qu'elle est en mesure d'élargir à très peu de frais le public qu'elle offre à ses annonceurs. Il peut y avoir aussi des économies au chapitre de l'exploitation et de la gestion si l'entreprise est propriétaire de plusieurs stations (de radio ou de télévision) ou encore si l'entreprise, qui exploite déjà des stations de télévision, possède en outre des stations radiophoniqes ou des journaux. C'est ce qu'on entend ici par propriété multiple. L'étude du CRTC, The Contemporary Status of Ownership and the Level of Concentration in the Canadian Broadcasting Industry, constate une tendance à la propriété par des groupes. En 1968, 38 % des stations de télévision appartenaient à des groupes, mais, dès 1975, la proportion avait atteint les 56 %, et 24 % des recettes de l'industrie passaient aux mains des groupes Baron et Télémétropole. En 1968, 64 % des stations de radio étaient la propriété de groupes: en 1975, le chiffre était de 81 %, les groupes Standard et Chum s'assurant 14 % des revenus globaux de l'industrie. De même, en 1975, les groupes dominants (Premier, Cablesystems, Nationale et Maclean-Hunter) canalisaient 41 % des recettes de l'industrie du câble.

Lorsqu'un groupe exploite différents canaux de communication, l'offre aussi bien que la demande en subissent le contre-coup. La propriété multiple affaiblit la concurrence puisque la télévision, la radio et les journaux se disputent normalement, à des degrés divers, les recettes de la publicité commerciale. Les marchés où la concurrence risque d'être le plus sensiblement amoindrie sont Regina, où le groupe Armdale est propriétaire de CKCK-TV, de CKOK-M.A. et du journal Leader Post, et London, où W.J. Blackburn ex-

45894

ploite CFPL-TV, CFPL-M.A., CFPL-M.F. et le journal London Free Press.

La concurrence pour la faveur des téléspectateurs canadiens

Étant donné que les stations de télévision "vendent" des publics en mesure de recevoir des messages publicitaires, il va de soi que la taille des auditoires influe sensiblement sur le loyer du temps réservé à la publicité et, partant, sur la rentabilité des stations. Comme il est normal, les stations situées dans les grandes agglomérations urbaines sont mieux placées que d'autres pour attirer des téléspectateurs en grand nombre.

Cependant, si l'on ajoute aux stations existantes une nouvelle station de télévision (soit traditionnelle, soit par câble), l'indice d'écoute des premières tendra à baisser. L'affiliation à un réseau influe aussi notablement sur les auditoires d'une station. L'affiliation au réseau CTV est plus fructueuse à cet égard que l'affiliation au réseau de la Société Radio-Canada, mais le réseau d'État, en revanche, est plus prometteur que les réseaux "indépendants" (parmi lesquels on range Global et TVA).

Depuis longtemps déjà, les radiodiffuseurs canadiens s'inquiètent overtement que nombre de téléspectateurs les délaissent en faveur des stations américaines. Les stations américaines dont les signaux sont directement captables sur les ondes trouvent faveur, en effet, auprès des téléspectateurs canadiens, à tel point, en fait, qu'ils en attirent un plus grand nombre que les stations canadiennes non affiliées à l'un des deux grands réseaux. Quant aux canaux américains accessibles uniquement par câble, ils connaissent peu de succès de ce côté-ci de la frontière.

L'influence de la structure du marché sur les tarifs publicitaires et la rentabilité

Les études antérieures sur la radio-télévision ont analysé les industries de ce secteur sur une base nationale, c'est-à-dire en considérant les stations de radio et de télévision comme étant en concurrence les unes avec les autres, indépendamment de leur situation géographique les unes par rapport aux autres. Bien que cette conception du problème puisse avoir son utilité à certaines fins, elle ne fournit pas une base convenable pour l'analyse économique. Les stations, soit de télévision, soit de radio, n'entrent en concurrence les unes avec les autres que si elles sont accessibles à un même groupe de spectateurs ou d'auditeurs.

Bien que nous n'ayons pas complètement rejeté l'analyse à l'échelle du pays (par exemple, nous examinons la propriété des stations tant sur le plan local que sur le plan national), c'est en déplaçant l'optique vers les marchés locaux que nous avons réussi à comprendre beaucoup mieux de quelle manière la structure des industries de la télévision et de la radio influe sur l'établissement de leurs tarifs et leur rentabilité.

Sans doute le résultat le plus important de notre travail aura-t-il été la détermination de l'influence primordiale que la concentration du marché exerce sur les tarifs et la rentabilité des entreprises de radiodiffusion. Pour la télévision, une hausse de 0,1 de l'indice Herfindahl relativement au marché d'une station entraînait une augmentation de plus de $ 25 du prix d'un message publicitaire de 30 secondes. Les indices Herfindahl pour les marchés de la télévision variant de 0,27 à 1 et le prix moyen d'une publicité de 30 secondes n'étant que de $271,50, il est clair que la puissance commerciale des stations situées dans des marchés locaux de haute concentration leur permet de relever substantiellement le loyer des temps d'annonce. De plus, ces stations atteignent des niveaux de bénéfices supérieurs aux profits des stations qui desservent des marchés plus concurrentiels.

Du point de vue économique, la télévision se présente essentiellement comme moyen de divertissement. L'augmentation des budgets consacrés à la programmation récréative se traduit par une augmentation des bénéfices, alors que l'augmentation des budgets consacrés aux informations diminue les bénéfices. Plus il y aura de programmes canadiens (relativement coûteux), moindres seront les profits; plus il y aura de programmes locaux (relativement peu coûteux), moindres seront les dépenses et plus élevés les profits. Il suffirait qu'une station consacre une heure de plus par jour, durant les périodes de "très grande écoute", à la diffusion de programmes canadiens pour voir ses dépenses augmenter du double ou à peu près.

L'influence des structures de la propriété sur les tarifs publicitaires et la rentabilité de la télévision

Notre étude a analysé la propriété de media différents tant au niveau des marchés locaux qu'à l'échelle du pays. Cependant, l'établissement des tarifs publicitaires obéit aux mêmes lois dans les deux cas. L'affiliation à un groupe qui exploite à la fois des stations radiophoniques et des stations de télévision accroît le prix des temps d'annonce, tandis que l'affiliation à un groupe propriétaire de stations de télévision et de journaux tend à le diminuer. Les stations qui ont la bonne fortune d'être en concurrence avec d'autres stations affiliées à des groupes nationaux de télévision et de radio sont, elles aussi, en mesure de relever leurs tarifs publicitaires. D'autre part, sur la base du coût des messages par téléspectateur, les stations qui appartiennent à la Société Radio-Canada, de même que leurs concurrentes, louent leurs temps d'annonce à meilleur marché que les stations des deux catégories susmentionnées.

Le taux moyen de rendement des 59 sociétés qui exploitent des stations de télévision dans les principaux marchés est de 32 %, soit 40 % pour les plus importantes d'entre elles, 45 % pour celles qui ont plusieurs stations de télévision et 20 % pour les entreprises qui sont propriétaires et de stations de télévision et de stations radiophoniques. Rien ne permet de croire, après une enquête poussée, que la radiodiffusion soit une industrie à risques. Par conséquent, on ne saurait expliquer des bénéfices au-delà d'un certain niveau de référence, mettons 13 %, du fait qu'ils se mesurent à l'importance exceptionelle du risque auquel s'exposent les investisseurs. Il semble bien que Lord Thomson savait de quel côté soufflait le vent.

Une des difficultés auxquelles on se heurte lorsqu'on tente d'isoler les facteurs déterminants de ces gros profits, c'est que les bénéfices sont comptabilisés globalement au niveau de l'entreprise, tandis que les influences qui déterminent les taux de rendement doivent être évaluées au niveau de chaque stations. Pour lever la difficulté, nous avons mesuré les profits au niveau des stations en adoptant la formule de la marge bénéficiaire, calculée de la façon suivante: la somme des revenus, moins le montant des dépenses, divisée par la somme des revenus. Cette approche mène à certains résultats inattendus. Alors que les sociétés propriétaires de plus d'une station de télévision enregistraient les taux de rendement les plus élevés, la marge bénéficiaire de leurs stations, considérées isolément, n'était pas supérieure à celle de toute autre station. Corollairement, bien que les entreprises propiétaires à la fois de stations radio-phoniques et de stations de télévision aient réalisé des bénéfices en-dessous du taux de rendement moyen, leurs stations, prises isolément, ont vu leurs recettes augmenter et leurs dépenses baisser. Par conséquent, elles on joui de meilleures marges bénéficiaires.

Il semble que les nouveaux arrivants sur le marché devraient se garder d'entrer en concurrence avec les stations des groupes de radio-télévision et de la Société Radio-Canada. Les concurrents des stations qui appartiennent à ces groupes voient leur marge bénéficiaire substantiellement réduite. Mieux vaut rechercher un marché où il existe une station dont la propriété soit détenue par un groupe télévision-journal. Une telle concurrence améliorera normalement la marge bénéficiaire de la nouvelle station.

La concurrence pour la faveur des auditeurs canadiens de la radio

Bien que, à l'instar des stations de télévision, les stations de radio "vendent" des auditoires prêts à recevoir des messages publicitaires, la nature de la concurrence qu'ils se livrent pour la faveur de ces auditoires diffère du tout au tout de la concurrence qu'on observe dans le domaine de la télévision. Ici, à l'exception de Radio-Canada, les stations ne sont pas affiliées à des réseaux, les stations américaines sont moins dans le jeu et la télévision par câble perd son importance. La concurrence pour l'écoute dans l'industrie de la radio semble essentiellement reliée à la localisation géographique de la station émettrice, à sa bande de fréquence et à la nature de sa programmation. Les stations situées hors des régions métropolitaines telles que les définit le recensement sont handicapées à cet égard, de même que les stations qui diffusent en modulation de fréquence. (La situation dans ce dernier cas change peu à peu.)

L'orientation des programmes n'a pas l'importance capitale
qu'on pourrait croire, sans doute parce que, en partie du moins,
la concurrence et les règlements tendent à établir l'équilibre
entre le nombre des programmes dits "populaires" et le nombre des
émissions d'autres catégories. Dans le cas de la radio M.F., les
programmes qui assurent un avantage aux stations sont ceux
qu'elles consacrent aux émissions dans les langues des groupes
minoritaires et à la musique classique et, dans le cas des stations M.A., les programmes qui font alterner l'ancien et le nou-
veau (l'anglais range ces stations dans la catégorie middle of the
road). D'un autre côté, la musique dite middle of the road, la
musique "dans le vent" et la musique de jazz constituent un handicap pour les stations M.F., tandis que les émissions dans les langues des groupes minoritaires et les émissions de musique country
et western désavantagent les stations M.A.

L'influence de la structure du marché sur les tarifs publicitaires et la rentabilité de la radio

Nous avons constaté que le loyer des temps d'annonce est éta-
bli principalement selon la taille de l'auditoire que la station
réunit dans sa localité d'origine. En règle générale, ces taux
plus élevés ne se traduisent pas par des profits plus élevés. En
fait, les dépenses qu'entraîne le rassemblement de vastes auditoires sont à ce point substantielles qu'elles balancent ou excè-
dent l'augmentation des revenus, ce qui, dans le cas des stations
les plus importantes, se traduit par un rétrécissement de la marge
bénéficiaire.

Comme pour la télévision, l'analyse au niveau du marché local
révèle que la concentration du marché influe largement sur les
tarifs publicitaires de la radio. Dans le cas d'un message de 30
secondes, par exemple, on estime qu'une hausse de 0,1 de l'indice
Herfindahl se traduira par une augmentation des taux d'environ $ 4
pour les stations M.A. (taux moyen: $ 41,43) et d'environ $ 5
pour les stations M.F. (taux moyen: $ 18,77).

Contrairement à la télévision, la radio semble être fondamen-
talement un moyen d'information. On a constaté que les dépenses
engagées dans la programmation des actualités contribuent autant,
sinon plus, à accroître les recettes et la rentabilité des stations de radio que les budgets qu'elles destinent aux émissions
récréatives.

L'influence de la structure de la propriété sur les tarifs publicitaires et la rentabilité de la radio

Les stations M.A. et les stations M.F. appartenant à des sociétés qui exploitent aussi des journaux vendent sensiblement plus
cher leurs temps d'annonce. Il en va de même des sociétés propriétaires de plus d'une station de radio, généralement par l'ap-
pariement M.A.-M.F., dans un marché particulier. D'autre part,
le fait d'exploiter un certain nombre de stations radiophoniques

qui desservent des marchés différents ne permet pas en soi aux entreprises propriétaires de hausser leur tarif. Rien d'ailleurs ne porte à croire que la propriété combinée de stations de radio et de stations de télévision ait quelque effet que ce soit sur le tarif publicitaire d'une station M.A.

Le taux de rendement global des 216 sociétés de radiodiffusion est de 18 %. Les entreprises qui possèdent plus d'une station réalisent en moyenne un taux de 20 %; celles qui exploitent à la fois des stations de radio et des stations de télévision ont, elles aussi, un taux de rendement de 20 %; les sociétés propriétaires et de stations radiophoniques et de journaux rapportent en moyenne 28 %.

Rien ne permet de conclure que la propriété détenue par des groupes nationaux ou la propriété multiple, quelle qu'en soit la structure, ait le moindre effet sur les marge bénéficiaires. D'un autre côté, les entreprises propriétaires à la fois d'une station de radio et d'une station de télévision ou d'une station de radio et d'un journal qui desservent le même marché constatent une réduction de la marge bénéficiaire de leur station radiophonique.

La nature de la programmation et les effets de la structure de l'industrie

Comme on l'a vu plus tôt, le rôle du programme de radio ou de télévision consiste à rassembler un auditoire prêt à recevoir des messages commerciaux. Si les coûts de divers programmes sont comparables et si, d'autre part, chaque auditeur ou téléspectateur a la même valeur aux yeux de l'annonceur, le radiodiffuseur, lui, voudra maximiser ses recettes publicitaires et ses profits en choisissant une combinaison de programmes propre à maximiser ses indices d'écoute. Dans le cas de la télévision, il a été clairement démontré que les émissions distrayantes - téléromans policiers ou comédies de situation d'origine américaine - sont aussi les plus recherchées du public. Au reste, il en coûte infiniment moins cher d'acheter des programmes de ce genre aux États-Unis que d'en réaliser de semblables au Canada. Par conséquent, les advantages économiques qu'offre l'importation de programmes réalisés aux États-Unis par rapport à ce que coûterait leur production au Canada en expliquent l'attrait pour les stations canadiennes. Il est évidemment dans l'intérêt des radiodiffuseurs d'offrir à leurs publics bon nombre de ces programmes populaires d'origine américaine. Même si l'on estime cet état de choses socialement déplorable, il ne serait guère raisonnable d'attendre des radiodiffuseurs du secteur privé qu'ils agissent volontairement à l'encontre des intérêts de leurs actionnaires.

La politique du CRTC a consisté jusqu'ici à contraindre ou à inciter les radiodiffuseurs à présenter des programmes auxquels, normalement, ils ne toucheraient pas. Un exemple de coercition, ce sont les règlements relatifs au contenu canadien. Cependant, et comme on devait s'y attendre, dans ces conditions de contrainte, les entreprises tentent de maximiser leurs profits en inscrivant des programmes canadiens à l'horaire, mais aux heures de moindre écoute, et en produisant le genre de programmes qui leur coûteront le moins cher. Un exemple de la politique de "séduction" du CRTC, c'est sa répugnance à prendre des décisions en matière de licences ou de télévision par câble qui puissent avoir des répercussions défavorables sur les bénéfices de la radiodiffusion privée. A ce qu'il semble, le CRTC considère que ces bénéfices sont nécessaires parce qu'ils assurent aux entreprises les moyens de réaliser des programmes canadiens de qualité. Reste à savoir, toute fois, si le degré de rentabilité des entreprises de radiodiffusion détermine en fait l'importance des budgets qu'elles consacrent à la programmation canadienne.

Il y a pourtant un élément structurel de l'industrie qui est de nature à stimuler la production de programmes différents: c'est la présence d'une société d'État. La Société Radio-Canada ne tire de la publicité commerciale que 20 % environ de ses revenus, sa principale source de financement lui venant des budgets annuels que lui vote le Parlement. Cependant, même ces 20 % exerceront vraisemblablement une influence sur sa programmation. Quant aux stations radiophoniques de Radio-Canada, elles ne diffusent pas de publicités commerciales.

Selon les données de 1974-1975, on constate que la programmation des stations de langue française et des stations de langue anglaise qui appartiennent à la Société Radio-Canada est mieux équilibrée dans l'ensemble et plus variée que celle de tout autre réseau canadien ou de tout autre groupe. On peut donc en conclure que Radio-Canada remplit son mandat à cet égard. Il ressort aussi de notre examen que la possibilité de recevoir une station de Radio-Canada ou de PBS ajoute plus aux options du téléspectateur que l'accessibilité d'une station privée. Il semble que les stations privées, qui doivent compter sur les revenus de la publicité commerciale et servir les intérêts de leurs actionnaires, ne soient pas en mesure d'assurer aux téléspectateurs la programmation équilibrée et variée, ni l'éventail des choix que la Loi sur la radiodiffusion estime souhaitables.

La télévision par câble

La télévision par câble exerce une influence marquée sur le genre des programmes que les Canadiens regardent au petit écran, étant donné que les signaux d'origine américaine sont captés sans frais de ce côté-ci de la frontière. Dans l'optique économique, cette situation élargit le marché des stations canadiennes mais fragmente leurs auditoires. La fragmentation ou dispersion des publics-cibles diminue la puissance commerciale et la rentabilité des entreprises de télévision.

L'analyse des coûts à la charge des sociétés de télécâble révèle qu'elles réalisent d'importantes économies de densité. En effet, à mesure que s'accroît le nombre de leurs abonnés par kilomètre de câble, leurs coûts par abonné diminuent. Ni la taille des entreprises de télécâble ni leur rentabilité ne semblent avoir quelque effet que ce soit sur les budgets qu'elles affectent à leur programmation locale.

Chapter 1

Introduction and Theoretical
Background

1.1 SCOPE OF THE STUDY

This study, funded under the University Research Grants Program of the federal Department of Communications, examines the current state of ownership and cross-ownership in the television, radio, and cable-television industries in Canada. It considers the effects of ownership and cross-ownership upon industry conduct and various measures of industry performance including profitability, audience size, and program quality. More specifically, the study examines and attempts to answer the following questions:

- What are the current ownership patterns (both at the local market and national levels) in the television, radio, and cable-television industries?

- What are the effects of ownership and cross-ownership on the conduct of firms in areas such as pricing and programming?

- What effects do the ownership patterns have on various performance measures such as profitability, audience size, and program choice land diversity?

The answers to these questions can be expected to have implications for public policy. This is important because there appears to be widespread dissatisfaction and concern with respect to the current state of broadcasting in Canada. Evidence of this is provided by the strong pressure recently for the appointment of a Royal Commission to examine broadcasting. The concerns seem to be numerous and many-sided and include:

(a) Concern with the extent of concentration in broadcasting and the effects of this concentration. This concern appears to have two facets. On the one side is the normative issue of the control of information and ideas, as well as decisions on program quality and diversity, resting in a few hands. On the other is the positive issue that centers on prices and efficiency in production.

(b) Concern with the role of the Canadian Broadcasting Corporation (hereafter CBC). Does it provide different programming?
Should it be permitted to buy popular American programs?   Should
it be required to phase out television advertising? Does a public
corporation have a role in broadcasting or is it a "waste" of taxpayers' money?

(c) Concern with Canadian content regulations and their effect on profitability.

(d) Concern with the effects of cable T.V.   Typically cable
imports some additional signals, often from the U.S., that are
unavailable "over-the-air." This increases the channel choice of
viewers but also fragments the audience in the market and hence
may affect the profitability of local stations.

(e) Concern with the role of the Canadian Radio-Television
and Telecommunications Commission (hereafter CRTC). Since the
CRTC both issues new broadcasting licenses and makes decisions on
the transfer of existing licenses, it controls the extent of group
ownership and cross-ownership. Through its Canadian content regulations as well as its control of the issue, transferal, and renewal of licenses, the CRTC has an influence on the programs
offered. The CRTC also issues licenses to cable companies, deter-
mines the rates they can charge and the signals they can distri-
bute. At a time when regulation itself is being increasingly
questioned in North America[1], there is the matter of whether
regulation of broadcasting, or at least regulation as currently
practised by the CRTC, is beneficial and desirable.

This study provides policy insights into many of the above
issues that are amenable to the analysis of positive economics.

1.2   ECONOMIC BACKGROUND AND FRAMEWORK FOR ANALYSIS

In economics it is usual to assume that the objective of the
firm is profit maximization. As there is no reason to believe
that this assumption is less valid for private companies in the
television, radio, and cable industries, than it is for firms in
other industries, we adopt the profit maximization assumption in
this study. Profits depend on the revenues and costs associated
with producing the product of the firm. The economic product of
television and radio companies is the audiences they produce in
order to provide a market for advertising messages. Cable T.V.
(CATV) on the other hand is a delivery system for television signals and the product it sells is the provision of signals unavailable "over-the-air" and/or improved reception of signals that can
be obtained "over-the-air."

The approach used in this study is the structure-conduct-performance paradigm of the industrial organization literature. We
refer to the structure-conduct-performance paradigm as an approach
or framework rather than a model since the paradigm offers an

operational matrix of actions and results rather than specific functional relationships from which one can formally determine equilibrium values resulting from firm decisions and market inter- action. Scherer[2] presents the basic paradigm in which causality runs from structure to conduct to performance with some feedback loops.

The elements of market structure include the number and size distribution of firms, the degree of product differentiation (real or imagined), the nature and height of entry, exist or mobility barriers, the nature and degree of vertical integration, and the nature of shape of the underlying cost structures. It is then argued that the conduct of firms is dependent upon these struc- tural characteristics. The dimensions of conduct include pricing behaviour, product strategies (such as differentiation via adver- tising or research and development), programming strategies, and perhaps strategies to limit competition. The performance of the industry which arises out of these structural and behavioural characteristics is evaluated in terms of technical efficiency (profitability and programming diversity and choice). This para- digm therefore allows one to both predict performance from basic economic and structural conditions as well as evaluate the struc- tural elements on the basis of performance.

We do not attempt an exhaustive application of the structure- conduct-performance paradigm, rather we focus on the ownership structure of the industries involved and examine the effect it, along with other structural characteristics, has on conduct and performance. Our approach is to assume that firms in these indus- tries are profit maximizers and the equations which are fitted are reduced forms which are completely specified and adequately de- scribe the firm or the marketplace. Since we do utilize reduced- form equations, the effects of joint ownership revealed with the use of "dummy" variables can be attributed to either demand or cost interdependence in the underlying (assumed) structural model. The choice of functional form is determined by both a priori rea- soning and "goodness of fit" statistics. Finally, in keeping with the spirit of the structure-conduct-performance paradigm, our re- duced-form equations have performance measures as dependent vari- ables and structural elements as explanatory variables. We argue that in the main, causality runs from structure, through conduct, to performance.

The industry structure on the demand side, depends on the be- haviour of consumers with their given tastes and preferences, and on the supply side in terms of the production technology. The basic conditions of demand include the price elasticity of demand, the growth of the market and the substitution possibilities be- tween various media as measured by the cross price elasticity of demand. In the case of the television and radio industries there is the interesting task of defining the market. Other studies, particularly in the U.S., have treated the market as a national one. We believe this is incorrect because the programming outputs of distant stations are not substitutable. We argue that the relevant market is the "signal shed," that area about urban areas in which consumers may substitute one signal for another, and we measure concentration accordingly. Similarly, we regard cable companies as monopolists in the geographic area over which they have the sole franchise.

Supply side considerations include the nature of the product and the technology of production and distribution. The technology of production and distribution differs between television and radio, which utilize the airwaves, and CATV which distributes its product through cable. Broadcasters of both radio and television signals produce what is basically a public good, that is, a product for which it is impossible to exclude anyone from consuming it and for which it is impossible to appropriate the value to consumers. The costs of producing the output are largely, not totally, fixed and the marginal cost of transmission or the marginal cost of serving one more consumer is approximately zero. There are therefore substantial economies of scale arising from the nature of production and the public good characteristics of the product. These economies arise at the level of the individual radio or television station. Operating and managerial economies may also occur when one firm owns more than one television station or when firms owning television stations also own radio stations or newspapers.

With these economies one would expect a move towards greater concentration in the television and radio industries and we provide evidence that this has occurred. The growth and concentration of economic power by way of multiple, or joint ownership is a central thesis of this study. We attempt to describe the level and extent of such joint ownership and its effects on the television and radio industries.

CRTC policy with respect to limiting (or permitting) concentration should reflect the trade-off between the benefits and costs of such concentration. The benefits of concentrating ownership within a medium may include economies of scale at the firm level in addition to those at the station level. Also, some argue that large groups have greater access to capital resources that may then be utilized to increase program quality and diversity. This is one of the hypotheses which we investigate. The costs of group ownership, with control resting in the hands of a few, include potential social abuses in terms of limitations on the freedom of expression and potential economic abuses. With respect to the latter, we would hypothesize that greater concentration within media results in higher prices (advertising rates) and excess profits (greater price-cost margins). However, it is interesting to note that, for the U.S., Levin found that group ownership does not result in higher advertising rates, that groups have only slight differences in profit margins suggesting little cost advantge, and that group stations earned quasi-rents comparable to those of single-owned stations.[3] Noll, Peck and McGowan argue though that these results are not surprising since there exists a limited number of VHF (very high frequency) allocations, the existence of three networks acts as a counterveiling force to large groups and there are a limited number of stations within each local market.[4]

The CRTC has tended to limit television groups to ownership of a single station in any one market. If the local market is the relevant locus of competitive forces this regulatory constraint would mean that stations belonging to groups have no more market power than single stations. While scale economies at the firm (group) level may exist, it is unlikely that they would be important enough to result in significant increases in profitability. The limited number of stations within each local market means that economic power in the local market can be expected to have a much more significant influence on profitability.

Only if a national market for television advertising is the relevant locus of competitive forces will the existence of national television groups serve to enhance market power. CTV, the leading Canadian private network, is owned by its member stations and hence does not act as a counterveiling force to large groups. However, all privately-owned television stations face competition from publicly-owned CBC stations for advertising revenues and competition for audiences from both imported U.S. signals and the CBC. Even in this case it would seem that group ownership may not result in significant economic power.

The above discussion has focused on television. One would expect that fewer advantages of group ownership accrue to radio groups. There are a larger number of stations within any market and the capital requirements for entry are minor relative to those of television. Furthermore, radio formats of music, involving a flat payment to performers or recording companies, reduce scale economies at the firm level and reduce the likelihood of the abuse of economic power. There still remains, for both television and radio, the question of group ownership limiting the flow of ideas or restricting diversity of views on various social and political issues.

Cross-media ownership also provides a structure in which economic as well as social abuse may occur. As Rosse, Owen and Gray note, "concentration of media ownership in local markets increases the potential for control over information, ideas and opinions and decreases the potential for diversity in sources of information, ideas and opinions."[5] Since television, radio, and newspapers are substitutes, to a greater or lesser degree, any cross-ownership within markets will allow monopoly pricing, excess profits, and the allocative inefficiencies resulting from such practices. Production similarities in the radio and television industries may permit firms with holdings in both of these industries to enjoy cost reductions.

We also investigate the implications of industry structure on programming performance. Programming performance is viewed in terms of balance, diversity, and number of options. A model, of the spatial competition variety, is developed which suggests that a television or radio industry comprised of profit maximizing private broadcasters obtaining their revenue from advertising will provide "inadequate" balance, diversity and choice of options. Inadequate is defined in the economic welfare sense that viewers could be made better-off at the same cost with a different program mix. Each broadcaster may obtain a larger audience, and hence probably a larger advertising revenue, from duplicating a popular program type and sharing the audience for this program type than from producing a different program type which has minority appeal. Obviously, however, the more competitors there are the greater the likelihood that one will obtain a larger audience by showing a minority program. Some argue that, for a given number of channels, a monopolist would provide more diversity and choice than competing broadcasters.[6] This view is based on the belief that a monopolist who shows a popular program type on one channel, can attract a larger total audience by offering a program of minority interest on the second channel. In doing so he will attract viewers who would not otherwise watch, rather than providing a second popular program that would attract most of its audience at the expense of the first channel.

In the case of the Canadian television industry, the economics of program purchase versus production reinforce the prediction of inadequate balance, diversity and choice. Programs with the highest audiences are mainly of a crime drama or situation comedy variety procured at low cost from the United States. Thus private broadcasters, if left to their own devices, would purchase the overwhelming majority of their programs from abroad. The primary influence of the CRTC in the area of programming has been to constrain this strategy by use of Canadian content regulations.

The Canadian system of broadcasting also includes a public broadcasting corporation, the CBC. The CBC television networks (English and French) do not rely exclusively on advertising revenue, receiving only about 20 percent of their income from this source. In radio, the CBC has both an AM and an FM station in many centers and does not broadcast any advertising messages. The major source of income for the CBC is the annual parliamentary appropriation. Under the Broadcasting Act (1968), the CBC has a mandate to provide balanced programming that appeals to different groups of people. Given its mandate and its diminished reliance on advertising revenue, one would expect the CBC to provide greater balance and diversity in programming.

Another complicating factor is that in most Canadian markets, there is competition for viewers from private U.S. television stations and often from a station associated with the Public Broadcasting System (PBS). These American signals may be available "over-the-air" or only by cable. The availability of the programming of U.S. stations can be expected to have an effect on the balance, diversity, and choice of programming offered to viewers in Canadian markets and may influence the type of programming selected by Canadian broadcasters.

1.3   OUTLINE OF THE STUDY

In this study which focuses on ownership and its attendant effects, we first investigate in Chapter 2 the broad characteristics of the television, radio, and cable-television industries. This serves to establish the relative importance of these industries within the economy as well as providing descriptive measures of the absolute size of each medium and relative sizes within media. Furthermore, it provides a description of the nature of these industries in which both public and private corporations compete.

Chapter 3 investigates, in turn, the ownership structure of the television, radio, and cable-television industries. Descriptions of ownership within and across industry are documented in extensive tables contained in an appendix. We then consider the characteristics of Canadian television and radio markets and provide a rationale for the selection of a sample of 14 major markets (rather than treating a national market) and the firms contained therein. The structure of each industry in each local market is characterized by a concentration measure. We argue that the most appropriate measure is the Herfindahl index and utilize it to construct measures on the basis of both audience and revenue data.

Having described the nature of the industry and its structural elements, we move on in Chapter 4 to 7 to investigate the conduct of television and radio firms, respectively. Estimates from reduced-form models are provided for audience demand equations. These estimates are then used in a simultaneous equation model of the determinants of price-advertising rates. These ad rates, we argue, are a function of ownership and market characteristics as well as variables indicating the degree of competition in the marketplace.

Performance characteristics of television and radio are evaluated in Chapter 8 to 11. Specifically, Chapter 8 considers alternative measures of profitability and includes an assessment of the return-risk performance of selected companies. Chapters 9 and 10 examine and attempt to explain the profit performance of the television and radio industries respectively. No analysis of rates of return in television is undertaken as most television stations are owned by corporations with significant non-television assets and asset information is provided only on a corporate level. Television price-cost margins are examined however. Radio profitability is evaluated in terms of both direct profit measures (rates of return) and price-cost margins. The balance, diversity and choice of programs is examined in Chapter 11. The analysis

considers program quality both across and within markets and by
network affiliation. We argue that the balance, diversity, and
choice of programs is a function of the number and type of station
as well as the method of financing the industry.

An analysis of the cable-television industry is contained in
Chapter 12. First, an overview of the industry is presented,
including financial and subscribed characteristics. A simultaneous equation model of the industry is estimated. This includes
estimates of demand, price, and cost equations. From the estimates we are able to investigate differences in the economics of
density and economies of scale and thereby determine the optimal
size of cable plant as well as their distribution in markets of
various sizes. The profitability of cable firms is also examined
with limited success. We are, however, able to examine the pricing practices which yield above-market rates of return. Finally,
a comparison is made between alternative pricing regimes and their
implications for industry profits.

Chapter 13 contains a summary and a discussion of the policy
implications arising out of estimates provided in the conduct and
performance analysis.

Notes to Chapter 1

1. See, for example, Economic Council of Canada, Responsible
    Regulation (Ottawa: Minister of Supply and Services Canada,
    1979).

2. F.M. Scherer, Industrial Market Structure and Economic Perfor-
    mance (Chicago: Rand McNally, 1970 and 2nd edition, 1979);
    see also Joe S. Bain, Industrial Organization, 2nd edition
    (New York: Wiley, 1968).

3. Harvey J. Levin, "Competition, Diversity, and the Television
    Group Ownership Rule," Columbia Law Review, Vol. 70, No. 5,
    May 1970, pp. 791-834.

4. Roger G. Noll, Merton J. Peck and John J. McGowan, Economic
    Aspects of Television Regulation (Washington, D.C.: The
    Brookings Institution, 1973).

5. J.N. Rosse, B. Owen and D. Grey, "Economic Issues in the Joint
    Ownership of Newspaper and Television Media," Memorandum 97,
    Research Centre in Economic Growth, Stanford University, May
    1970.

6. See, for example, Noll et al. op. cit.

Chapter 2

An Overview of the Television, Radio and Cable-Television Industries in Canada

The central focus of regulation of the mass media in Canada has been with what might be termed its "normative" roles. Specifically, there has been an emphasis on the use of the media to protect and promote a Canadian identity.[1] With the emphasis on the "social" use of the media, and the resulting restrictive licencing and content regulation, little attention has been paid to the economic ramifications of this type of regulation, that is, the effects on program quality, firm profitability, costs and pricing decisions. Excessive profits are a problem in that they result in substantial transfers of income from all Canadians to those fortunate enough to possess broadcasting licenses. They are evidence of inefficient allocation of resources, and they may provide the basis for an undue concentration of economic and political power.

We have already suggested that because of the nature of the product, there are economies of scale in both radio and television broadcasting. Under competitive conditions, entry of firms would reduce audience sizes and hence advertising rates.[2] With the nature of the cost function, the equilibrium structure in each industry would be characterized by a large number of firms (limited by both market size and the spectrum available) with differentiated programming.[3] However, with regulation an artificial barrier to entry is created that allows firms to increase prices and reap monopoly profits. These excess profits - excessive relative to the no entry barrier case - are rents to licenses held by individuals or groups fortunate enough to be protected. These rents may then be utilized to expand either vertically or horizontally within the industry thereby giving rise to even greater profits and substantial economic power.

Bigness and economic power are not synonymous. For example, the single consumer goods store in a small town is certainly not large yet it has substantial control over prices and other economic variables because of its dominant position in the market. Thus a firm that is large in terms of employment, assets or sales may not have substantial economic power. However, size does tend to confer political as well as economic advantages due to control over certain economic resources. The broadcasting industry may have even a greater advantage relative to size because of the volume of its output and its influence over ideas and information. It is the focus of this study to examine the economic effects of ownership and cross- ownership and thus, among other things, the effects of regulation on size and the extent of rivalry within the industry.

Below we examine, the absolute size of each industry and the relative size of firms within each. This descriptive exercise is useful not only to set the stage for the analysis that follows in the subsequent chapters, but also to see the importance of television, radio and cable-television in the Canadian economy and the relative sizes of the public and private sectors in broadcasting.

2.1   TELEVISION

Private television in 1975 consisted of a total of 65 corporations which controlled a total of 189 stations. CTV affiliates totalled 157, with 6 TVA (French language) affiliates, 6 Global stations, 14 independents, and 6 stations of OECA. These television corporations received total revenues of $234 million, incurred total operating expenses of $194 million, and owned $98 million in net tangible assets (property, plant and equipment net of accumulated depreciation).

The public corporation, the CBC, had a total of 234 affiliates and owned and operated another 238 stations. Of these stations, the English network reaches 91 percent of the population while the French network reaches 68 percent. The CBC in 1974, received a total of $233 million in Parliamentary appropriations, gross advertising revenues provided an additional $60 million. Since the CBC is not a profit maximizing firm, but rather is concerned with Canadian content, it expends substantially more on programming. The private television sector spent approximately 48 percent of the CBC's total expenses where on programming - 47 percent of which was for salaries and wages.

Table 2.1 provides a summary of financial statistics for private television in 1975. These figures, developed from Statistics Canada data, are arranged by size of firm where size is defined by total revenues. This method of measuring size is poor since revenues vary with both prices and quantities sold. Utilizing this method two firms with the same amount of assets and the same share of audience would be ranked in different classes if one were in a small and the other was in a large market. This results from the higher price which the firm in the larger market is able to charge since it has a larger audience. It is therefore not clear that one is not ranking markets as well as firms with the revenue measure. This criticism is somewhat mitigated when we note that the average net assets from firms in the largest (revenue) size class is more than six times the average for the next size class. There

Table 2.1

FINANCIAL SUMMARY, PRIVATE TELEVISION, CANADA 1975

(in millions of dollars)

	Stations by Revenue Group				
	$4.5 and over	$1.8 to $4.5	$1.0 to $1.8	Under $1	Total
Number of corporations	6	17	16	16	65
Total revenue	152.412	48.005	22.746	10.408	233.571
Non-programming operating expenses	52.008	19.122	9.701	5.646	86.476
Programming expenses	64.807	21.186	7.122	3.198	96.313
Total operating expenses	116.815	40.308	16.823	8.844	182.789
Depreciation	6.553	2.168	1.467	1.012	11.200
Total expenses	123.368	42.476	18.290	9.856	193.989
Net operating profits before tax	29.044	5.528	4.457	.551	39.580
Provision for income tax	15.467	2.998	2.134	.410	21.010
Net operating profits after tax	13.577	2.530	2.322	.141	18.571
Net tangible assets[1]	68.743	12.136	8.776	8.245	97.900

Note:

1. Property, plant and equipment net of accumulated depreciation at August 31, 1975. The comparable figure for the CBC, including both television and radio, was $142,154,753 and for CBC was $212,243,000.

Source: Statistics Canada, Radio & Television Broadcasting, Cat. No. 56-204, 1975 (annual).

is not, however, this correspondence when one ranks the average net assets per firm for the remaining three size classes.

The table suggests that large firms have substantially greater net operating profit than do mid-size firms. However, when measured as a return on assets large and mid-size firms have approximately the same profitability while small firms (column 4 of Table 2.1) have a significantly lower rate of return. These results reflect two phenomena. First, there are economies of scale arising from the initial threshold investment required for production and small plants seem to suffer from not reaping most of these economies. Second, large firms in bidding for an increased audience share by improved programming (either through own production or bidding for high quality foreign programs) thereby allowing greater revenues through higher ad rates, face large cost increases. The result is that the additional cost of increasing audience size may be greater than the additional increment in revenues. Finally, one must consider the impact of Canadian content rules which tend to increase costs since programs must be produced in-house or bought from Canadian networks rather than being purchased at low cost abroad. For example, the CBC paid on average $15,596 per hour to produce its own programs while paying only $4,718 per hour on average for purchased programs. Local stations paid $2,940 per hour for CBC-produced programs while paying $187 per hour for procured programs. If budget constraints reduce the quality and hence the audience to domestic programs, revenues will fall while expenses rise, thereby squeezing profits. Since one can expect larger firms to operate in larger markets with one or more American channels, they may face greater distortions from Canadian content rules than small firms operating in small markets where there are fewer substitutes.

If one compares Table 2.1 and 2.2, it is clear that the private television industry has approximately twice the amount of assets as the private radio industry, one quarter the number of corporations, only slightly more total revenues but substantially higher profits than does the radio industry. The assets, revenues and profits and therefore the economics power is concentrated in significantly fewer hands in television than in radio. This concentration of power is even more significant if one takes account of the substantial cross-ownership between the two media.[5]

2.2 RADIO

In 1975 there were a total of 282 private radio stations operating within Canada, ranging in size, measured by revenue, from less than $100,000 per year to over $2 million per year. The average revenue for radio stations was approximately $750.000

Table 2.2 indicates that the private radio industry had total revenues of $208 million, incurred total operating expenses of $171 million, obtained $15 million in net operating profits after tax. Net tangible assets (property, plant and equipment net of

Table 2.2

FINANCIAL SUMMARY, PRIVATE RADIO, CANADA 1975

(in millions of dollars)

	Stations by Revenue Group										
	$1.7 and Over	$1 to $1.7	$.7 to $1	$.58 to $.7	$.434 to $.58	$.349 to $.434	$.273 to $.349	$.184 to $.273	$.107 to $.184	Under $.107	Total
Number of corporation	28	28	29	29	28	28	29	28	28	28	282
Total revenue	85.190	36.272	22.903	18.434	13.932	10.618	8.825	6.312	4.090	1.663	208.239
Non-programming operating expenses	42.895	19.099	12.522	10.929	8.271	6.237	5.538	3.577	2.655	1.233	112.953
Programming expenses	21.543	10.267	6.867	5.479	4.176	3.283	2.854	1.906	1.401	.393	58.169
Total operating expenses	64.438	29.366	19.389	16.408	12.447	9.520	8.392	5.483	4.056	1.626	171.122
Depreciation	1.688	1.250	.741	.546	.482	.449	.368	.301	.175	.137	6.138
Total expenses	66.126	30.616	20.130	16.954	12.929	9.969	8.760	5.784	4.231	1.763	177.260
Net operating profits before tax	19.064	5.655	2.773	1.480	1.003	.648	.065	.529	-.141	-.100	30.978
Provision for income tax	10.157	2.858	.797	.588	.318	.359	.128	.114	.028	.013	15.359
Net operating profits after tax	8.907	2.798	1.976	.893	.685	.289	-.063	.415	-.168	-.113	15.619
Net tangible assets[1]	12.808	9.101	5.199	4.139	4.136	3.884	3.079	2.816	1.952	1.397	48.511

Note:

1. Property, plant and equipment net of accumulated depreciation at August 31, 1975. The comparable figure for the CBC, including both television and radio was $212,243,000.

Source: Statistics Canada, Radio and Television Broadcasting, Cat. No. 56-204, 1975 (annual).

accumulated depreciation) amount to $48.5 million. This brief quantitative assessment provides some indication of the magnitude of resources controlled by and generated from radio licence holders. This is by no means a complete picture because of the existence of group ownership within and across media.

In addition to the private sector in radio, the public Canadian Broadcasting Corporation owned and operated 50 AM and 30 FM radio stations. As of 1975, the CBC also had over $200 million in radio and television net assets (see the note to Table 2.1).

Our data indicate that radio firms are less profitable than TV firms. The criticisms developed above regarding the method by which size classes are constructed are also applicable in radio. Despite these, it is evident that profits (and profitability) increase with size. This result occurs for, although there are some economies of scale due to the nature of the product, there are also lower entry barriers in the form of absolute capital requirements. Thus there are a larger number of firms in any radio market than is the case for television. There is also room for more radio stations than television stations in the spectrum. Finally, we note that between size classes the relative proportions spent on programming and operation increase in approximately the same proportion as revenues. For example, between the second largest and the largest size class, each expense category increases by approximately 2.1 times while revenues increase by a factor of 2.3. Profitability, as measured by a return on assets, also approximately doubles.

There are a larger number of firms in radio than television and a wider variance in firm size. This would reflect differences in economies of scale, market sizes, and the ability of the spectrum to accommodate more radio than television signals. Furthermore, the lower average profitability of radio relative to television reflects both a larger number of competitors in the radio sector and a higher cross elasticity of demand between radio and media other than television.

2.3   CABLE TV

In 1975 there were 423 cable systems in Canada, however, 35 were non-operational. The 388 operating systems were controlled by 304 business organizations; 47 percent were single-owned and 53 percent group- owned. The group-owned systems obtained 77 percent of the gross revenue or approximately $122 million, while the single-owned systems obtained 23 percent of gross revenues.

Table 2.3 depicts the macro characteristics of the cable television industry in 1975. Total revenues were $158 million, significantly less than both radio and television, but total operating expenses ($83 million) were also significantly less (less than half) than those of radio or television. CATV total assets are significantly larger than radio or television, at 150 million,

Table 2.3

FINANCIAL SUMMARY, CABLE TELEVISION, CANADA 1975

(in millions of dollars)

					Stations by Total Assets						
	$4.7 and Over	$2.48- $.45	$1.19- $2.48	$.65- $1.19	$.45- $.65	$.305- $.45	$.218- $.305	$.147- $.218	$.105- $.147	$.105 and Under	Total
Total revenue	86.052	27.95	14.741	9.418	6.58	4.872	3.579	2.527	1.952	1.093	158.768
Non-programming operating expenses	39.156	12.774	7.584	5.24	4.145	3.055	2.172	1.648	1.164	.808	77.242
Programming expenses	3.112	1.339	.512	.465	.164	.208	.132	.133	.091	.012	6.152
Total operating expenses	42.270	14.113	7.584	5.705	4.311	3.263	2.305	1.763	1.256	.820	83.396
Depreciation	18.330	5.252	3.086	1.766	.912	1.133	.720	.426	.401	.196	32.226
Total expenses	60.600	19.365	10.670	7.471	5.221	4.396	3.625	2.189	1.657	1.016	115.622
Net operating profits before tax	19.156	5.654	2.765	1.154	1.603	.63	.293	.058	.176	.061	30.987
Provision for income tax	9.679	2.706	1.166	.834	.430	.182	.149	.076	.066	.023	15.315
Net operating profits after tax	9.476	2.947	1.599	.319	1.173	-.119	.143	-.018	.110	.038	15.671
Net tangible assets	83.306	23.696	14.893	7.635	7.793	3.976	2.920	1.983	2.273	1.133	149.612

Source: Statistics Canada, Cable Television, Catalogue No. 56-205 (1975).

a large portion of which is in the trunk cable and drop-offs.   The net after tax profits amounted to $15.7 million in 1975, approximately the same as in the television and radio industries.   The distribution of revenues and expenses over firm sizes is similar to that of radio and television, however, it is notable that large firms are more profitable than the medium size and small firms.

Cable has made substantial inroads in the markets it serves in Canada.   In 1975, 66 percent of the homes passed by cable were also cable subscribers and 45 percent of all homes in Canada were cable subscribers.

2.4 CONCLUSIONS

This overview shows that fairly modest pools of economic resources employed in Canadian broadcasting are generating growing revenues and large amounts of profit.   In 1975 all 65 private television stations, 282 radio stations and 388 cable TV systems combined had revenues of $600.6 million and net tangible assets of $296.0 million.   On the basis of revenues, these entitites combined ranked only 48th on the list of the 100 largest non-financial Canadian companies in 1975/76.[5]   In contrast, the largest company on the list, George Weston Limited, had revenues of $5,047 million and assets of $1,248 million.   The revenues of all private television radio and cable T.V. operators in 1975 were only slightly greater than Woodward Stores Ltd. - a Vancouver-based department store chain.   Nevertheless, it is important to recognize that the importance of broadcasting in Canadian life cannot be adequately measured solely, or even principally, by economic statistics.

The data in this chapter reveal a big variation in the size firms in both cable and radio while not in television.   Furthermore, there is evidence of substantial within-media group and cross-media ownership.   It is to this question we now turn in the chapters that follow.   That is, how have ownership patterns influenced the magnitude and distribution of economic power and what are the implications for certain performance measures, such as, price and profits?

Notes to Chapter 2

1.   See, for example, Robert E. Babe, Canadian Television Broadcasting Structure, Performance and Regulation (Ottawa: Economic Council of Canada, 1979).

2.   The relationship between audience size and advertising rates is fully discussed in Chapter 4.

3. See Roger G. Noll, Merton J. Peck and John J. McGowan, <u>Economic Aspects of Television Regulation</u> (Washington, D.C.: The Brookings Institution, 1973).

4. The issue of cross-ownership is discussed in Chapter 3.

5. See Royal Commission on Corporate Concentration, <u>Report</u> (Ottawa: Minister of Supply and Services Canada, 1978), pp. 15-17, Table 2.1.

Group Ownership, Cross-Ownership and Concentration in the Television, Radio and Cable-Television Industries

The structure of the television, radio and cable-television industries in Canada is characterized by large group holdings. These group holdings may or may not have significant economic ramifications. The element of structure with which we are principally concerned is the level of concentration in the relevant market. In order to evaluate this we present an analysis of ownership patterns and group holdings and in later chapters attempt to identify the impact of group ownership with and across media on certain economic performance and programming performance measures.

We first present a description of the holdings of the large media groups in television, radio and cable. This provides an indication of the potential market power of these groups on a nation-wide basis and within any specific metropolitan market area. This suggests the two dimensional nature of the potential effects of the economic power arising from ownership concentration. On the one hand, we are able to determine the absolute size of the groups and the financial resources that they control, on a national basis. This is important if such firms are able to achieve economies at the firm, as distinct from station, level from such things as producing or buying programs which are then used on a network basis. Alternatively, they may through vertical integration of their members obtain substantial monopsony (buyer) power in industries that provide inputs for various media such as programs. Finally, information on aggregate holdings provide some indication of the relative economic power wielded by the various groups and of their potential influence on the flow of ideas.

The second dimension of concentrated ownership is the economic power that firms have, within a particular local market, to influence prices and revenues and whether different types of within or across-media groups are able to extract substantial profits. This market distinction is crucial since a group may be small in the national market but wield great economic power in a metropolitan market within which it operates since it may, for example, be the only station in that market.

After describing the group ownership patterns, we develop the rationale for the definition of the market for which concentration

measures are constructed as well as a discussion of the appropriate measure of concentration.

The Canadian Radio-Television and Telecommunications Commission (CRTC) issues licences to individuals or corporate entities
to undertake to receive and transmit broadcasts. In order to properly define group holdings, a definition of corporate control
must be established. Following the recent CRTC ownership study,
we define "corporate control" as more than half of the voting
shares of an enterprise, or the largest single ownership interest
in the voting shares, whichever is applicable.[1] This definition
implies control is exercised only through voting stock. Other
control arrangements could be voting trust agreements or the holding of debt in a corporation which has a high debt/equity radio.

The ownership control is divided into three categories:

• Single plant firm: one in which no more than one plant of
  the same medium is controlled;

• Group ownership: a multi-plant firm in which more than one
  plant in the same medium but not necessarily the same market,
  is controlled; and

• Group cross-ownership: a multi-plant firm controlling plants
  in more than one medium (again, not necessarily in the same
  market).

Information on the radio, television, and cable-television
revenues and assets of media group owners was obtained from Volume
Two of the report of the CRTC Ownership Study Group.[2] Information on group holdings outside these industries was obtained from
The Financial Post, "Report on Media," May, 1976.[3]

3.1 OWNERSHIP IN THE TELEVISION INDUSTRY

In September 1975 there were 64 private commercial television
stations in Canada. These included parent, full-time and part-
time, program-originating stations and excluded rebroadcasters.
Of the 64 stations, 28 were owned by firms which owned only a single television station while the remaining 36 were group-owned.
Therefore, in 1975 56 percent of stations were group owned, a dra-
matic increase from 1968 when 38 percent of private TV stations
were group owned. The average gross revenue in 1975 was $3.4 mil-
lion for a groupowned station and $2.8 million for a single-owned
station.

Television groups vary widely in size. The leading four ownership groups, Baton, Télé-Métropole, Southam-Selkirk and B.C.
Television (Western Broadcasting), together account for 40 percent
of industry revenue. The size of the market in which a group's
stations are located is an important determinant of a group's
relative size. For example, the top two groups, Baton, and Télé-

Métropole, which own CFTO-TV in Toronto and CFTM-TV in Montreal respectively, account for 24 percent of total industry revenue.

The top ten groups, consisting of a total of 21 television stations, account for 65 percent of total industry revenue. Tables 3.1 - 3.15 and 3.18 to 3.23 show for each group owner the television stations, AM and FM radio stations, newspapers, and cable systems owned, as well as indicating the market in which each is located. Holdings in other industries are noted at the foot of the table.

3.2 OWNERSHIP IN THE RADIO INDUSTRY

In 1975 there were 376 private, program-originating AM-FM radio stations. This total excludes non-commercial stations and CBC stations. Eighty-one percent of all private radio stations were group owned. This represents a sizeable increase from the situation of 1968 when 64 percent were group owned and 36 percent were singles. This large percentage is partly a result of the common occurrence of AM-FM twins. The average gross revenue of a group-owned radio station was $585,000 compared to $456,000 for a single-owned station.

The 10 largest radio groups accounted for 44 percent of all radio industry revenues in 1975. As in the case of television, a large proportion of this concentration of revenue resulted from the location of group-owned stations in major markets. For example, the two largest groups, Standard and CHUM, account for 14 percent of industry revenue. The Standard groups holdings (see Table 3.9) include CFRB-AM in Toronto and CJAD-AM in Montreal. CHUM (see Table 3.6) owns CHUM-AM in Toronto, CFUN-AM in Vancouver, CFRW-AM in Winnipeg and CFRA-AM in Ottawa.

The holdings of the 10 largest radio groups, which account for 74 radio stations, and 44 percent of total radio industry revenue, are shown in Table 3.1, 3.3, 3.4, 3.6, 3.9 and 3.11-3.15. We note that the four largest, and the eighth largest, radio groups are owned by concerns which were in the top ten television groups, the reader is referred to the earlier description of group holdings. These groups which have major holdings in both the television industry and the radio industry are the Standard group (Table 3.9), CHUM group (Table 3.6), the Western group, (Table 3.4), the Southam-Selkirk group (Table 3.3), and the Baton group (Table 3.1).

3.3 OWNERSHIP IN THE CABLE-TELEVISION INDUSTRY

In 1976 there were 188 "large" (i.e., greater than 1,000 subscribers) companies which accounted for 98 percent of cable subscribers while 124 small companies represented the remainder. Tables 3.16 and 3.17, complied by the federal Department of Communications, show subsribers and other operating characteristics of the large firms.

MEDIA OWNERSHIP

TABLE 3.1	BATON GROUP, 1975				
Market	Television Stations	AM Radio Stations	FM Radio Stations	Newspapers	Cable Systems
Toronto	CFTO				
Ottawa		CFGO			
Windsor		CKLW	CKLW		
Saskatoon		CFQC			

Other interests:
o Subsidiary: Glen-Warren Productions Ltd. (100%)

TABLE 3.2	TÉLÉ-METROPOLE GROUP, 1975				
Market	Television Stations	AM Radio Stations	FM Radio Stations	Newspapers	Cable Systems
Montreal	CFTM				
Chicoutimi, Que.	CJPM(50%)				

Other interests:
o Subsidiaries: Paul L'Anglais Inc.
J.P.L. Productions Inc.

TABLE 3.3	SOUTHAM-SELKIRK GROUP, 1975				
Market	Television Stations	AM Radio Stations	FM Radio Stations	Newspapers	Cable Systems
Vancouver	CHAN (41%)[1]	CKWX		Vancouver Province	
Victoria	CHEK (41%)[1]				
Hamilton	CHCH			Hamilton Spectator	
Edmonton		CJCA	CJCA	Edmonton Journal	
Calgary	CFAC	CFAC		Calgary Herald	
Victoria		CJVI			
Lethbridge	CJOC	CJOC			
Kelowna	CHBC(33%)				
Blairmore, Alta.		CJPR			
Vernon, B.C.		CJIB			
Grande Prairie		CFGP			
Ottawa					Ottawa Cablevision Ltd. (35%)
Thunder Bay					Lake Superior Cable-vision Ltd. (33%)
Winnipeg					Greater Winnipeg Cablevision Ltd. (50%)

Other interests:
o Subsidiaries: Radio Sales & Marketing Ltd.
  All Canada Radio & Television Ltd.   Robert Lawrence Productions
  Selkirk Communications Ltd. (owns 43%   (Canada) Ltd.(60%)
    of London Broadcasting Co., England)   Selcom Inc.(65%)
  British Columbia Broadcasting   o Affiliate:
    System Ltd.(41%)   Beacon Broadcasting Ltd.,
  Quality Records Ltd.   England(30%)
[1] Majority of shares in CHAN/CHEK are owned by Western Broadcasting group.

TABLE 3.4	WESTERN BROADCASTING GROUP, 1975				
Market	Television Stations	AM Radio Stations	FM Radio Stations	Newspapers	Cable Systems
Vancouver	CHAN	CKNW	CFMI		
Victoria	CHEK				
Winnipeg		CJOB	CJOB		
Hamilton		CHML	CKOS		
Calgary		CHQR			

Other interests:
 o Subsidiaries:
  Western Productions Ltd.
  Western Broadcasting (Sports) Ltd.
  Northwest Sports Enterprises Ltd.
  and Vancouver Hockey Club Ltd.,
  both 69% owned.

British Columbia Television Broadcasting System Ltd.(50%).
Little Mountain Sound Co.(50%).
 o Other Interests:
  Harlequin Enterprises Ltd.(16%).
  Toronto *Star* (about 188,000
  non-voting B shares).

TABLE 3.5	MUTIPLE ACCESS GROUP, 1975				
Market	Television Stations	AM Radio Stations	FM Radio Stations	Newspapers	Cable Systems
Montreal	CFCF	CFCF	CFQR		

Other Interests:
 Champlain Productions Ltd.
 Unstated interests held in Alexander
 Pearson and Dawson Inc. and
 Paul Mulvihill Radio Ltd.

AGT Data Systems(99%), which owns
the computer group.
 o Subsidiary:
  TCC Inc. Texas(51%).

TABLE 3.6	CHUM GROUP, 1975				
Market	Television Stations	AM Radio Stations	FM Radio Stations	Newspapers	Cable Systems
Toronto		CHUM	CHUM		
Vancouver		CFUN			
Ottawa		CFRA	CFMO		
Winnipeg		CFRW	CHIQ		
Halifax	CJCH(51%)	CJCH			
Peterborough		CKPT(80%)			
Moncton/ Charlottetown	CKCW				
Barrie	CKVR				
Sydney	CJCB(50%)				
Saint John	CKLT				

Other Interests:
 o Subsidiaries:
  National Security Systems Ltd.
  Goldfarb Consultants Ltd.(82%)
  Intertask Ltd.(58%),
  Accu-Tab Computer Services Ltd.
 o Franchise:
  "Music by Musak."

TABLE 3.7	TÉLÉ-CAPITALE GROUP, 1975				
Market	Television Stations	AM Radio Stations	FM Radio Stations	Newspapers	Cable Systems
Montreal		CKLM			
Quebec City	CFCM CKMI	CHRC	CHRC		

Other Interests:
  Télé-Capital Unicorn Ltd.
  Immeubles Télé-Capital Ltd.
  Cine Capital Distributers Ltd.(51%)
  Les Productions du Verseau Inc.(40%)
  Cinevideo Inc.(40%)

TABLE 3.8	IWC-SLAIGHT GROUP, 1975				
Market	Television Stations	AM Radio Stations	FM Radio Stations	Newspapers	Cable Systems
Toronto	CKGN	CFGM			
Montreal		CFOX(80%)			
Sarnia		CHOK			

Other Interests:
  o Subsidiaries:
  Barrie Cable TV Ltd.
  Orillia Cable TV Ltd.
  Terra Communications Ltd.
  Global Communications Ltd.(control).

TABLE 3.9	STANDARD GROUP, 1975				
Market	Television Stations	AM Radio Stations	FM Radio Stations	Newspapers	Cable Systems
Toronto		CFRB	CKFM		
Montreal		CJAD	CJFM		
Ottawa	CJOH(52%)				

Other Interests:
  o Subsidiaries:
  Standard Broadcast Sales Co.
  Canadian Standard Broadcast
    Sales Inc.
  Standard Broadcast Productions Ltd.
  Standard Sound Systems Co.
  Standard Broadcasting Realty Ltd.
  Standard Broadcasting Co., England
  St. Clair Productions Ltd.

  Broadcast Marketing Services Ltd.,
    England(75%)
  Bushnell Communications Ltd.(52%)
  o Associated minority interests in England:
  Capital Radio Ltd.
  Radio City (Sound of Merseyside) Ltd.
  North East Broadcasting Co.
  Plymouth Sound Ltd.
  Bradford Community Radio Ltd.
  Radio Trent Ltd.

TABLE 3.10	BLACKBURN GROUP, 1975				
Market	Television Stations	AM Radio Stations	FM Radio Stations	Newspapers	Cable Systems
London, Ont.	CFPL	CFPL	CFPL	London Free Press	
Wingham, Ont.	CKNX	CKNX			

Information on other holdings not available.

Canada in 1975 had 350 cable television systems. Group-owned systems constituted 53 percent of the total while 47 percent were individually-owned. The group-owned systems had 77 percent of total revenues. The average gross revenue ($643,000) of group-owned system was approximately three times that of a single-owned system ($230,000).

The largest group, Premier, controls eight systems (see Table 3.18) and accounts for 13 percent of total Canadian cable television revenues. The four largest groups, Premier, Cablesystems, Nationale and Maclean-Hunter, account for 41 percent of total revenue. The cable-television and broadcasting industry assets of the ten largest cable groups, which account for 64 percent of overall cable-television revenues, are described in the Tables 3.3, 3.11, 3.14 and 3.18-3.24.

3.4   MARKET-BY-MARKET CONCENTRATION

A first step in analyzing the effect of ownership structure on various conduct and performance measures is to examine structural measures of concentration. The well utilized paradigm of structure-conduct-performance of the industrial organization literature (discussed in Chapter 1) suggests a more or less unidirectional causality from structure to conduct to performance.[4] Furthermore, it suggests that permanent improvement in behaviour or conduct with resulting changes in performance is best achieved by modifications to market structure.

The structural measures are not measures of "rivalry" per se, but are indicators of the likelihood of rivalry. It is therefore desirable at the outset to distinguish between "structural competition" and "behavioural competition." We describe as competitive those industries characterized by large numbers of firms that have no market power. That is, competition refers to the structural characteristics of the industry such as the number and size distribution of firms whereas rivalry we take to mean as the conduct or behaviour of firms operating in the same market. Therefore, structural measures only suggest that rivalry is more or less likely to occur, they are not measures of rivalry. For example, the four-firm concentration ratio is a structural measure of competition. The higher this ratio is (i.e., the higher the percentage of industry sales of assets accounted for by the largest four firms) the greater the market power of those firms. Economic theory suggests that firms with market power are less likely to engage in vigorous competition (particularly price competition) with other firms in the industry. Thus, if we find from our concentration measures that there is little competition in a market, this only suggests that less rivalry will occur. In order to measure the actual amount of rivalry we must examine the conduct or behaviour by looking at, for example, their pricing and output policies.

The principal dimensions of market structures are the number and size distribution of firms and degree of product differentiation within the market place. This suggests that a measure of competition must take account of the first two elements and that care must be taken in properly defining the relevant market; for the structural measure overall is a measure of potential <u>market</u> power. As we noted above, one must also not confuse bigness and market power; they are not synonymous.

In defining the market one must take account of substitution possibilities in both consumption and production. On the consumption side, if consumers are willing to substitute one good for another, both should be included in the relevant market. In the case of supply, firms will be market competitors if they employ similar skills and capital equipment and if there are no important barriers preventing firms from entering each other's product lines. As well, one needs to consider import competition, the existence of local or regional markets (as opposed to the national market) and product ties. Finally, market power is understated if markets are defined to include products that are not substitutable, if the market is defined too broadly (for example, defining a market as national when the appropriate one is regional or local), or if producers have significant product ties, brand loyalties or franchising activities. Market power is overstated if substitutes are excluded and significant import competition is excluded.

Structural measures of competition can be characterized in terms of concentration measures. A large number of such measures exist, but few have the preferred properties to truly reflect market competition. Hall and Tideman have noted that the most desirable properties of a concentration measure include: that it be a unidimensional, unambiguous measure; that it depend on, and is sensitive to, the relative size distribution and changes therein of firms within an industry and not on industry size; that it should be a decreasing function of the number of firms in the industry; and that it should have a range between zero and one.[5]

The best of a number of measures, and one which can be calculated relatively easily, is the Herfindahl index (H) defined as follows:

$$H = \sum_{i=1}^{n} S_i^2$$

where S is the i firm's market share and n is the total number of firms in the industry. H ranges in value from 0 (perfect competition) to 1 (monopoly, i.e., a single seller). If all firms within the industry are of equal size, H varies inversely with the number of firms. If the number of firms is held constant, an increase in the degree of inequality of firm size will result in a rise in H.

TABLE 3.11　　MACLEAN-HUNTER GROUP, 1975

Market	Television Stations	AM Radio Stations	FM Radio Stations	Newspapers	Cable Systems
Toronto		CKEY			
Calgary		CFCN(60%)			
Kitchener		CHYM	CHYM		
Chatham		CFCO			

o Subsidiaries:
Maclean-Hunter Cable TV Ltd.(62%)
Combined Communications Ltd.
Westbourne-Maclean-Hunter (Proprietary)(70%)
Design Craft Ltd.
Co-operative Book Centre of Canada Ltd.
Macmillan Co. of Canada
I.D.C. Publishing Co.
Metro Toronto News Co. Ltd.
Professors Den Bookstores of Canada Ltd.
Somerset Specialties Ltd.
Telephone Communications Canada Ltd.(51%)
Maclean-Hunter Ltd. (Britain)
Maclean-Hunter Pulishing Corp. (U.S.)

o 50% owned:
Trans Canada Expositions Ltd.
KEG Productions Ltd.
Quality Service Programs Inc.
Sinnott News Co.
Tarifmedia SA, Paris
Media-Daten, Verlagsgesellschaft m.b.h., Frankfurt
Media-Daten, Oesterreichisches G.m.b.h., Vienna
Media-Daten, Zurich
Datie Tariffe Pubblicitarie S.p.A., Milan
Corena Ltda, Sao Paulo
o Owned by Subsidiaries:
International Exposition Services Inc.(50%)
Paul Mulvihill Ltd.(49%)

TABLE 3.12　　CIVITAS GROUP, 1975

Market	Television Stations	AM Radio Stations	FM Radio Stations	Newspapers	Cable Systems
Montreal		CJMS	CKMF		
Ottawa		CJRC			
Quebec City		CJRP			
Trois-Rivieres		CJTR			
Sherbrooke		CJRS			

Information on other holdings not available.

TABLE 3.13   TÉLÉMÉDIA-BEAUBIEN GROUP, 1975

Market	Television Stations	AM Radio Stations	FM Radio Stations	Newspapers	Cable Systems
Montreal		CKAC			
Hull		CKCH	CKCH		
Quebec City		CKCV			
Trois-Rivieres		CHLN			
Sherbrooke		CHLT	CHLT		
		CKTS			
Rimouski, Que.		CJBR/CJBM	CJBR		

Information on other holdings not available.

TABLE 3.14   MOFFAT GROUP, 1975

Market	Television Stations	AM Radio Stations	FM Radio Stations	Newspapers	Cable Systems
Vancouver		CKLG	CKLG		
Winnipeg	CKY	CKY	CKY		
Edmonton		CHED(45%)			
Calgary		CKXL	CHFM		
Moose Jaw		CHAB			

Other Interests:
Relay Communications Ltd.(50%)
Winnipeg Vidcon Ltd.(80%)

				Newspapers	
				Media Tours Ltd.(90%)	
				Sibbald Arms Ltd.(45%)	

TABLE 3.15   STIRLING GROUP, 1975

Market	Television Stations	AM Radio Stations	FM Radio Stations	Newspapers	Cable Systems
Westmount (Montreal)		CKGM	CHOM		
Windsor		CKWW	CJOM		
St. John's, Nfld.		CJON			
Grand Bank		CJOX			
Grand Falls		CJCN			
Gander		CJCR			

Information on other holdings not available.

Table 3.16

CABLE TV COMPANIES IN CANADA, 1976
(Arranged in Descending Order of Magnitude of Total Subscribers)

Company Name	Locations of Systems Operated by Each Company
1. Canadian Cablesystems (Metro) Ltd.	Toronto, Burlington, Mississauga, Kitchener-Cambridge, Hamilton Cornwall, London, Brantford, Newmarket, Oshawa, Bowmanville, Ont., and Calgary, Alta.
2. Vancouver Cablevision (1976) Ltd. (A Division of Canadian Wirevision Ltd.)	Vancouver, Burnaby, Richmond and U.B.C. Endowment Lands, B.C.
3. National Cablevision Ltd.	Montreal, Ville de Laval, Ascot County, Cap-de-la-Madelaine, Chateauguay-Candiac, Sherbrooke and Victoriaville, Que.
4. Cable T.V. Ltd.	Montreal and Ville de Laval, Que.
5. Winnipeg Videon Ltd.	Winnipeg and Pinawa, Man.
6. Rogers Cable TV Ltd.	Toronto, Ont.
7. Ottawa Cablevision Ltd.	Ottawa, Ont.
8. Coaxial Colourview Ltd.	Toronto, Ont.
9. MacLean-Hunter Cable TV Ltd.	Toronto, Ajax-Pickering, Collingwood, Guelph, Hamilton, Huntsville, London-Lambeth, Midland-Penetanguishene, Mississauga-Streetsville, North Bay, Meaford-Owen Sound, St. Catherines, and Thunder Bay, Ont.
10. Skyline Cablevision Ltd.	Ottawa, Ont.
11. York Cablevision ltd.	Don Mills, Ont.
12. Victoria Cablevision Ltd.	Victoria (includes Oak Bay, Saanich and Esquimalt), B.C.
13. Calgary Cable TV Ltd.	Calgary North, Alta.
14. Q.C.T.V. Ltd.	Edmonton West, Alta.
15. Western Cablevision Ltd.	New Westminster, B.C.
16. Capital Cable TV Ltd.	Edmonton East, St. Albert, Sherwood Park, Fort Saskatchewan, Leduc and Spruce Grove, Alta.
17. North West Community Video Ltd.	North and West Vancouver, Nelson, Robson-Castlegar and Nanaimo, B.C.
18. Keeble Cable Television Ltd.	Toronto and Mississauga, Ont.
19. Greater Winnipeg Cablevision Ltd.	Winnipeg East, Man.
20. Télé-Cable de Quebec Inc.	Quebec City, Que.
21. C.U.C. (Scarboro) Ltd.	Part of Metropolitan Toronto, Ont.
22. Coquitlam Cablevision Ltd.	Coquitlam (includes Port Coquitlam, Ioco, Port Moody, Maple Ridge and Whonnock), B.C.
23. La Belle Vision (1972) Inc.	Trois-Rivieres and Shawinigan, Que.
24. Bramalea Telecable Ltd.	Brampton-Bramalea, Ont.
25. Halifax Cablevision Ltd.	Halifax, N.S.
26. Mountain Cablevision Ltd.	Hamilton-Wentworth, Ont.
27. Graham Cable TV Ltd.	Parts of Metropolitan Toronto, Ont.
28. Express Cable TV Ltd.	North Vancouver, B.C.
29. Videotron Ltée.	Beloeil-McMasterville, Buckingham, Mont-Laurier, Gatineau-Templeton and St. Jerome, Que.
30. Classic Communications Ltd.	Richmond Hill, Parts of the Towns of Markham, Vaughan and Whitchurch-Stouffville, Ont.

Source: Department of Communications, Statistical Information Services, Ottawa.

The most widely-used measure is the four or eight-firm concentration ratio. This measures the proportion of total industry
sales, output, employment or assets held by the largest four or
eight firms in the industry. This measure is weak, however, since
it fails to be sensitive to the total number of firms in the industry. Furthermore, recent evidence shows that concentration
ratios are generally a poor proxy for the Herfindahl index, particularly in the case of highly concentrated industries.[6]

Alternative measures include the Lorenz curve and Gini coefficient. The latter measures the degree of inequality of firms
while the former graphs the percentage of total industry output,
sales, etc., accounted for by various number of firms. (It is a
cumulative frequency distribution.) While these are useful descriptive measures, they contain two major disadvantages. The
Lorenz curve and Gini coefficient provide paradoxical answers if
only a few firms exist in the industry but are of equal size, and
the Gini coefficient is quite sensitive to the definition of the
number of firms in the industry.

The first important factor in developing concentration measures for the television and radio industries is the definition of
the market. Other studies, particularly those in the United
States, have treated the market as a national one. In our view
this is not correct since the programming outputs of distant stations are not substitutable on either the demand or supply side.
The relevant market is the "signal shed," that area about urban
areas in which consumers may substitute one signal for another.
We therefore develop concentration measures of competition for 14
market areas for television and 16 market areas for radio. Similarly, whereas the cable-television industry can be analysed on a
national basis, each firm has a monopoly position in its local
market (which may be a city or even part of a city), and it therefore makes little sense to calculate concentration measures for
the cable industry as a whole.

The measure of market share used in the calculation of Herfindahl indices may be based on either revenue or audience data.
Revenue share is the station's share of the total revenue of all
stations within the signal shed; audience share is the station's
proportion of weekly viewing hours for all stations within the
signal shed. The use of revenue shares in the concentration measure will over-state concentration somewhat since "import competition" is not taken into account. The magnitude of this bias is
not expected to be large. Audience share measures implicitly take
account of import competing signals.

Herfindahl indices for the various television and radio markets have been calculated using both revenue share and audience
share data. Preliminary estimates of the determinants of prices,
profitability, revenues and costs were developed using first the
revenue Herfindahl and then the audience Herfindahl index. Despite the differences in the two measures, the substitution of one

Table 3.17

SUBSCRIBER AND OTHER OPERATING CHARACTERISTICS OF CANADA'S LARGEST CABLE TELEVISION COMPANIES, 1976

(All values in thousands)

	Largest 5 Companies (1 - 5)	Largest 10 Companies (1 - 10)	Largest 20 Companies (1 - 20)	Largest 30 Companies (1 - 30)	All Companies (1 - 188)*
Total No. of Subscribers	1,019	1,533	2,028	2,284	3,086
Total Operating Revenues	62,671	93,928	126,501	142,628	194,776
Total Operating Expenses	32,634	48,567	67,175	76,058	105,348
Pretax Profit	14,113	21,074	28,073	30,556	35,369
Net Income	6,940	10,840	15,100	16,508	17,894
Total Assets	128,890	195,112	249,655	274,059	384,142
Net Fixed Assets	75,982	104,717	146,289	164,688	235,865

* Excludes those licensees having less than 1,000 subscribers. The latter group has only 2% of total subscribers.

Source: Department of Communications, Statistical Information Services, Ottawa.

for the other had little effect on the results. Therefore, to permit comparability with previous work which has used revenue based concentration measures, the final estimates prepared and presented in later chapters use a revenue, rather than audience Herfindahl index.

Market areas defined by signal shed are the appropriate measure of plant concentration since they account for substitution possibilities on both the demand and supply sides. In the following sections concentration measures on a market-by-market basis are developed for the television industry. Corresponding concentration measures for radio are discussed in section 3.6.

3.5   TELEVISION MARKETS

Before examining television markets some consideration is warranted concerning whether it is appropriate to distinguish between a television industry and a radio industry or whether both should be regarded, for purposes of analysis, as part of a "media industry" which should also include newspapers. The argument for regarding them as competitors in a media industry is that television, radio and newspapers all sell essentially the same product, namely audience/readership exposure to advertising messages. They are all competing for advertising revenue. As Levin[7] has noted, however, the different media are also partly complementary in the sense that each of the media is best suited to a particular type of advertising message. Radio is more effective than newspapers for bringing brand names and a few important characteristics of a product to the attention of consumers. Television is considered the most effective all round advertising medium, but it is still inferior to newspapers for providing information of any depth. Another complementary aspect is that radio and newspapers carry primarily local advertising whereas television also has substantial national advertising. Thus advertising campaigns often involve the purchase of time/space in each of the three media.

As the different media are partly complementary as well as partly competitive, we feel justified in adopting the usual approach of analyzing television broadcasting and radio broadcasting as separate industries. In our discussion of the individual markets, however, we will note any cross-ownership among the different media within the same geographic market as this presumably reduces competition for the advertising dollar in general.

We have argued that the relevant market is defined by the signal shed. A Census Metropolitan Area (CMA) provides a reasonable approximation of a signal shed and is a convenient choice because BBM audience data is available on this basis. When selecting markets it was decided to include all CMAs in Canada with populations of over 200,000. To improve regional representation, St. John's and Regina were added to the sample which also included Halifax, Quebec City, Montreal, Ottawa-Hull, Toronto, Hamilton,

TABLE 3.18   PREMIER GROUP, 1975

Market	Television Stations	AM Radio Stations	FM Radio Stations	Newspapers	Cable Systems
Toronto					York Cablevision
Toronto, Miss.					Keeble Cable(90%)
Oakville					Oakville Cablevision
Vancouver					Canadian Wirevision
Coquitlam					Coquitlam Cablevision
Saanich					Victoria Cable
Camp Borden					Borden Cable

Other interests:
Albion Cablevision Ltd., Britain(75%)
Marlin Communal Aerials Ltd., Ireland(87%)
Delta-Benco Ltd.(24%)
Northwest Sports Enterprises Ltd.(11½%)
Vancouver Professional Soccer Ltd.(7%)
Stuart Plastics Ltd.(80%)

TABLE 3.19   CABLESYSTEMS GROUP, 1975

Market	Television Stations	AM Radio Stations	FM Radio Stations	Newspapers	Cable Systems
Toronto, Burlington, Miss.					Metro Cable
Kitchener, Stratford					Grand River Cable TV
Hamilton					Hamilton Co-Axial
London, Ont.					London Cable TV
Cornwall					Cornwall Cablevision
Kingston					Kingston Cable TV(50%)
Chatham					Chatham Cable TV(50%)
Oshawa, Bowmanville					Pine Ridge Cable
Newmarket, Brantford					Jarmain Cable TV

Other Interests:
Alberni Cable Television Ltd.(20%)
Bushnell Communications Ltd.(6.3%)
Tele-Capital Ltd.(18%)
Edmonton World Hockey Enterprises Ltd.(30%)
Cableshare Ltd.(50%)
Agra Industries Ltd.(2%)

TABLE 3.20   NATIONALE GROUP, 1975

Market	Television Stations	AM Radio Stations	FM Radio Stations	Newspapers	Cable Systems
Montreal, Sherbrooke					Nationale Cablevision
Victoriaville,					
Ville de Laval,					
Cap Madelaine					
Quebec City					Télécable de Quebec Inc.
Rouyn-Noranda, Malartic,					Cablevision du Nord
Val d'Or					de Quebec

No data available on other interests.

TABLE 3.21   ROGERS GROUP, 1975

Market	Television Stations	AM Radio Stations	FM Radio Stations	Newspapers	Cable Systems
Toronto		CFTR	CHFI		Rogers Cable
Toronto					Co-axial Colourview
Hamilton		CHAM			
Sarnia		CKJD			
Leamington		CHYR			Rogers Management
Brampton					Bramelea Telecable

No data available on other interests.

TABLE 3.22   CABLECASTING GROUP, 1975

Market	Television Stations	AM Radio Stations	FM Radio Stations	Newspapers	Cable Systems
Toronto					Graham Cable TV
Winnipeg					Greater Winnipeg Cablevision Ltd.(50%)
Calgary					Calgary Cable TV(64%)
Sarnia, Wallaceburg					Huron Cable TV Ltd.(33%)
St. Thomas					Allview Cable Service Ltd.

TABLE 3.23   SHAW GROUP, 1975

Market	Television Stations	AM Radio Stations	FM Radio Stations	Newspapers	Cable Systems
Edmonton, Leduc, Fort Sask, Spruce Grove					Capital Cable
Revelstoke					Revelstoke Cable TV
Kelowna					Kelowna Cable
Penticton, Hedley					Penticton Cable TV
Woodstock					Western Cable TV

No data available on other interests.

TABLE 3.24   CABLE TV LTD., 1975

Market	Television Stations	AM Radio Stations	FM Radio Stations	Newspapers	Cable Systems
Montreal, Ville de Laval					Cable TV Ltd.

Kitchener, London, Windsor, Winnipeg, Edmonton, Calgary, Vancouver, and Victoria. Because of overlapping signals within major metropolitan areas, Hamilton and Victoria were dropped as television markets. We elaborate on this below.

In order to measure concentration, using the Herfindahl index discussed above, the television stations in the market must be identified. Broadcasting is unusual in the sense that some stations, often available by cable only, that are not competing for advertising revenue in a market are nevertheless competing for audience, and hence presumably affect the advertising rates and revenues in that market. Thus a station that sells time to advertisers in a market has two types of competitors; stations that are direct competitors for advertising revenue and stations that are competing for audience only. Both types of competition may influence the advertising rates and hence profits of firms, although the mechanisms are different. Stations competing for audience will include both the stations that compete for revenue and the additional stations that obtain a significant audience share. The two levels of competition can be reflected in concentration measures using revenue and audience shares respectively.

3.5.1   Identification of Stations Competing for Revenue

The following criteria were adopted for determining whether a station is a revenue competitor in a market. Subject to the provisos that the station sells advertising time and accounts for one percent or more of the Total Hours Tuned (All persons age 2+, Monday through Sunday) in the Market CMA[8], the station is included if

(a) It is physically located in the CMA[9], or
(b) It is physically located outside the CMA but within Canada and
  (i) Over 50 percent of the Total Hours Tuned (All persons age 2+, Monday through Sunday) to the station are in the CMA[10], or
  (ii) The CMA is the single target market (in terms of total hours tuned) for the station and 20 percent to 50 percent of the Total Hours Tuned (All persons age 2+, Monday through Sunday) to the station are from the CMA.

The effect of the provisos are to exclude station CICA in Toronto, because it does not advertise and to exclude CBC French stations in Toronto, Winnipeg, and Edmonton because they have an audience share of less than one percent. The stipulation, in criterion (b), that the station be located inside Canada probably results in the exclusion of a few U.S. stations, for example KVOS (Bellingham) which is heard in Vancouver, that would otherwise qualify. The reason for this criterion is that revenue information for American stations is not available, hence it would be impossible to compute their revenue share or include them in the calculation of the Herfindahl index based on revenue.

The reasons for choosing criteria (a) and (b) (i) are self evident; most of the advertising messages on stations that qualify under these criteria are obviously aimed at the CMA market. It was thought, however, that on their own these criteria were too restrictive. They would exclude, for example, a station with 49 percent of its audience in the CMA, 11 percent in another CMA, and the remaining 40 percent evenly divided among eight other markets. Obviously, most of the advertising on such a station would be targeted at the CMA. It was decided that a station should be included if the CMA is its largest single market and if at least 20 percent of its Total Hours Tuned are from the CMA. The 20 percent figure is obviously arbitrary, but some lower limit is necessary to exlude stations whose audience is spread so thinly that it would be unreasonable to suppose that most of the advertising messages carried are aimed at one particular CMA.

In the application of these criteria, problems were encountered because of overlap between the Toronto and Hamilton markets, and between the Vancouver and Victoria markets. The Department of Communications identifies CHCH as the sole station located in Hamilton. Hence, including Hamilton CMA as a separate market would entail, under criterion (a), allocating CHCH to this market. However, 52.3 percent of the audience (Total Hours Tuned) of CHCH is accounted for by Toronto CMA and only 14.6 percent by Hamilton CMA. Presumably its audience in Toronto CMA is responsible for considerably more advertising revenue than its audience in Hamilton CMA. Thus it was decided that it would be misleading to retain Hamilton CMA as a separate market. One possible treatment would be to redefine the market as Toronto CMA/Hamilton CMA. For CHCH, and CBLT this alternative would make a lot of sense as Hamilton CMA is the second largest audience for these stations. It is obvious though that CITY, with only 0.5 percent of its audience in Hamilton CMA, is not aimed at the Hamilton market. With this in mind, and also considering that all the other stations, including CHCH, have less than 15 percent of their audience in Hamilton, it was decided instead to omit Hamilton CMA as a television market. With Hamilton CMA omitted, CHCH qualifies, under criterion (b) (i), as a revenue station in the Toronto CMA market.

CHEK, the sole station located in the Victoria CMA, is a similar case to CHCH. It seemed undesirable to retain Victoria CMA as a separate market because only 22 percent of CHEK's audience is from Victoria CMA. Redefining the market as Vancouver CMA/Victoria CMA was rejected because Victoria is not an important market for the Vancouver stations: for CBUT it comprises 9.2 percent of its audience while for CHAN it is only 4.3 percent (smaller even than Kamloops). This permitted CHEK to qualify as a revenue station, under criterion (b) (ii), in the Vancouver CMA market.

The only other problem encountered in assigning stations was the treatment of CKGN (Global). In essence, Global network is a single station, with production centered in Toronto, which has a number of re-broadcast facilities. As it reports as a single entity to the Department of Communications, its revenues are not sub-divided by re-broadcast facility. Hence, employing criterion (b) (ii), it was decided to include Global in its largest single market, Toronto CMA. The only other treatment possible would have been to pro-rate the revenue according to the Global audience in the different markets, i.e., Toronto, 30.6 percent, Ottawa-Hull, 15.8 percent, London, 4.2 percent, Kitchener, 3.9 percent, Windsor, .75 percent. However such a scheme assumes a one to one correspondence of audience and revenues that, as we discussed earlier, is unlikely to be the case.

The stations assigned to the television markets as revenue competitors are shown in Appendix 3.1; for convenience each market is ordered from East to West. With the exception of cases already discussed, all the stations are physically located within the CMA of the market to which they are assigned. These tables also include the name of the group, using the abbreviations and definitions provided in the footnote to Appendix 3.1. The revenue Herfindahl index for the market in question is shown at the top of each of these tables. To permit easier inter-market comparisons of revenue Herfindahl indices, they are also listed by market in Table 3.25. To maintain confidentiality the revenue Herfindahl index for each market was calculated by the staff of the federal Department of Communications. For this reason, the revenue share of each station is not known to the authors and cannot be reported in the tables.

An upward bias exists in the revenue Herfindahl index calculated for some markets because the calculation excluded revenue from advertising aimed at the market from television stations not assigned to the market. Thus some of CKGN's advertising revenue will come from advertising aimed at Ottawa-Hull but it will not be reflected by the revenue Herfindahl for that market. Canadian advertising on U.S. stations comes under the same category. It is believed that approximately $20-22 million in advertising was spent by Canadians on U.S. television and radio stations in 1974 with about 75 percent of this spent in Buffalo (aimed primarily at Toronto) and Bellingham (aimed at Vancouver).[11]

3.5.2 Identification of Stations Competing for Audience

The criterion used to identify competitors for audience in a market was to include all stations that account for one percent or more of the Total Hours Tuned (All persons age 2+, Monday through Sunday) as identified from BBM data. A side effect of the one percent rule is that Vancouver is the only market that includes a PBS station as an audience competitor. The additional audience competitors are listed for each market in Appendix 3.1 The audience share[12] of each station is also shown and the audience Herfindahl index indicated at the top of the table. To permit easier inter-market comparisons and also comparison with revenue

Table 3.25

HERFINDAHL INDICES BY MARKET, 1975:   TELEVISION

Market CMA	Herfindahl Index	
	Revenue	Audience
St. John's	.60	.51
Halifax	.62	.39
Quebec	.64	.35
Montreal	.39	.30
Ottawa-Hull	.50	.21
Toronto	.27	.13
Kitchener	1.00	.15
London	1.00	.18
Windsor	1.00	.20
Winnipeg	.52	.26
Regina	.74	.62
Edmonton	.39	.28
Calgary	.54	.33
Vancouver	.63	.19

Table 3.26

OUT OF MARKET STATIONS ASSIGNED AS REVENUE COMPETITORS, 1975

Station	Location	Market Assigned	Criteria	
			b(i)[1]	b(ii)[2]
CFDR	Dartmouth	Halifax	*	
CFLS	Levis	Quebec	*	
CFGL-FM	Laval	Montreal	*	
CKVL	Verdun	Montreal	*	
CKVL-FM	Verdun	Montreal	*	
CHLO	St. Thomas	London	*	
CFTH	Galt	Kitchener		*
CFAM	Altona	Winnipeg	*	
CFRY	Portage-la-Prairie	Winnipeg		*
CFCW	Camrose	Edmonton		*
CKNW	New Westminster	Vancouver	*	
CFMI-FM	New Westminster	Vancouver	*	
CJJC	Langley	Vancouver	*	

Notes:

[1] Outside the CMA but within Canada and over 50 percent of the Total Hours Tuned (All persons age 2 + Monday through Sunday) to the station.

[2] Outside the CMA but within Canada and the CMA is the largest single market (in terms of total hours tuned for the station and 20 to 50 percent of the Total Hours Tuned to the station are from the CMA.

Herfindahl index for the same market, the audience Herfindahl indices are also listed by market in Table 3.25.

3.5.3 Competition and Concentration in the Markets

An examination of the individual markets reveals that certain markets have similar characteristics. St. John's and Regina are isolated markets that are not served by cable. As such they are the only markets with no additional audience competitors. With two revenue and two audience competitors the Herfindahl indices based on both revenue and audience indicate a high level of concentration. Regina actually exhibits a higher revenue and a higher audience concentration than any of our other markets. In addition, there is cross-ownership in both markets. In St. John's the Stirling Group owns both CJON-TV and CJON-AM. In Regina, the Armdale Group includes CKCK-TV and CKCK-AM as well as the Leader Post newspaper. It is interesting to note that in both St. John's and Regina the revenue Herfindahl index is greater than the audience Herfindahl index. This indicates that the market power in terms of revenue of CJON-TV in St. John's and CKCK-TV in Regina is greater than their audience share would suggest.

Kitchener, London, and Windsor each have a revenue Herfindahl index of 1.00. Because there is only one station in the market, these stations have a low audience Herfindahl index reflecting substantial audience competition both from Canadian and American stations. The U.S. networks, in fact, regard Windsor as part of the Detroit market. These are the prime examples of markets where the revenue Herfindahl index alone would give a misleading impression. The London market exhibits an interesting case of cross-ownership. The W.J. Blackburn Group owns CFPL-TV, CFPL-AM, CFPL-FM and the London Free Press newspaper. Obviously its control of the advertising outlet in the area is quite substantial.

Montreal, Ottawa-Hull, and to a lesser extent Quebec City, are markets where a significant portion of the audience watch television stations which broadcast in the minority language for that market. This raises questions as to the extent to which French language and English language stations compete with one another. For example, if Francophones view only French stations and Anglophones view only English stations, there would be two television markets in each such city. Audience analyses conducted by the CBC, however, indicate that while Anglophone viewing of French television is very low the converse is not true.[13] English language and French language stations compete for the Francophone audience. As a result, only in Ottawa-Hull where this is the minority audience is there likely to be a downward bias in the reported Herfindahl index. Quebec City, where such a bias would be least, is the only market which exhibits cross-ownership with the Télé-Capitale Group controlling CFCM-TV, CHRC-AM and CHRC-FM. CBC has two revenue stations in both Montreal and Ottawa-Hull. As such it is a multi-plant operation within the same market and, for purposes of calculating the Herfindahl indices, the market share of the corporation as a whole is used.

Vancouver is the only market where a private group owns more than one television station. The Western Broadcasting group includes CHAN-TV and CHEK-TV as well as radio stations CKNW-AM and CFMI-AM. Consistent with our treatment of CBC in the Montreal and Ottawa-Hull markets, the market shares of CHAN-TV and CHEK-TV are combined for purposes of calculating the Herfindahl indices. With Western Broadcasting having only one revenue competitor, CBUT, the revenue Herfindahl index is high. As indicated earlier, however, this figure is biased upwards because the effect of KVOS (Bellingham) as a revenue competitor is ignored. The substantial audience competition from U.S. stations results in a low audience Herfindahl index.

Toronto is the least concentrated market with the lowest revenue Herfindahl index and the lowest audience Herfindahl index. This is despite an upward bias in the revenue Herfindahl index because substantial revenue competition from Buffalo stations is not accounted for.

Of the other markets, Edmonton with a third independent station, CITV, has the lowest revenue concentration, while Winnipeg, with four additional audience competitors as compared to one for Edmonton, has the lowest audience concentration. Calgary, with two revenue competitors and two additional audience competitors, has a somewhat higher revenue Herfindahl index and audience Herfindahl index that the other two markets. Substantial cross-ownership exists in Calgary where the Southam-Selkirk Group owns CFAC-TV, CFAC-AM, and the Calgary Herald newspaper. In Winnipeg, the Moffat Group control CKY-TV, CKY-AM and CKY-FM.

3.6   RADIO MARKETS

The Census Metropolitan Area is an appropriate and convenient definition of market area for radio as well as television. For each market it is necessary, for the reasons given in the previous discussion of television markets to identify both the stations that are competing for advertising revenue and the additional stations that are competing for audience only. Competition for advertising revenue will also be affected by media cross-ownership occurring within a market.

3.6.1   Identification of Stations Competing for Revenue

The criteria adopted for determining whether or not a station is a revenue competitor in a market are similar to those employed for television. Subject to the provisos that the station is a commercial operation that sells advertising time and accounts for one percent or more of the Total Hours Tuned (All persons age 2+, Monday through Sunday) in the Market CMA[14], the station is included if:

(a) it is physically located in the CMA[15], or
(b) it is located outside CMA but within Canada, and
     (i)   over 50 percent of the Total Hours Tuned (All persons age 2+, Monday through Sunday) to the station are in the CMA[16]; or
     (ii) The CMA is the single largest market (in terms of total hours tuned) for the station and 20 to 50 percent of the Total Hours Tuned (All persons age 2+, Monday through Sunday) to the station are from the CMA.

CBC radio stations were phasing out commercial advertising in 1974 and are not included as revenue competitors. The provisos also resulted in the exclusion of religious stations VOAR and VOWR in St. John's, provincially owned CKUA-AM and FM in Edmonton, and all student radio stations. In contrast to television, a significant number of stations, not identified by the Department of Communications as located in the market, are included under criteria b(i) or b(ii). These stations are listed in Table 3.26 together with their actual physical actual location[17] and assigned markets.

In the application of the criteria it was found that the overlap between the Toronto and Hamilton markets and the Vancouver and Victoria markets is not nearly as pronounced for radio as television. None of the Hamilton stations would qualify as a revenue competitor in Toronto, and none of the Victoria stations would qualify as a revenue competitor in Vancouver. As a consequence, retaining Hamilton and Victoria as distinct markets does not pose a problem.

The stations assigned to the radio markets as revenue competitors are shown in Appendix 3.2 at the end of this chapter, arranged in order from East to West. The format is the same as that employed for television markets. To simplify inter-market comparisons, the revenue Herfindahl indices, calculated by the Department of Communications, are listed by market in Table 3.27. In general, revenue competition from American stations is less important in radio than in television. The Windsor market is probably the only one where it is substantial enough for our calculation of the revenue Herfindahl, calculated by the federal Department of Communications, which ignore such competition, to be biased upwards significantly.

3.6.2 Identification of Stations Competing for Audience

The criterion used to identify audience competitors is to include all stations with one percent or more of the Total Hours Tuned (All persons age 2+, Monday through Sunday) in the CMA. As CBC stations located in the market were not included as revenue competitors, they now appear as additional audience competitors. Stations assigned as audience competitors are listed in Appendix 3.2 and their audience shares indicated. The audience Herfindahl indices are reported by market in Table 3.27.

Table 3.27

HERFINDAHL INDICES BY MARKET, 1975:   RADIO

Market CMA	Herfindahl Index	
	Revenue	Audience
St. John's	.52	.34
Halifax	.35	.27
Quebec	.43	.27
Montreal	.13	.11
Ottawa-Hull	.28	.22
Toronto	.27	.19
Hamilton	.48	.26
Kitchener	.44	.13
London	.35	.25
Windsor	.61	[1]
Winnipeg	.25	.29
Regina	.37	.29
Edmonton	.22	.21
Calgary	.25	.22
Vancouver	.18	.14
Victoria	.34	.16

Note:

[1] An audience Herfindahl for Windsor is not included because, although U.S. stations have nearly 40 percent of this market, BBM do not provide the audience data for U.S. radio stations.

A problem with the BBM radio audience data used to apply this criterion is that the Total Hours Tuned to U.S. stations is not given. Hence we cannot identify American stations with one per- cent or more of the audience and cannot use their market share as an input in the calculation of the audience Herfindahl index. With cable not a factor for radio, the consequence of this is pro- bably serious only for the Windsor market. In Windsor the audi- ence shares, of all Canadian stations received, amount to just over 60 percent of the total. Presumably the remainder is ac- counted for by American stations. Under the circumstances, an audience Herfindahl index based on Canadian stations only would be misleading, hence none is reported.

3.6.3   Competition and Concentration in the Markets

For most markets the revenue Herfindahl index and audience Herfindahl index are lower for radio than for television (see Table 3.25 and 3.27). This reflects the greater number of compe- titors. The larger markets again tend to have the lower concen- tration. Montreal has the lowest revenue and the lowest audience Herfindahl index although this may be misleading as there is a question concerning the extent to which stations broadcasting in different languages are really competing. If we ignore the un- usual Windsor market, we find St. John's has the highest concen- tration in both revenue and audience terms.

Within most of our markets, radio-radio cross- ownership is found. This usually, but not always, involves common ownership of an AM and FM station. In the calculation of Herfindahl indices, the market shares of such stations are combined before squaring. This kind of cross-ownership can be noted immediately from the media ownership tables as the same group name will appear for both stations. Cases of cross-ownership within a market which involved ownership of a radio station and a television station have already been identified in the previous section. The only remaining cross-ownership within a market is of the radio-newspaper (ex- cluding television) variety and all involve the Southam-Selkirk Group. This Group owns CKOY-AM and FM and the Ottawa Citizen in Ottawa-Hull, CJCA-AM and FM and the Edmonton Journal in Edmonton, and CKWX and the Vancouver Province in Vancouver.

3.7   SUMMARY

The audience and revenue concentration measures for radio and television calculated in this chapter as well as the development of the appropriate market definitions are the elements character- izing the structure of the broadcast sector in Canada.

The concentration measures within media indicate greater con- centration and therefore greater potential market power than in radio. The measures should also be interpreted as a minima since they do not capture cross-ownership. To the extent that cross-

ownership exists, concentration will be increased as will the
attendant potential market power.

The structural measures calculated in this chapter are used
in the evaluation of industry performance. We include structural
measures as well as cross-ownership variables when investigating
profits and price-cost margins in Chapter 9 and 10.

In the next two chapters, we examine the forces that influence television station and radio station audience size.

Notes to Chapter 3

1. Canadian Radio-television and Telecommunications Commission,
   The Contemporary Status of Ownership and the Level of Concen-
   tration in the Canadian Broadcasting Industry, Background
   Study II to the Report of the Ownership Study Group (Ottawa:
   CRTC, 1978).

2. Canadian Radio-television and Telecommunications Commission,
   Ownership of Private Broadcasting: An Economic Analysis of
   Structure, Performance and Behaviour, Report of the Ownership
   Study Group (Ottawa: CRTC, October 1978).

3. The Financial Post, May 1, 1976, p. S4.   More recent data may
   be found in The Financial Post, September 22, 1979, pp. S16-
   S17.

4. See Joe S. Bain, Industrial Organization, 2nd edition, (New
   York: Wiley, 1968).

5. M. Hall and N. Tideman, "Measures of Concentration," Journal
   of the American Statistical Association, Vol. 62, No. 1,
   March, 1967, pp. 162-168.

6. R. Schmalensee, "Using the H index of Concentration with Published Data," Review of Economics and Statistics, Vol. 59,
   1977, pp. 186-193 and J.C. Hause, "The Measurement of Concentrated Industrial Structure and the Size Distribution of
   Firms," Annals of Economic and Social Measurement, Vol. 6,
   1977, pp. 73-107.

7. H.J. Levin, Broadcast Regulation and Joint Ownership of Media,
   (New York: New York University Press, 1960).

8. Identified from BBM Television Circulation Report by Area,BBM
   Coverage and Circulation Report: Television, October 28 -
   November 10, 1974.

9. As identified by the federal Department of Communications.

10. Identified from BBM Television Station Coverage Report, BBM Coverage and Circulation Report: Television, October 28 - November 10, 1974. This is also the source for all subsequent figures in this chapter of audiences for individual stations.

11. Howard B. Turetsky, Broadcasters: Canada Versus the United States, Report prepared by Faulkner, Hawkins and Sullivan for the Department of Communications (April 17, 1975).

12. The audience share of a station is the Total Hours Tuned (All persons age 2+, Monday through Sunday) to the station in the CMA divided by the Total Hours Tuned to All Stations in the CMA.

13. Canadian Broadcasting Corporation, Patterns of Television Viewing in Canada (Ottawa: Canadian Broadcasting Corporation, Research Department, 1973).

14. Identified from BBM Radio Circulation Report by Area, BBM Coverage and Circulation Report: Radio, October 28 - November 10, 1974. This is the source for all market CMA audience figures employed in this chapter.

15. As identified by the federal Department of Communications.

16. Identified from BBM Radio Station Coverage Report, BBM Coverage and Circulation Report: Radio, October 28 - November 10, 1974. This is the source for all audience breakdowns for individual stations in this chapter.

17. The physical locations of these stations were obtained from Canadian Radio-Television Commission, List of Broadcasting Stations in Canada, (Ottawa: Information Canada, 1975).

APPENDIX 3.1

TELEVISION MARKETS IN CANADA, 1975

Stations in the Mkt. for Rev. Purposes	Call Sign Addn'l Stations Competing for Aud. Share	Name of Group for Can. Sta- tions (if applic.)	Nature of Group [2]	Audience Share
ST. JOHN'S CMA		Revenue H = .60, Audience H = .51 [1]		
1 CJON		STIRLING	TT-RR-TR	.57
2 CBNT		CBC		.43
HALIFAX CMA		Revenue H = .62, Audience H = .39		
1 CJCH		CHUM	TT-TR-RR	.54
2 CBHT		CBC		.28
3	WEMT			.09
4	WLBZ			.07
QUEBEC CITY CMA		Revenue H = .64, Audience H = .35		
1 CFCM		TÉLÉ-CAPITALE	TR-RR	.44
2 CBVT		CBC		.39
3 CKMI		TÉLÉ-CAPITALE	TR-RR	.05
4	CFTM	TÉLÉ-METROPOLE	TT	.07
5	WMTW			.01
6	CKTM	H. AUDET	TT	.01
7	WCAX			.01
MONTREAL CMA		Revenue H = .39, Audience H = .30		
1 CFTM		TÉLÉ-METROPOLE	TT	.378
2 CBFT)		CBC		.35
3 CBMT)				
4 CFCF		Multiple Access	TR-RR	.18
5	WCAX			.04
6	WPTZ			.02
7	WMTW			.02

Notes:

[1] Market Herfindahl Indices.

[2] The abbreviations used to denote the nature of a group are as follows:
    TT denotes a group with more than one television station.
    TR denotes a group with at least one television station and at least one
        radio station.
    RR denotes a group with more than one radio station, (includes AM plus FM).
    N   denotes a group which includes at least one newspaper as well as at
        least one television or radio station.

APPENDIX 3.1 cont'd.

Stations in the Mkt. for Rev. Purposes	Call Sign Addn'l Stations Competing for Aud. Share	Name of Group for Can. Stations (if applic.)	Nature of Group [2]	Audience Share
OTTAWA-HULL CMA		Revenue H = .50, Audience H = .21		
1 CJOH		STANDARD	TR-RR	.24
2 CBOT)		CBC		.33
3 CBOFT)				
4 CFVO				.05
5	WWNY			.14
6	CKGN	IWC-SLAIGHT	TR-RR	.14
7	CFTM	TÉLÉ-METROPOLE	TT	.02
8	WPTZ			.02
9	CFCF	Multiple-Access	TR-RR	.02
10	CKWS	THOMSON-DAVIES	TT-TR-RR	.02
TORONTO CMA		Revenue H = .27, Audience H = .13		
1 CFTO		BATON	TT-TR-RR	.20
2 CBLT		CBC		.18
3 CITY				.04
4 CHCH		SOUTHAM-SELKIRK	N-TT-TR-RR	.15
5 CKGN		IWC-SLAIGHT	TR-RR	.06
6	CICA			.01
7	WKBW			.12
8	WBEN			.10
9	WGR			.09
10	WUTV			.02
11	CKVR	CHUM	TT-TR-RR	.02
KITCHENER CMA		Revenue H = 1.00, Audience H = .15		
1 CKCO		ELECTROHOME	TR-RR	.28
2	WKBW			.11
3	CHCH	SOUTHAM-SELKIRK	N-TT-TR-RR	.15
4	WBEN			.10
5	CFPL	BLACKBURN	N-TT-TR-RR	.11
6	WGR			.09
7	CKGN	IWC-SLAIGHT	TR-RR	.09
8	CBLT	CBC		.03
9	CFTO	BATON	TT-TR-RR	.02
LONDON CMA		Revenue H = 1.00, Audience H = .18		
1 CFPL		BLACKBURN	N-TT-TR-RR	.36
2	CKCO	ELECTROHOME	RR-TR	.15
3	WICU			.10
4	WSEE			.08
5	CHCH	SOUTHAM-SELKIRK	N-TT-TR-RR	.08
6	CKGN	IWC-SLAIGHT	TR-RR	.07
7	WJET			.06
8	WXYZ			.03
9	WJBK			.02
10	WEWS			.02

APPENDIX 3.1 cont'd.

Stations in the Mkt. for Rev. Purposes	Call Sign Addn'l Stations Competing for Aud. Share	Name of Group for Can. Stations (if applic.)	Nature of Group [2]	Audience Share
WINDSOR CMA		Revenue H = 1.00, Audience H = .20		
1 CKLW				.19
2	WJBK			.25
3	WXYZ			.22
4	WWJ			.21
5	WKBD			.07
6	CKGN	IWC-SLAIGHT	TR-RR	.01
WINNIPEG CMA		Revenue H = .52, Audience H = .26		
1 CKY		MOFFAT	TR-RR	.30
2 CBWT		CBC		.33
3	KCND			.23
4	KXJB			.06
5	WDAZ			.04
6	KTHI			.03
REGINA CMA		Revenue H = .74, Audience H = .62		
1 CKCK		ARMADALE	N-TR-RR	.75
2 CBKRT		CBC		.24
EDMONTON CMA		Revenue H = .39, Audience H = .26		
1 CFRN		RICE	RR-TR	.37
2 CBXT		CBC		.28
3 CITV				.28
4	KXLY			.10
CALGARY CMA		Revenue H = .54, Audience H = .33		
1 CFCN				.41
2 CFAC		SOUTHAM-SELKIRK	N-TT-TR-RR	.38
3	KREM			.10
4	KXLY			.09
VANCOUVER CMA		Revenue H = .63, Audience H = .19		
1 CHAN)		WESTERN	TT-RR-TR	.29
2 CHEK)				.21
3 CBUT		CBC		.21
4	KVOS			.15
5	KOMO			.13
6	KING			.11
7	KIRO			.08
8	KCTS			.01
9	KSTW			.01

APPENDIX 3.2

RADIO MARKETS IN CANADA, 1975

Call Sign Stations in the Mkt. for Rev. Purposes	Addn'l Stations Competing for Aud. Share	Name of Group for Can. Stations (if applic.)	Nature of Group [2]	Audience Share
ST. JOHN'S CMA		Revenue H = .52, Audience H = .34 [1]		
1 CJON		STIRLING	TT-RR-TR	.34
2 VOCM		J.V. BUTLER	RR	.42
3	CBN	CBC		.21
4	VOWR			.01
HALIFAX CMA		Revenue H = .35, Audience H = .27		
1 CHNS)				
2 CHFX (FM))		L.F. DALEY	RR	.34
3 CHNX (SW))				
4 CJCH		CHUM	TT-TR-RR	.29
5 CFDR				.25
6	CBH	CBC		.10
QUEBEC CITY CMA		Revenue H = .42, Audience H = .27		
1 CJRP		CIVITAS	RR	.25
2 CKCV		TÉLÉMEDIA-BEAUBIEN	TT-TR-RR	.02
3 CFLS				.05
4 CHRC (AM))				
5 CHRC (FM))		TÉLÉ-CAPITALE	TR-RR	.43
6 CFOM				.10
7	CBV)			
8	CBV (FM))	CBC		.12
MONTREAL CMA		Revenue H = .13, Audience H = .11		
1 CFCF)				
2 CFQR (FM))		MULTIPLE ACCESS	TR-RR	.16
3 CFOX		IWC-SLAIGHT	RR	.01
4 CJAD)				
5 CJFM)		STANDARD	RR	.13
6 CJMS		CIVITAS	RR	.16
7 CKMF(FM)				
8 CKAC		TÉLÉMEDIA-BEAUBIEN	TT-TR-RR	.11
9 CKGM)				
10 CHOM (FM))		STIRLING	TT-TR-RR	.12
11 CKVL)				
12 CKVL (FM))		TIETOLMAN	N/A	.14
13 CFGL (FM)				.07
14	CBM)			
15	CBM (FM))			
16	CBF)	CBC		.08
17	CBF (FM))			

[1], [2] See footnotes in Appendix 3.1

Note: N/A indicates this information was not available.

APPENDIX 3.2 cont'd.

Stations in the Mkt. for Rev. Purposes	Call Sign Addn'l Stations Competing for Aud. Share	Name of Group for Can. Stations (if applic.)	Nature of Group [2]	Audience Share
OTTAWA CMA		Revenue H = .28, Audience H = .22		
1 CFGO		BATON	TT-TR-RR	.09
2 CFRA)				
3 CFMO (FM))		CHUM	TT-TR-RR	.39
4 CJRC		CIVITAS	RR	.10
5 CKOY)				
6 CKBY (FM))		SOUTHAM-SELKIRK	N-TT-TR-RR	.13
7 CKCH)				
8 CKCH (FM))		TÉLÉMEDIA-BEAUBIEN	TT-TR-RR	.10
9	CBO)			
10	CBO (FM))	CBC		.15
11	CBOF)			
12	CHOM (FM)	STIRLING	TT-RR-TR	.02
TORONTO CMA		Revenue H = .27, Audience H = .19		
1 CKFM (FM))				
2 CFRB)		STANDARD	RR	.35
3 CFTR)				
4 CHFI (FM))		ROGERS	RR	.14
5 CHIN (AM))				
6 CHIN (FM))		LOMBARDI	RR	.02
7 CHUM (AM))				
8 CHUM (FM))		CHUM	TT-TR-RR	.17
9 CKFH				.02
10 CKEY		MACLEAN-HUNTER	RR	.12
11	CBL)			
12	CBL (FM))	CBC		.08
13	CJBC)			
14	CFGM	IWC-SLAIGHT	TR-RR	.04
15	CKDS (FM)	WESTERN	TT-TR-RR	.02
HAMILTON CMA		Revenue H = .48, Audience H = .26		
1 CHAM		ROGERS	RR	.10
2 CHML)				
3 CKDS (FM))		WESTERN	TT-TR-RR	.47
4 CKOC		ARMADALE	N-TR-RR	.111
5	CFRB)			
6	CKFM (FM))	STANDARD	RR	.12
7	CBL	CBC		.04
8	CFGM	IWC-SLAIGHT	TR-RR	.03
9	CHUM (AM))			
10	CHUM (FM))	CHUM	TT-TR-RR	.05
11	CHFI (FM))			
12	CFIR)	ROGERS	RR	.03

APPENDIX 3.2 cont'd.

Stations in the Mkt. for Rev. Purposes	Call Sign Addn'l Stations Competing for Aud. Share	Name of Group for Can. Stations (if applic.)	Nature of Group [2]	Audience Share
KITCHENER CMA		Revenue H = .44, Audience H = .13		
1 CHYM)				
2 CHYM (FM))		MACLEAN-HUNTER	RR	.21
3 CKKW)				
4 CFCA (FM))		ELECTROHOME	RR	.20
5 CFTJ				.02
6	CFRB)			
7	CKFM (FM))	STANDARD	RR	.16
8	CFTR)			
9	CHAM)	ROGERS	RR	.13
10	CHFI (FM))			
11	CBL)	CBC	RR	.06
12	CKOS (FM))			
13	CHML)	WESTERN	TT-RR-TR	.05
14	CHUM (AM))			
15	CHUM (FM))	CHUM	TT-RR-TR	.04
16	CJOY (AM))			
17	CJOY (FM))	SLATER-METCALF	RR	.03
18	CKOC	ARMADALE	N-TR-RR	.02
19	CKPC (AM))			
20	CKPC (FM))	R.D. BUCHANAN	RR	.02
LONDON CMA		Revenue H = .35, Audience H = .25		
1 CFPL (AM))				
2 CFPL (FM))		W.J. BLACKBURN	N-TT-TR-RR	.43
3 CJBK				.22
4 CKSL				.10
5 CHLO				.05
6	CFCA (FM)	ELECTROHOME	RR	.05
7	CBL	CBC		.03
8	CJOM (FM))			
9	CKWW)	STIRLING	TT-TR-RR	.02
10	CKLW	BATON	TT-TR-RR	.01
WINDSOR CMA		Revenue H = .61, Audience H [3]		
1 CKLW)				
2 CKLW (FM))		BATON	TT-TR-RR	.25
3 CKWW)				
4 CJOM (FM))		STIRLING	TT-TR-RR	.25
5	CBE	CBC		.09
6	CHYR	ROGERS	RR	.01

Note:

[3] See Table 3.27.

APPENDIX 3.2 cont'd.

Stations in the Mkt. for Rev. Purposes	Call Sign Addn'l Stations Competing for Aud. Share	Name of Group for Can. Stations (if applic.)	Nature of Group [2]	Audience Share
WINNIPEG CMA		Revenue H = .25, Audience H = .29		
1 CFRW (AM))				
2 CFRW (FM))		CHUM	TT-TR-RR	.14
3 CJOB (AM))				
4 CJOB (FM))		WESTERN	TT-TR-RR	.49
5 CKY (AM))				
6 CKY (FM))		MOFFAT	TR-RR	.10
7 CKRC		ARMADALE	N-TR-RR	.10
8 CFAM		KROCKER FAMILY	RR	.06
9 CFRY				.02
10	CBW (AM))			
11	CBW (FM))	CBC		.07
REGINA CMA		Revenue H = .37, Audience H = .29		
1 CJME		RAWLINSON FAMILY	TR-RR	.29
2 CKCK		ARMADALE	N-TR-RR	.38
3 CKRM)				
4 CFMQ (FM))		G.G. GALLAGHER	RR	.24
5	CBK	CBC		.06
EDMONTON CMA		Revenue H = .22, Audience H = .21		
1 CFRN (AM))				
2 CFRN (FM))		RICE	RR-TR	.14
3 CHED		MOFFAT	TR-RR	.32
4 CHQT				.24
5 CJCA (AM))				
6 CJCA (FM))		SOUTHAM-SELKIRK	N-TT-TR-RR	.15
7 CFCW				.06
8	CBX	CBC		.06
9	CKUA (AM))			
10	CKUA (FM))			.02
CALGARY CMA		Revenue H = .25, Audience H = .22		
1 CFCN		MACLEAN-HUNTER	RR	.20
2 CFAC		SOUTHAM-SELKIRK	N-TT-TR-RR	.24
3 CHQR		WESTERN	TT-TR-RR	.22
4 CKXL)				
5 CHFM)		MOFFAT	TR-RR	.27
6	CBR	CBC		.04

APPENDIX 3.2 cont'd.

Call Sign				
Stations in the Mkt. for Rev. Purposes	Addn'l Stations Competing for Aud. Share	Name of Group for Can. Stations (if applic.)	Nature of Group [2]	Audience Share
VANCOUVER CMA		Revenue H = .18, Audience H = .14		
1 CFUN		CHUM	TT-TR-RR	.08
2 CHQM (AM))				
3 CHQM (FM))		Q BROADCASTING	RR	.16
4 CJOR				.18
5 CJVB				.03
6 CKWX		SOUTHAM-SELKIRK	N-TT-TR-RR	.07
7 CKLG (AM))				
8 CKLG (FM))		MOFFAT	TR-RR	.13
9 CKNW)				
10 CFMI (FM))		WESTERN	TT-TR-RR	.23
11 CJJC				
12	CBU (AM))			
13	CBU (FM))	CBC		.05
14	CBUF (FM))			
VICTORIA CMA		Revenue H = .34, Audience H = .16		
1 CKDA)				
2 CFMS (FM))		D. ARMSTRONG	RR	.19
3 CJVI		SOUTHAM-SELKIRK	N-TT-TR-RR	.25
4 CFAX				.20
5	CKLG (AM))			
6	CKLG (FM))	MOFFAT	TR-RR	.12
7	CJOR			.06
8	CBU (AM))			
9	CBU (FM))	CBC	TT-TR-RR	.05
10	CFUN	CHUM	TT-TR-RR	.02
11	CKNW)			
12	CFMI (FM))	WESTERN	TT-TR-RR	.01

Chapter 4

Television Station Audience Size

Broadcasters of both television and radio signals produce
what is basically a public good - a product for which it is impossible (or inefficient) to exclude additional consumers and for
which it is impossible to charge individual consumers for the
benefit they receive. Since privately-owned stations are unable
to recapture directly from their consumers (viewers) funds to
cover their broadcasting expenses they must find other sources of
revenue. The most important of these alternative sources, in
Canada, is advertising revenues from the sale of air time for
commercial purposes.

Since advertising is the prime source of revenue, broadcasters are not in business to produce programs. They are in
business to produce audiences. These audiences, or rather, the
means of access to them are then sold to advertisers. Firms in
the television industry, the sellers of television time, engage in
both program competition for audience and in price competition
(i.e., the level of advertising rates). Each of these is examined
in turn.

In this chapter we examine the influence of market structure
on the size of audience obtained by a television station. These
audience size results are then used in subsequent chapters to
analyze the pricing of 30 second prime time commercials and television station price-cost margins.

One of the prime determinants of the audience size of a particular television station is the number of potential viewers, or
the population, in the station's market. For a given standard of
programming, the larger the potential audience of a station, the
larger the actual audience size that can be expected.

Audience size is not a direct function of population, however, since as the market grows additional over-the-air television
broadcasting stations can be expected to emerge. Cable system
subscribers may be presented with a further set of options. Although additional choice may serve to somewhat expand the total
audience viewing all stations, the principal effect of new en-

trants can be expected to be a fragmentation of the audience of existing stations.[1] This type of audience fragmentation analysis would argue that, other things being equal, the audience of a particular television station is a function of the population in the market divided by the number of stations. But all stations do not compete on equal terms. The principal differences relate to non-local location, cable-only reception, and type of programming.

First, stations located in distant markets, whether these be cities in the U.S. or Canada, are unable to adapt their programming either in timing or content to the exigencies of the local market.[2] Signal reception may also be impaired.

Second, distant stations available only via cable, although they may overcome reception difficulties, face a different type of handicap in that they are limited in their potential audience to a subset of the overall market, i.e., viewers in cable-equipped households.

The third difference between stations relates to the nature of their programming. CTV affiliates could be expected to be in the most advantageous position because of their relative freedom from programming constraints. CBC owned and affiliated stations may be handicapped by their greater public affairs/public service orientation both in their competition for English-speaking audiences with CTV and Global affiliates and in their competition with TVA affiliates for French-speaking audiences.[3] Independent stations, in turn, may suffer programming handicaps in that they lack the network advantage of having their programming costs spread over a large number of stations.

4.1 ECONOMETRICS AND ECONOMIC MODELS

In order to understand complex industries such as television, radio, and cable-television it is necessary to focus attention on only the important economic variables. These must be defined and the relationships between them specified in what are termed economic models. Econometric techniques provide a way of measuring these economic relationships.[4]

The estimated models improve our understanding of the industries, not only permitting the testing of hypothesized relationships but also revealing hitherto unsuspected relationships. In addition, the estimated model can be used to predict the value of certain variables in the future (forecasting), and simulate the impact of various policies on certain economic variables of interest (policy evaluation).

We have constructed, from economic theory, models to try and understand the important and significant variables influencing audience size, ad rates, and profits. To estimate the models we have used regression analysis, the most common of econometric techniques.

Economic relationships are measured with the use of regression techniques. The most general model could be expressed as

$$Y = \alpha + \beta X + u$$

where Y represents a dependent variable, such as a television station's ad rate, X is an explanatory variable, such as audience size, α and β are parameters we wish to estimate, and u is a stochastic disturbance term (random variable) which represents unmeasurable influences. This model basically says that the value of Y is determined by the values of X and by the value of the disturbance term u. The "way" X and u determine Y is governed by the value of α and β.

What we wish to do is obtain estimates of α and β, which for the given values of X, best predict the value of Y. If we have estimates of α and β, say $\hat{\alpha}$ and $\hat{\beta}$ we could predict Y, as $\hat{Y}$;

$$\hat{Y} = \hat{\alpha} + \hat{\beta} X.$$

Recalling that $\hat{Y}$ is an estimate of the true value of Y, the difference between Y and Y is an error term, e. Therefore,

$$e = Y - \hat{Y}$$

where e represents the amount by which $\hat{Y}$ either under or over predicts Y. These errors are known as residuals. One can express the residuals with the knowledge that $\hat{Y} = \hat{\alpha} + \hat{\beta} X$, as

$$e = Y - \hat{\alpha} - \hat{\beta} X.$$

We clearly want a model with predicts Y as accurately as possible or, alternatively, we wish to minimize the amount by which $\hat{Y}$ deviates from Y. The method by which we achieve this is to minimize the sum of the squared residuals and this is known as the principle of least squares. More formally, we select values of $\hat{\alpha}$ and $\hat{\beta}$ which

$$\text{minimize } \Sigma e^2 = \Sigma (Y - \hat{\alpha} - \hat{\beta} X)^2$$

For the simple model used in this illustration, the value of $\hat{\alpha}$ and $\hat{\beta}$, using the least squares principle, will be given by

$$\hat{\alpha} = \overline{Y} - \hat{\beta}\overline{X}$$
$$\hat{\beta} = \Sigma [(Y-\overline{Y})(X-\overline{X})]/\Sigma(X-\overline{X})^2$$

where $\overline{Y}$ and $\overline{X}$ are the mean (average) values of Y and X.

To return to our ad rate example let us hypothesize that a television station's ad rate depends not only on the size of audience the station can supply to an advertiser but also on the average income of that audience. If X_1 represents audience size and

X_2 represents average income then the relationship can be expressed as

$$Y = \alpha + \beta_1 X_1 + \beta_2 X_2 + u$$

Computer programs using the method of least squares can be used to estimate this relationship, providing values of all parameters. We are interested primarily in the estimated values of $\hat{\beta}_1$ and $\hat{\beta}_2$. $\hat{\beta}_1$ is interpreted as the change in ad rate (Y) for a one unit changes in audience (X_2) assuming the average income (X_2) is held constant. Similarly, $\hat{\beta}_2$ is the change in ad rate (Y) for a one unit change in average income (X_2) holding the audience (X_1) constant. Thus if $\hat{\beta}_1 = .002$ than a 1,000 unit change in audience can be expected to result in a 2 unit change in ad rate.

Once $\hat{\alpha}$ and $\hat{\beta}$ have been estimated they are tested for their reliabiblity using tests of significance. The most frequently used test in this research is the t-test which applies to individual coefficients. The purpose of the test statistic is to determine if $\hat{\alpha}$ and $\hat{\beta}$ are truly significantly different from zero (or some other critical value) or whether the value obtained is pure chance. Since $\hat{\alpha}$ and $\hat{\beta}$ are estimates we can only say with some "probability" that the estimated value is not equal to zero. The coefficients $\hat{\alpha}$ and $\hat{\beta}$ are generally expressed as being statistically significant at the 90%, 95% or 99% level. This means that if the coefficient is significant at the 90% (.90) level, there is only a probability of .1 that it will be outside of the narrow range of

$\hat{\beta} \pm 2$ times the standard error of $\hat{\beta}$.

Another measure of "reliability" for the whole equation is the R^2, also called the coefficient of determination. The R^2 varies between 0 and 1. An R^2 of .60, for example, signifies that 60 percent of the variation in the dependent variable (y in our example) is "explained" by $\alpha + \hat{\beta} X$. The higher the R^2 the better the model fits and the more reliable is the model for predictive purposes.

4.2 MODEL SPECIFICATION

In Appendix 4.1 to this chapter a model is developed which permits an estimation of the relative importance of the various determinants of television station audience size.

4.3 THE DATA

The nature and sources of the data used to test this model are described in Appendix 4.2 to this chapter.

4.4 EMPIRICAL RESULTS

The determinants of television station audience size are estimated first using data on a station's audience in its local CMA and then using data for total audience from all areas. Before turning to the results if may be worthwhile to consider the interpretation to be given these audience measures.

The average local market audience for all 56 stations was 334,675; the average total audience over the 35 stations for which it was available was 741,817. These are figures for "seven day average of total hours tuned 6 p.m. - 1 a.m. by all persons aged 2 and over". Thus, for example, in the case of CFRN in Edmonton a market audience of 369,200 implies that each of the 523,480 residents of Edmonton watches the station, approximately 0.7 hours per evening (369,200/523,480).

4.4.1 Television Station Local Market Audience

The results of the estimation of the determinants of television station audience size over a sample of 56 stations, using local market audience data, are shown in Table 4.1. The estimated equation accounts for 72 percent of the variation in size of local market audience achieved by a station. Local market audience includes only viewers within the local CMA and excludes viewers in all other areas. All estimated co-efficients with the exception of the constant term are statistically significant at the 95 percent level of confidence.

The "handicap" variables consist of seven mutually exclusive categories, i.e., any particular station can fall in one, and only one, of these categories. Therefore the audience for each type of station can be viewed as having three components - some constant or absolute number of viewers accruing to any station plus some share of potential audience less some negative share of potential audience according to its category. For example, Table 4.1 shows an American over-the-air station can be expected to attract an audience of 27,693 (statistically insignificant from zero) plus 4.26 times potential audience less a handicap of 2.67 times potential audience. In other words, over-the-air U.S. stations can expect a market audience of some constant amount plus a net of 1.59 times potential audience. Over-the-air non-local Canadian stations, on the other hand, attract only the constant amount plus an almost negligible .03 times potential audience. The net share of potential audience attracted by stations available in Canadian markets via cable-only is extremely small amounting to .40 times potential in the case of U.S. stations plus .27 times potential in the case of non-local Canadian stations.

The net shares of potential audience attracted by local Canadian stations are much larger than those of non-local Canadian stations and cable-only U.S. stations. In the strongest market position are CTV affiliates which attract a net 3.04 times poten-

Table 4.1

REGRESSION RESULTS: TELEVISION STATION

LOCAL MARKET AUDIENCE, 1975

Independent Variables:		Size of Coefficient (t-statistic)	
Constant		27,693	(.53)
(POP/N)	Potential audience	4.26	(8.57)**
(POP/N)(OU)	Over-the-air U.S.	-2.67	(4.24)**
(POP/N)(OC)	Over-the-air non-local Canadian	-4.23	(2.38)**
(POP/N)(CU)	Cable-only U.S.	-3.86	(7.04)**
(PUP/N)(CC)	Cable-only non-local Canadian	-3.99	(4.21)**
(POP/N)(CB)	Local CBC owned or affiliated	-1.62	(2.89)**
(PUP/N)(CT)	Local CTV affiliated	-1.22	(1.97)**
(POP/N)(IN)	Local Canadian independent	-3.00	(4.44)**
Dependent variable: market audience		Mean = 334,675	
n = number of stations		56	
R²		.72	

  * Significant at the 90 percent level of confidence.
 ** Significant at the 95 percent level of confidence.

Table 4.2

REGRESSION RESULTS: TELEVISION STATION

TOTAL AUDIENCE, 1975

Independent Variables:		Size of Coefficient (t-statistic)	
Constant		241,779	(2.12)**
(POP/N)	Potential audience	6.67	(7.18)**
(PUP/N)(CB)	Local CBC owned or affiliated	-3.78	(3.66)**
(POP/N)(CT)	Local CTV affiliated	-3.01	(2.65)**
(PUP/N)(IN)	Local Canadian independent	-5.42	(4.39)**
Dependent variable: total audience		Mean = 741,817	
n = number of stations		35	
R²		.66	

  * Significant at the 90 percent level of confidence.
 ** Significant at the 95 percent level of confidence.

tial viewers. CBC owned and affiliated stations trail slightly at 2.64 times potential. Local Canadian independent stations, including Global and TVA affiliates, however, attract only a net 1.26 times potential audience, smaller by .33 than U.S. stations available over-the-air.

For an example of what these estimates mean, consider the Edmonton market. There are four stations with one percent or more of total prime-time CMA audience: CFRN a CTV affiliate, CBXT a CBC station, CITV a local independent Canadian station and KXLY a cable-only American station based in Spokane, Washington. With an Edmonton population of 523,480 and four stations the potential audience available to each is 523,480/4 or approximately 131,000. Since the constant term was not estimated to be significantly different from zero it may be ignored and the audience for each of these stations calculated using only the net share values estimated above. Using our regression equation we would estimate an audience of approximately 393,000 for CFRN, the CTV affiliate (3.04 x 131,000). The actual audience was 369,200.

In the case of CBXT, the CBC station net audience share value leads to an estimated audience of (2.64 times potential 131,000) approximately 346,000. (Actual audience 239,400.) The estimated audience of CITV, the Canadian independent is (1.26 times potential 131,000) approximately 165,000. (Actual audience 277,000). For KXLY, the cable-only U.S. station the estimate is (.40 times potential 131,000) approximately 52,400. KXLY's actual audience was only 9,640 because at this stage cable-television was available to only parts of Edmonton and, since it offered only one U.S. channel, had a low penetration rate.

4.4.2 Total Audience

The findings on the relative attractiveness of CTV, CBC, and independent station programming are corroborated by the results of an analysis of the determinants of total audience. Total audience differs from local market audience in that it includes all viewers wherever they reside as opposed to only those living in the station's Census Metropolitan Area. Data on total audience was gathered for only the 35 Canadian stations broadcasting from one of the major markets covered in this study. Accordingly, variables for U.S. and non-local Canadian over-the-air stations and for cable-only U.S. and Canadian stations were eliminated from equation 4 (see Appendix 4.1).

The results are shown in Table 4.2. The estimated equation accounts for 66 percent of the variation in total audience achieved by a station. All estimated co-efficients, including the constant term (241,779) are significant at the 95 percent level of confidence.[5]

Total audience of a typical station represents a capture of 6.67 times potential audience within the station's CMA less a "handicap" ranging from 5.42 times potential in the case of Canadian independents to 3.78 times potential and 3.01 times potential for CBC and CTV stations respectively. The net capture of potential audience ranges from 1.25 times potential for independents to 2.91 times potential for CBC owned and affiliated stations and 3.66 times potential for CTV affiliates.

These findings indicate that, whether the measure is local market audience or total station audience, CTV affiliates attract the largest audiences in the leading markets in Canada. CBC owned and affiliated stations trail modestly in ability to attract viewers with independents at a distinct competitive disadvantage.

4.5 CONCLUSIONS

Audience is a significant economic variable in the television industry because, as we have argued above, what television stations produce and sell is exposure to an audience. The ability of stations to attract viewers plays an important role in determining the prices they are able to charge advertisers as well as total revenues and profits.

The results adduced in this chapter demonstrate that ownership, or more precisely network-affiliation, is an important determinant of television station audience size. Aside from some constant number of viewers common to all stations, CTV affiliates attract within their CMA 3.04 times potential viewers where the latter is defined to be the population of the CMA divided by the number of stations. CBC owned and affiliated stations attract 2.64 times potential; local Canadian independents, including Global; and TVA affliates attract only 1.26 times potential.

The choice, balance, and diversity of program offerings of CTV, CBC, and Canadian independent stations are examined in detail in Chapter 11. The relative attractiveness of these offerings can, however, be inferred from the evidence in this chapter. CTV network offerings attract the largest proportion of potential viewers. The higher Canadian content and greater public affairs/ public service orientation of the CBC appear to have a discernable negative but notsevere impact on prime time audience size. In part this reflects the success of the CBC's strategy of including some American programming with high audience ratings in their prime time schedule. On the other hand, Canadian independent stations, unable to spread programming costs over a larger number of network stations, appear to be in a weak competitive position. Their limited ability to attract viewers may also reflect the start-up problems of the Global network.

American stations available over-the-air in leading markets are revealed to be strong competitors for audience attracting 1.59 times potential audience. These stations that are not subject to Canadian content and other regulatory constraints would clearly afford strong competition for television advertising revenue in major Canadian markets were it not for the non-deductability of such expenditures for Canadian income tax purposes. Canadian stations located outside major markets show little ability to attract viewers in those markets. This holds true whether they are received over-the-air or via cable-only. Presumably this weak showing results from the fact that in most cases such stations are only able to provide a duplication of either CTV or CBC network services.

The small audiences attracted by American stations available via cable-only contrast sharply with those of U.S. stations available over-the-air. This contrast demonstrates the magnitude of the competitive disadvantage resulting from the cable-only reception handicap. Part of this disadvantage stems from restriction to an audience of cable subscribers, a sub-set of all potential viewers; part from the ability of Canadian stations to schedule episodes of popular American series to appear prior to their appearance on competing American channels. The magnitude of the cable-only handicap has significant public policy implications. It suggests that permitting additional American (and non-local Canadian) channels to be carried by cable systems may have only minor effects in terms of fragmenting the audience of existing Canadian broadcasters in those markets.

Notes to Chapter 4

1. The Canadian Broadcasting Corporation concludes, "There is no evidence that, in general, people who become cable viewers, and who are hence able to avail themselves of the additional channels that cable TV brings, spend any more time watching television than they did before." Cable TV and Audience Fragmentation: At Year End 1971 (Ottawa: Canadian Broadcasting Corporation, Research Department, 1972).

2. The most significant timing problems occur when the city from which signals originate is in a different time zone from that of the city in which they are received. For example, the "Tonight Show" which is broadcast at 11:30 local time in the U.S. appears at 10:30 in certain Eastern Canadian markets, at 11:30 in other Canadian cities and at 12:30 in Edmonton and Calgary because of importation across time zone boundaries.

3. The expected Canadian content handicap arises from the basic economies of program production versus purchase discussed in Chapter 11. The problem is that a programming expenditure of a certain sum must cover full costs in the case of a Canadian production, but it need only amount to a small proportion of the total cost when an American program is purchased. Therefore, stations with higher Canadian content, but similar over-

all programming expenditures, will be presenting offerings
with much lower production value per segment.

4. Two excellent sources to which the interested reader is directed are: Jan Stewart, Understanding Econometrics (London:
Hutchinson & Co. Ltd., 1976); and M.D. Intriligator, Econometric Models, Techniques and Applications (Englewood Cliffs,
N.J.: Prentice-Hall, 1978).

5. This increase in magnitude, and the statistical significance
of the constant term is to be expected because of the lack of
any measure of potential audience for areas outside the station's Census Metropolitan Area.

Appendix 4.1

TELEVISION STATION AUDIENCE SIZE: MODEL SPECIFICATION

The model used to estimate the determinants of television station audience size attempts to capture the principal aspects of the discussion in the text.[1] First, the model makes a station's audience size depend on the number of potential viewers in its market and on the total number (including cable) of competing signals it faces. Second, the model allows for differences in the physical location of stations distinguishing between local stations, Canadian stations located in distant markets and U.S. stations. Canadian stations located in distant markets and American stations are further differentiated according to whether they are available over-the-air or via cable-only. Finally, the model allows for differences in the network affiliation of local Canadian stations.

If all television stations in a market broadcast from the same location, have similar reception availability, and have access to the same program materials, they should achieve the same audience size. The audience size achieved by each such station can be expected to vary in direct proportion to the potential audience available to it.

If AUD is the prime time audience achieved by the station, N the number of stations in the market, and POP the population in the market,

$$AUD = a_0 + a_1(POP/N) \tag{1}$$

If $a_0 = 0$ and $a_1 = .50$, in a four station market with 2000 homes the audience of each station would be 250.

If one or more of these four stations does not broadcast from the local area it may be handicapped in attracting viewers. Such a station may be either a Canadian station located in a distant market but available over the air or a U.S. station available over the air. Even though they are available over the air, and regardless of network affiliation, stations which do not broadcast from the local market may face some handicap in attracting viewers. These may result from an inability to tailor program content to local tastes, scheduling problems which result in many offerings being seen first on local stations, or simply impaired reception because of distance.

Consider the case where one of the stations is an American channel available over the air. If the reduction in audience a station experiences as a result of being a U.S. over-the-air channel does not affect the audience of its competitors,

$$AUD = a_0 + a_1(POP/N) + a_2(POP/N)(OU) \tag{2}$$

where OU is a variable taking the value 1 if a station is a U.S. over-the-air channel and zero otherwise. According to this equation, the audience reduction of an over-the-air U.S. station varies according to the audience a station would have attained had it had no handicap.

In our example, if the audience of a U.S. over-the-air station is smaller than that of a typical Canadian station located in the market by the amount $a_2 = -.20$, the audience in this market of such a station would decline by $(-.20)(500)$ or 100 viewers. Each typical Canadian station would continue to attract an audience of 250 but the U.S. over-the-air station would attract only 150 viewers.

Canadian stations not located in the local market, but available over the air can be included in the model in a parallel fashion using a variable OC taking on a value of 1 for such a station and zero otherwise.

Certain of the stations that do not broadcast locally face an additional handicap in that they are available only to cable subscribers, a sub-set of the total market. The model can be generalized to treat the cable-only handicap of both U.S. stations and distant Canadian stations by defining variables CU and CC which take on the value 1 for a station falling in the respective category, zero otherwise.

$$AUD = a_0 + a_1(POP/N) + a_2(POP/N)(OU)$$
$$+ a_3(POP/N)(OC) + a_4(POP/N)(CU)$$
$$+ a_5(POP/N)(CC) \tag{3}$$

Local stations, although they do not face the handicaps imposed by an out-of-market location or limitation to an audience of cable-subscribers, are not by any means equally situated regarding ability to attract audience. They offer different types of programming which have various degrees of attractiveness to potential viewers. If each station's programming were completely individualized it would, of course, be impossible to categorize and hence to analyze along this dimension. Fortunately, there is some degree of commonality in program offerings, principally as a result of network affiliation. Local television stations, if they broadcast in the English language will, with the exception of a few independent stations, be affiliated with either the CBC or CTV networks. French language stations may be either CBC affiliates, independents, or TVA affiliates. CBC and CTV each offer a venue of programs which are identifiable and distinct from that offered by independents and TVA affiliates. If the programming of either of the major networks is relatively less attractive than the programming offered by independents and TVA affiliates, then the affiliates of this network will be handicapped in attracting audiences. This handicap can be analyzed using the approach developed above to deal with non-local location and cable-only reception.

The program content of a particular station can be described using a variable taking on the value of 1 if it is in the category described (zero otherwise):

CBC = CBC owned or affiliate
CT = CTV affiliate
IN = Local Canadian independent station (including affiliates of Global and TVA networks).

When the program offerings of local stations are distinguished in this way, and non-local location and cable-only reception are taken into account, an estimating equation of the following form results.

$$AUD = a_0 + a_1(POP/N) + a_2(POP/N)(OU)$$
$$+ a_3(POP/N)(OC) + a_4(POP/N)(CU)$$
$$+ a_5(POP/N)(CC) + a_6(POP/N)(CB)$$
$$+ a_7(POP/N)(CT) + a_8(POP/N)(IN)$$

$$(4)$$

Note to Appendix 4.1

1. For a somewhat similar approach, used to estimate program rates for television time see Stanley M. Beson, The Value of Television Time and the Prospects for New Stations (RAND Corp.: Santa Monica, Cal., 1973).

Appendix 4.2

TELEVISION STATION AUDIENCE SIZE: THE DATA

Once a market's population is known, the principal data problems arise in determining which U.S. and non-local Canadian stations should be considered as competitors for audience share. All
non-local stations must then be classified as to their availability over-the-air or via cable only. Finally, the network affiliation of local stations must be identified.

The Census Metropolitan Area (CMA), as defined by Statistics
Canada, was used to define each market area. The 1974 population
of each Census Metropolitan Area was obtained from BBM Coverage
and Circulation Report: Television.[1]

Following the methodology developed in Chapter 3, the number
of stations to be included in the market as competitors for audience share was determined by including all stations with one percent or more of the total prime-time CMA audience. Local market
audience for each station was measured by seven day average of
total hours tuned 6:00 p.m. to 1 a.m. by all persons two years of
age and over living in the station's CMA. Total audience for each
station was based on the corresponding data for all markets in
which the station was received. Audience information was obtained
from BBM Coverage and Circulation Report: Television.[2]

It was possible to decide whether American stations and non-
local Canadian stations were available over-the-air or via cable-
only on the basis of information in the CBC report, Cable TV and
Audience Fragmentation at Year End 1971.[3] A station was classified as over-the-air if the proportion of off-the-air viewing of
the station in the market CMA is 50 percent or more of the proportion of all viewing of the station in the market CMA.

The network affiliation of local stations was obtained from
the CRTC catalogue of cable television systems in Canada[4] sup-
plemented as required by unpublished data on program categorization supplied by the CRTC Economic Planning and Analysis
Branch.[5]

Notes to Appendix 4.2

1. Bureau of Broadcast Measurement,BBM Coverage and Circulation
    Report: Television October 28 - November 10, 1974 (Toronto:
    BBM, 1974).

2. Ibid.

3. Canadian Broadcasting Corporation, Cable TV and Audience Fragmentation: At Year End 1971 (Ottawa: CBC Research, 1972).

4. Canadian Radio-Television Commission, Cable Television Systems in Canada, (Ottawa: Information Canada, 1975).

5. CRTC categorization of programs September 29, 1974 - September 27, 1975, unpublished data supplied by CRTC Planning and Analysis Branch, Ottawa.

Chapter 5

The Pricing of Television Commercial Time

The industrial organization structure-conduct-performance paradigm argues that the conduct (or behaviour) of firms in an industry is largely dependent on the market structure, including the ownership structure, of the industry. Market conduct includes pricing behaviour, product strategies such as differentiation via advertising or research and development, and strategies to limit competition. In this chapter we concentrate on an examination of pricing behaviour in the television industry. The purpose of the analysis is to identify, and measure the impact of, the various factors, including elements of market structure, affecting the pricing of 30 second prime time television commercials.

5.1 TELEVISION ADVERTISING RATES

The price of a 30 second prime time television commercial may appear to be a simple concept, but actually there are two ways of looking at this price, depending on what one thinks is being priced. Is the advertiser buying 30 seconds of air time on a television station or is he buying a certain number of audience exposures to his commercial message? If the former, then the simple dollar price attached to the 30 second commercial is the relevant variable. If the latter, then some price per thousand viewers should be considered. Since analysis of each of these prices promises to yield its own insights both are examined in this chapter.

The relationship between ownership structure and pricing behaviour is of primary interest in this study but ownership structure cannot be treated in isolation. The complex interrelationship between advertising rates and audience sizes must be properly treated. The impact of factors such as market concentration, population, and income levels must be considered. Finally, ownership structure, both in terms of group ownership and cross-ownership arrangements can be brought into the picture.

5.1.1   The Competitive Position of the Firm

A firm's competitive position in the markets in which it operates can clearly be expected to influence its pricing behaviour.
A television station's audience, both in its local CMA and elsewhere, as well as its share of total market revenues, all provide
indications of this competitive position.

Since advertisers are concerned with the purchase of audience
exposures to their message increases in audience size can be expected to exert an important influence in raising the price of
television commercial time. This follows, however, only so long
as the dependent variable is the price of a 30 second commercial.
When the price variable is re-defined on a price per thousand audience exposure basis, audience is eliminated as an explanatory
variable.

Another factor complicating the role of audience size is the
possibility that all audience exposures may not be of equal value
to advertisers. Consideration of demographic factors such as age
and sex is beyond the scope of this study, but it is possible to
consider separately the role of audience drawn from within the
station's local CMA as opposed to audience drawn from other areas.
Separate examination of local market audience, audience outside
the local market, and total audience provides some insight into
the nature of the demand function firms face in the television
industry, specifically in respect to the importance advertisers
place on targetting their advertising to a station's local CMA.

A television station's share of total market revenue provides
another indication of its competitive position. Whether a large
revenue share should be expected to be associated with higher or
lower prices is not entirely clear however. One possibility is
that stations with large shares of total market revenue should be
considered to be in a strong market position on that account and
therefore be able to extract higher prices. Alternatively, at-
taining and maintaining a large market share may call for strong
competitive tactics, amongst them the offering of reduced rates on
commercials.

5.1.2   Local Market Characteristics

Certain local market characteristics such as market population, average income levels, and the degree of seller concentration are elements of market structure common to all competitors in
that market. Population in a station's market area provides one
measure of potential audience or of total market size. Since
commercial time must be sold prior to the time of broadcast, advertising rates may be influenced by such a measure of potential
audience.

The income level of a station's audience is also of concern
to advertisers. Increases in the income level of the audience

increase buying power and can be expected to increase the rates which can be charged for commercial time.

In the analysis of market concentration the traditional industrial organization theory should apply. Markets characterized by a small number of firms and a high concentration of television advertising sales revenue would be expected to exhibit prices higher than the competitive norm because of the market power wielded by each of the leading sellers. Even if there is no formal collusion in the setting of advertising rates, when television advertising revenues are concentrated in a few hands firms become much more interdependent. They become less willing to cut prices or otherwise compete vigorously for advertising customers because of their recognition that such actions harm their rivals and may stimulate retaliatory competitive responses. Under such conditions, all the leading firms may be worse off than if they follow parallel strategies.

5.1.3 Ownership Structure

When the analysis of the setting of advertising rates is conducted on a market-by-market basis, there are two ways of looking at ownership structure. The first is to consider only the pattern of ownership within the local market, i.e., whether two television stations in the market are owned by a group owner or whether a local television station is cross-owned by the owners of a local newspaper or radio station. The second is to examine the implications for the local market of the pattern of ownership of the broadcasting industry across Canada, i.e., whether a television station in the market is owned by a group owner with another television station anywhere in Canada or whether a local television station is cross-owned by the owners of a newspaper or radio station anywhere in Canada. (Refer to Tables 3.1 to 3.15 in Chapter 3.)

Consider first group ownership (television/television) using a market based definition of ownership structure. Multiple holdings of television stations in a single market would serve to reduce the number of competitors for the television advertising dollar in the local market. This could be expected to increase the interdependence of the remaining stations and to produce a tendency toward higher advertising rates. In actual fact, regulatory constraints imposed by the CRTC have tended to make group ownership at the local market level uncommon.

It is, however, still possible that group ownership considered on a nation-wide basis may affect pricing behaviour. The question becomes this: if groups are restricted to one television station per market, and hence cannot affect concentration in individual markets, what influence can group ownership have on advertising rates? One possibility is that such ownership (other things being equal) reduces the cost of collusion and hence increases its likelihood. This would happen if group ownership in-

creased the probability that two firms operating in any given market would also compete in some other market. If collusion is more
worthwhile where is applies to more than one market, or if firms
pair off as competitors in a number of markets, then advertising
rates in excess of the competitive norm should be expected.

Alternatively, if important groups of advertisers consider
viewers in different cities to be close substitutes for one another then the market power of stations in a particular city may be
limited by the potential competition offered by stations in alternative cities. Groups, since they could influence the level of
advertising rates in a number of cities simultaneously, could
possibly have an enhanced ability to raise prices. This effect
appears problematic since, as a general proposition, broadening
the definition of the relevant market serves to reduce concentration. It seems unlikely that collusion which is unprofitable in a
narrowly-defined market would become profitable in a more broadly-
defined one.

In addition to the potential effects of group ownership,
cross-ownership arrangements among newspapers, television stations, and radio stations may influence pricing. Take the case
where one firm owns both a newspaper and a television station in
the same market (CMA). If the demand for television time depends
in part on the price of newspaper space and the demand for newspaper space depends in part on the price of television time then
such a firm will alter the price of both newspaper space and television time from the price that would have been obtained had they
been priced independently.[1] If these effects were very important, the distinction between the market for television time and
newspaper advertising space would blur and a single market for
advertising time and space would result. On the other hand, if
newspapers, radio, and television are not close substitutes then
definitions implying separate markets become useful and cross-
ownership effects of this type become less important.

If radio, television and newspapers all compete for the advertising dollar and the single market definition becomes more appropriate, cross-ownership amongst media may increase interdependence amongst firms and facilitate collusive pricing arrangements.
The same demand (and cost) interrelationships that were operative
in pricing decisions internal to the firm apply at the inter-firm
level. The gains from conscious parallel action or collusion are
determined by the nature and extent of the demand (and) cost interrelationships. If the demand for, say, TV commercial time were
elastic but the supply inelastic, the effect of collusion or conscious parallelism would be minimal.

The same reasoning applies to cross-holdings involving both
radio and TV stations in the same market. Of course, the empirical significance of these effects must be examined. As Peterman
states:

One cannot simply assert that effects exist. They may not because the interrelations in demand (and costs) are not worth taking into account, collusion may not be feasible or worthwhile, and the joint firm may have little influence on the supply of radio audiences, so that joint ownership has no independent effect on TV rates.[2]

Cross-ownership defined on a nation-wide basis should also be examined. Where advertising buyers consider audiences in one city to be a close substitute for those in another, and coverage in one medium to be a close substitute for coverage in another, cross-owned holdings in television, radio and newspapers may influence the setting of advertising rates in the manner discussed above. Conglomerate ownership of a television station should not, however, be expected to influence advertising rate-setting.

5.2 MODEL SPECIFICATION

There has been some controversy over the most appropriate approach to modeling the determinants of television and radio advertising rates.[3] This controversy hinges on the nature of the relationship between audience and advertising rates. Owen, who has argued that advertising rates and audience size are codetermined, examines advertising rates as a function of only area population, income, and various joint ownership variables.[4] Lago argues that effects of advertising rates on audience size in the same time period (via programming expenditures) can be expected to be minor.[5] But even if there is significant interdependency, he argues it can be dealt with by using a two-stage least squares model that acknowledges joint dependency but is able to produce an unbiased estimate of the audience-advertising rate relationship. The analysis that follows adopts Lago's approach.

As in subsequent chapters, a formal structural model that examines separately demand and supply side influences and permits the determination of equilibrium values is not used. It is assumed that firms in the television industry are profit maximizers and the equations which are fitted are reduced forms that are completely specified and adequately describe the firm's competitive position in the market, local market characteristics and ownership structure. Since reduced form equations are used, the effects of joint ownership revealed with the use of dummy variables can be attributed to either demand or cost interdependence in the underlying (assumed) structural model. The choice of functional form depends on both a priori reasoning and "goodness of fit" statistics. In keeping with the structure-conduct-performance paradigm we argue that, in the main, causality runs from structure to conduct.

First, audience estimates are prepared using the methodology developed in the analysis of television station audience size but allowing for the possible influence on audience size of various

additional determinants of advertising rates. These fitted audience values are then used as one of the independent variables in
the estimation of advertising rates. A detailed explanation of
the development of the television advertising rate model is contained in Appendix 5.1.

5.3   THE DATA

The nature of the data used to test the models developed in
Appendix 5.1, and the sources of this data are described in Appendix 5.2.

5.4   EMPIRICAL EVIDENCE

Two distinct and different approaches have been adopted for
the analysis of ownership structure viz. market defined variables
and nationally defined variables. Accordingly, the empirical evidence on the determinants of television advertising rates is presented separately for each approach.

5.4.1   Empirical Evidence Using Market Defined Ownership
        Variables

The results of the estimation of television station advertising rates using market defined ownership variables are shown in
Table 5.1. The results of estimating the 30 second advertising
rate model and the advertising rate per 10,000 audience hours
model are shown in equations 1 and 2 respectively in the table.

These and subsequent tables do not present estimated coefficients for all variables included on an a priori basis in the
models developed in Appendix 5.1. Such results were estimated but
the application of goodness to fit tests to these preliminary results influenced the final functional form estimated. Variables
found to be both statistically insignificant and lacking in explanatory power (in the sense of adding to R^2) have been excluded.
Results presented in all cases reflect the estimation of a functional form reflecting the elimination of such variables one after
another on a step-by-step basis. The average price of a 30 second
commercial, considering all 34 stations in our sample, was
$271.50. Equation 1 accounts for 65 percent of the variation be-
tween stations in 30 second ad rates. The constant term is statistically insignificant. The average rate per 10,000 hours of
market audience was $9.02. Equation 2 accounts for 56 percent of
the variation in these rates. The constant term, significant at
the 95 percent level, represents a flat rate per 10,000 audience
hours of $16.79.

In equation 1, contrary to expectations, market audience
proved to be statistically insignificant. Possibly, in this case,
population provides a better proxy for potential audience. Audience outside the station's Census Metropolitan Area, on the other
hand, was significant at the 90 percent level of confidence. An

Table 5.1

TELEVISION STATION ADVERTISING RATE ESTIMATES
USING MARKET DEFINED OWNERSHIP VARIABLES[1]

Dependent Variable	Eqn. 1 Rate	Eqn. 2 Rate per 10,000 hrs. market audience
Independent Variables:		
Constant	-204.99 (1.03)**	16.79 (3.14)
Fitted market audience	.0000032 (.03)	
AUDE (audience outside CMA)	.00021 (1.66)*	
SHR (revenue share)	152.07 (2.11)**	-12.74 (2.50)**
HRF (revenue Herfindahl)		15.77 (2.66)**
POP (population)	.000076 (2.47)**	-.0000014 (1.81)*
INC (income)	.059 (1.32)	
TRM (TV/radio in market)	78.41 (1.96)**	
TNM (TV/news in market)	-83.79 (1.45)	-4.68 (1.93)*
CBC (CBC owned)		-14.11 (3.34)**
CCBC (competes with CBC owned)		-5.95 (1.54)
Mean value of dependent variable	271.50	9.02
R^2	.65	.56
n = no. of stations	34	34

[1] Figures in parentheses are t-statistics.

* Significant at the 90 percent level of confidence.
** Significant at the 95 percent level of confidence.

increase of 1,000 in this extra-market audience led to a $0.21 increase in ad rates.[6]   Since advertising rates per ten thousand are based on market audience the latter cannot be used as an explanatory variable in equation 2.   As would be expected, there was no evidence of a statistical relationship between the size of a station's audience outside its local CMA and its ad rate per 10,000 market audience.

The market share results in equation 1 indicate that an increase of 10 percentage points in a firm's share of total market revenue is associated with a $15.21 increase in its ad rate.   On the other hand, this same increase is associated in equation 2 with a $1.27 reduction in rate per 10,000 hours of market audience.   These results indicate that while firms with large market shares are able to charge higher rates for commercial time, possibly as a result of increased market power, these increases are not fully commensurate with the increased audiences they are able to offer advertisers.

Population, presumably as a measure of potential audience, was significant in equation 1 at the 95 percent level of confidence with an increase of 100,000 in market population leading to a $7.60 increase in ad rate.   The corresponding increase in ad rates per 10,000 was $0.14 (significant at the 90 percent level). The level of per capita income was not significant in either equation.

Market concentration, as measured by the revenue Herfindahl index, had no discernable influence on the pricing of 30 second ad rates in equation 1.   In equation 2, however, a 10 percentage point increase in the Herfindahl index was found to be associated with a $1.58 increase in ad rates, on a per 10,000 hours market audience basis.   This is evidence that firms operating in concentrated markets tend, either as a result of collusion or merely recognized interdependence, to charge more on a per 10,000 basis than firms operating in less concentrated markets.   This finding, it should be noted, is in no way contradictory to the positive influence which market share was found to have on rates for 30 second spots. Even although stations with large shares of total market revenue, and audience, may cut their rates per 10,000 viewers they should still be expected to have higher rates per <u>unit of time</u>.

Television/radio cross-ownership at the local market level was the only statistically significant element of ownership structure.   The results in Table 5.1 indicate that television stations whose owners also operate a radio station in the same market charge $78.41 more for a 30 second spot commercial. This would be equivalent to a 29 percent increase on the average rate of $271.50.

Television/radio cross-ownership in the local market does not appear to affect the setting of rates per 10,000 hours of market

audience. Television/newspaper cross-ownership in the local market contributes to a $4.68 (significant at the 90 percent level)
rate reduction however. Similarly, the results show that CBC
owned stations quote rates $14.11 lower than others (95 percent
level of confidence). Both of these are large effects in relation
to the mean value of $9.02 per 10,000 hours of market audience.

5.4.2 Empirical Evidence Using Nationally Defined Ownership Variables

Nationally defined ownership variables reflect group and
cross-ownership patterns for Canada as a whole. Ownership of, for
example, a newspaper anywhere in Canada, by the owners of a local
television station serves to qualify that station as television/
newspaper cross-owned. Redefinition of the ownership variables in
this fashion focuses the analysis on the pricing implications of
national ownership patterns rather than local market ownership
patterns. The results of the estimation of television station advertising rates using these nationally defined ownership variables
are shown in Table 5.2. The results of estimating the 30 second
ad rate model and the ad rate per 10,000 model are shown in equations 1 and 2 respectively in the table. Reported results reflect
reestimation after variables with little explanatory power and insignificant coefficients have been eliminated.

Equation 1 accounts for 73 percent of the variation in 30
second ad rates. All variables reported were significant at the
95 percent level of confidence. The constant term implies a flat
ad rate of minus $744.34.

Examination of the estimated results for equation 2 reveals
that it was able to account for 62 percent of the variation in ad
rate per 10,000 hours of market audience. The constant term is
insignificant.

In equation 1 it is estimated that an increment of 1,000 to a
television station's total audience in all markets is associated
with a $0.15 increase in its 30 second ad rate. Therefore, using
Edmonton as an example, the 130,000 difference in audience between
CFRN (369,200) and CBXT (239,400) would account for an ad rate
differential of $19.50. Again, audience cannot be included as an
explanatory variable in equation 2.

When nationally defined ownership variables are incorporated
in the analysis there is no evidence of any statistical association between a firm's share of market revenues and its price for a
prime time 30 second commercial. In equation 2, however, firms
with larger shares of market revenue again tend to quote lower
rates per 10,000. A 10 percentage point increase in revenue share
was associated with an $0.89 decrease in ad rate per 10,000 (sig-
nificant at the 90 percent level) where the average rate per
10,000 hours of market audience is $9.02.

Table 5.2

TELEVISION STATION ADVERTISING RATE ESTIMATES
USING NATIONALLY DEFINED OWNERSHIP VARIABLES[1]

Dependent Variable	Eqn. 1 Rate per 30 second ad	Eqn. 2 Rate per 10,000 hrs. market audience
Independent Variables:		
Constant	−744.34 (2.88)**	.23 (.02)
Fitted total audience	.00015 (5.50)**	
SHR (revenue share)		−8.95 (1.75)*
HRF (revenue Herfindahl)	267.17 (2.63)**	11.79 (2.03)**
INC (income)	.15 (3.27)**	.0038 (1.89)*
TT (national TV/TV group)		−4.92 (1.98)**
TR (national TV/radio)	220.63 (3.91)**	
TN (national TV/news-paper)	−209.20 (3.05)**	
CBC (CBC owned)		−10.10 (3.99)**
CON (conglomerate owner)		−10.88 (3.42)**
CTR (competes with national TV/radio)	128.38 (2.20)**	
CTN (competes with national TV/news-paper)	−164.79 (2.10)**	
CCON (competes with conglomerate)		−6.23 (2.64)**
Mean value of dependent variable	271.50	9.02
R^2	.73	.62
n = no. of stations	34	34

[1] Figures in parentheses are t-statistics.

* Significant at the 90 percent level of confidence.
** Significant at the 95 percent level of confidence.

Each $1,000 increment in average income is estimated in equa-
tion 1 to result in a $150 increase in the 30 second ad rate. The
corresponding increase in ad rates on a per 10,000 basis, in equation 2, is $3.80 (significant at the 90 percent level). A 10 per-
centage point increase in the revenue Herfindahl index is associated with an increase of $26.72 in each firm's 30 second ad
rate. The corresponding increase in the case of ad rates on a per
10,000 basis is $1.18.

In equation 1, as was the case when market-defined variables
were used, television/radio and television/newspaper cross-ownership result in large changes in ad rates. Again the effects are
roughly equal in size but opposite in direction with television/
radio cross-ownership estimated to increase 30 second ad rates by
$220.63 and television/newspaper cross-ownership to decrease them
by $209.20. Both changes should be viewed in relation to the
$271.50 average rate. What is new and revealing in the equation 1
results is the demonstrated effect which these cross-ownership
arrangements have on the pricing policy of competitors. Stations
competing with a television/radio cross-owned station were found
to charge an estimated $128.38 more on that account (all other
things being equal) while those competing with a television/news-
paper cross-owned station were forced to reduce their ad rate by
an estimated $164.79.

Four ownership structure variables are significant - all at
the 95 percent level of confidence. All are associated with decreases in ad rates per 10,000. The results indicate that membership in a national television/television group results in a $4.92
reduction in a station's per 10,000 ad rate; that CBC ownership
reduces ad rates by $10.10 and conglomerate ownership by $10.88.
Stations forced to compete with a conglomerate-owned television
station suffered reduction of $6.23 in their ad rates per 10,000.

5.5 CONCLUSIONS

One of the basic premises of industrial organization theory
is that the pricing decision of firms are affected by the economic
conditions of the markets in which they operate. In this chapter
we have tried to identify such links between market structure and
market conduct in the case of Canadian television.[7] The elements of market structure considered fall in three classes: (1)
characteristics of the local market for television advertising
such as market concentration, market population, and average incomes, (2) description of the individual firm's place within that
market such as its audience size and share of market revenue, and
(3) ownership structure both from the local market and national
perspective. Each of these classes will be discussed in turn.

5.5.1 Local Market Characteristics

The most significant finding here has been the identification
of the important role which market concentration plays in the

pricing of television commercial time. Our results indicate that an increment of .10 in the market revenue Herfindahl index is associated with a $26.70 increase in 30 second ad rates (mean $271.50) or an increase of from $1.20 to $1.60 in the 30 second ad rate per 10,000 hours of market audience (mean $9.02). The magnitude of this influence can be better appreciated by recalling that revenue based Herfindahl indices in major Canadian markets vary from .272 in the case of Toronto to 1 in a city such as London – see Table 3.25 in Chapter 3. Thirty second commercials would therefore be priced some $175 higher and rates per 10,000 would be some $8.50 to $11.00 higher in the latter two cities, as compared to Toronto, on account of market concentration alone (holding all other factors constant).

Population is of statistical significance in the setting of ad rates only in an analysis using market-defined ownership variables. There a 100,000 increment in the population of the station's Census Metropolitan Area is associated with a $7.60 increase in the 30 second spot rate and a $0.14 decrease in the rate per 10,000 (see Table 5.1). These changes are minor in relation to the respective mean values but are consistent in that a larger population, with a larger potential audience, should be expected to permit the charging of a higher rate per unit of time whereas cost savings or competitive conditions in such a city may simultaneously be resulting in reductions in rates expressed on a per 10,000 basis.

As predicted on theoretical grounds, advertising rates both on a 30 second and on a per 10,000 basis are directly related to levels of market income. The effects are best demonstrated in the analysis using nationally-defined ownership variables where a $1,000 increment in average income results in rate increases of $150 in the ad rate and $3.80 in the rate per 10,000 hours of market audience (Table 5.2).

5.5.2   The Competitive Position of the Firm

The effects of audience size on a station's pricing policy could only be evaluated in the case of 30 second spot rates as audience size is itself involved in the calculation of rates per 10,000. When nationally-defined ownership variables were used the expected direct relationship between a station's audience size and its ad rate was supported with an increment of 1000 in a station's total audience adding $0.15 to its rate. In the analysis using market defined ownership variables, an increase of 1000 in a station's audience outside its CMA led to a $0.21 ad rate increase, but audience within the CMA had no discernable influence. Overall, these results should probably be viewed as an affirmation of audience size as a statistically significant but minor determinant of advertising rates.

The theoretical analysis above suggested that a firm's share of total market revenue might provide a useful supplementary measure of its market power, in which case firms with higher market shares could be expected to charge higher ad rates. Our results do not support this in that higher shares of market revenue are associated with lower ad rates when these are expressed on a per audience exposure basis. Stations with higher shares do seem to charge more for a 30 second spot ($15.20 per 10 percentage points of share in the market-defined ownership variable analysis), but on a per 10,000 basis they are lower by from $0.90 to $1.27 per 10 percentage points of share. This is consistent with an elastic demand for televison advertising spots priced on a per audience exposure basis. Charging less per audience exposure results in higher revenue.

5.5.3 Ownership Structure

The implications of ownership structure on the setting of advertising rates has been analyzed using two different sets of ownership variables. Proper interpretation of the results of this analysis requires careful consideration of the nature of and relationship between these two characterizations of ownership structure. On the one hand, the two sets of variables constitute two different prisms, or windows on reality – the one focused on the local market, the other on the ownership structure of the nationwide Canadian television industry. On the other hand, since the market definition ownership variables are a sub-set of the nationally defined ownership variables, the results of the two analyses should to some extent be interrelated and mutually supportive. But it must not be forgotten that once the analysis shifts away from the area of local market competition to a national market a quite different interpretation may be required to explain seemingly similar results.

Consider, for example, the case of group holdings of television stations. The results above have indicated that stations owned by such groups charge rates per 10,000 some $4.92 lower than firms with a single television station (Table 5.2). This finding was, of course, based on nationally defined ownership variables since television/television group holdings at the local market level have been forestalled by regulation. It supports the conclusions of the theoretical analysis that there was very little reason to suspect that national television groups would be able to exact higher advertising rates than owners of single stations. But note that it would be completely fallacious to similarly conclude that group holdings at the local market level would serve to reduce advertising rates. Group holdings at the local market level would increase market concentration and our findings above on market concentration show unequivocally that higher concentration is associated with much higher advertising rates.

Conglomerate ownership was examined only in the national analysis since the concept is of little interest at the local market level. Although there is little reason to expect conglomerate ownership to affect advertising rates in either an upward or a downward direction, our results indicate that it is associated with a $10.88 decrease in rate per 10,000 and, furthermore, that stations competing with conglomerate owned stations are forced to reduce rates per 10,000 by $6.23 (Table 5.2). This is strong evidence that conglomerate-owned television stations are active price competitors.

Similarly, our results demonstrate that publicly owned CBC stations charge lower rates per 10,000 than do privately owned stations (by $10.10 in the national analysis; by $14.11 in the local market analysis).

Although television/radio cross-ownership has no discernible influence on ad rate on a per 10,000 basis, it is associated with higher 30 second rates in both the market analysis ($78) and the national analysis ($220). Since the average 30 second rate for all 34 stations is only $271.50 increases of this magnitude are evidence of significant deviations from the competitive norm. Further support is provided by the findings that the presence of a national television/radio group owned station in the market is associated with an increase of $128 in the 30 second ad rate of each competing station.

On the other hand, ownership by a television/newspaper group has an equally large but negative effect on 30 second ad rates, reducing them by $209 for a national group. Stations competing against members of national television/newspaper groups are in turn forced to cut 30 second ad rates by $165. In addition, there is evidence that local television/newspaper cross-ownership is associated with a $4.68 lowering of rates on a per 10,000 basis.

Overall, when we focus on the ownership structure of the local market itself, CBC ownership, television/newspaper cross-ownership, and competition against a CBC station are all associated with lower advertising rates on a per 10,000 basis. In the case of 30 second rates, local television/radio groups are associated with increases; local television newspaper groups with decreases.

When variables are defined on the basis of national rather than local market, ownership patterns, television/radio cross-ownership, and competition with such stations is associated with higher 30 second ad rates while the converse is true for television/newspaper cross-ownership. Membership in a television/television group, CBC ownership, conglomerate ownership, or competition with a conglomerate owned station are all associated with decreases in advertising rates on a per 10,000 audience hours basis.

Notes to Chapter 5

1. This result depends on the demand curves faced by the firm in each market being less than perfectly elastic and the interdependencies of demand being of a significant magnitude. See R.H. Coase, "Monopoly Pricing With Interrelated Costs and Demands", Economica, Vol. 13, N.S. 278, November 1946, pp. 278-294.

2. John L. Peterman, "Concentration of Control and the Price of Television Time," American Economic Review, Vol. LXI, No. 2, May 1971, p. 76.

3. For a complete review or this debate see Walter S. Baer, Henry Geller, Joseph A. Grundfest, and Karen B. Possner, Concentration of Mass Media Ownership: Assessing the State of Current Knowledge (Santa Monica, Cal.: RAND, 1974).

4. Bruce M. Owen, "Empirical Results on the Price Effects of Joint Ownership in the Mass Media" (Stanford: Stanford University Research Centre in Economic Growth, Memorandum No. 93, November 1969), as cited by Armando M. Lago, "The Price Effects of Joint Mass Communication Media Ownership," Antitrust Bulletin, Vol. 16, 1971, p. 790.

5. See Lago, op. cit., pp. 789-813.

6. Total audience, the sum of market audience and extra-market audience, was also investigated as an explanatory variable. It proved to be statistically insignificant.

7. The results here may be usefully contrasted with Lago's American study (op. cit., p. 803) which found that only income, population, and audience size were statistically significant - ownership structure variables were unimportant.

Appendix 5.1

THE PRICING OF TELEVISION COMMERCIAL TIME: MODEL SPECIFICATION

In order to allow for possible joint dependency between audience size and advertising rates audience estimates were prepared first using the methodology developed in the analysis of television station audience size but allowing for the possible influence on audience size of various additional determinants of advertising rates. Format variables were included for only CBC network (owned or affiliated), CTV network, and independent since no U.S. or cable-only stations were included in the advertising rate data analyzed.

These fitted audience values were then used as one of the independent variables in the estimation of advertising rates. When ownership variables are defined on a market-by-market basis the model used to estimate these fitted audience values (FAUD) takes the form:

$$
\begin{aligned}
FAUD = {}& a_0 + a_1(POP/N) + a_2(POP/N)(CB) \\
& + a_3(POP/N)(CT) + a_4(POP/N)(CN) + a_5 AUDE \\
& + a_6 SHR + a_7 POP + a_8 INC + a_9 HRF \\
& + a_{10} TTM + a_{11} TRM + a_{12} TNM + a_{13} CBC \\
& + a_{14} CTTM + a_{15} CTRM + a_{16} CTNM + a_{17} CCBC
\end{aligned}
\tag{1}
$$

Where ownership structure is defined on a nation-wide basis (see below) the appropriate changes in the group and cross-ownership variables in equation (1) must be made. The additional variables are defined below.

This approach allows for interdependency between advertising rates and audience size. Since N includes all stations with one percent or more of local prime time audience it also permits consideration in the audience equation of the audience fragmentation effect of U.S. and non-local Canadian stations, while permitting the exclusion of such stations, where they are not competitors for advertising revenue in the local market, from measures of competitive conditions and ownership structure in that market. Since such stations are not based in the markets under consideration data on them is also excluded in the estimation of advertising rates, revenues, and profits.

A5.1   COMPETITIVE POSITION OF THE FIRM

The use of FAUD as a determinant of advertising rates implies a target-audience approach by buyers of commercial time since only the local market audience affects advertising rates. Many television stations have large numbers of viewers outside their local CMA. The role these extra viewers play in rate setting can be examined by including in the model a variable AUDE representing the excess of total viewing audience of a station over its audience in the local CMA.

A firm's share (SHR) of aggregate television station revenues (or audience) for the market provides an additional indication of its competitive position. Where RATE is the price of a 30 second commercial in prime time, FAUD is the <u>fitted</u> value of the average prime time local market audience achieved by the station, AUDE is the station's audience drawn outside its local CMA, and SHR is its share of overall television advertising revenues in the market, then

$$RATE = a_1 + a_1FAUD + a_2AUDE + a_3SHR \qquad (2)$$

A5.2 LOCAL MARKET CHARACTERISTICS

The Herfindahl summary index (HRF) measures concentration for a market as the sum of squared firm sizes. THese sizes can be measured as a proportion of either total television station revenue, or audience, for the market depending on which is felt to provide a better indicator of competitive conditions. Since the Herfindahl index is calculated at the market level, a single value of the measure will apply to all firms in a given market. This value reflects the extent of interdependence amongst firms and the consequent expected effect on the general level of advertising rates.

Population of the market area (POP) in which the station operates may have an influence on advertising rates which is separate from its effect on audience size. Increases in the level of average incomes in the market area can be expected to increase advertising rates. Incorporating these structural variable describing local market characteristics results in

$$RATE = a_0 + a_1FAUD + a_2AUDE + a_3SHR$$
$$+ a_4POP + a_5INC + a_6HRF \qquad (3)$$

A5.3 OWNERSHIP STRUCTURE

The analysis above has indicated that, while continuing to consider advertising rate setting at the local market level, ownership structure can be considered at two different levels. The first, presumably more relevant for the purposes of economic analysis, is to examine ownership structue only in terms of the individual local market. Information on the ownership structure of individual markets permits evaluation of the degree of competition for audiences and for advertising revenues in these markets. The second approach would examine the competitive implications of ownership structure where group ownership and cross-ownership holdings located anywhere in Canada are considered. Once ownership structure is incorporated into the rate-setting model both approaches can be accommodated through an appropriate transformation of the structure variables.

Four principal dimensions of ownership structure can be identified. Consider first the definition of these on the individual
local market basis. Instances where two television stations in a
given market have a common owner (television/television in market
denoted as TTM) can be identified.[1] Ownership of a television
station by the owner of a radio station in the same market (tele-
vision/radio in market denoted as TRM) is one potentially important category of cross-ownership; ownership of a television station by the owners of a newspaper in the same market (television/
newspaper in market denoted as TNM) is another. Public ownership
(denoted CBC) can also be identified.

Since these variations in ownership structure influence the
degree of competition they can be expected to influence not only
the market behaviour of the firms characterized by multi and
cross-ownership, but the market behaviour of their competitors
also. This requires the inclusion of variables representing competition from a firm owning two television stations in a market
CTTM, compeititon from a firm owning both a radio station and a
television station in the market CTRM, and competition from a firm
owning both a television station and a newspaper in the market
CTNM. Competition with a CBC-owned station can be denoted by
CCBC.

Analysis of ownership structure on this market-by-market basis results in an estimating equation of the form

$$\begin{aligned}
RATE = {} & a_0 + a_1 FAUD + a_2 AUDE + a_3 SHR \\
& + a_4 POP + a_5 INC + a_6 HRF + a_7 TTM \\
& + a_8 TRM + a_9 TNM + a_{10} CBC + a_{11} CTTM \\
& + a_{12} CTRM + a_{13} CTNM + a_{14} CCBC
\end{aligned} \qquad (4)$$

Each of the ownership structure characteristics is described by a
dummy variable taking the value 1 when the characteristic applies
in the case of the firm at hand, zero otherwise.

When the dependent variable is re-defined as advertising
rate per 10,000 hours local market audience (ADPM) the estimating
equation becomes

$$\begin{aligned}
ADPM = {} & a_0 + a_1 AUDE + a_2 SHR + a_3 POP \\
& + a_4 INC + a_5 HRF + a_6 TTM + a_7 TRM \\
& + a_8 TNM + a_9 CBC + a_{10} CTTM + a_{11} CTRM \\
& + a_{12} CTNM + a_{13} CCBC
\end{aligned} \qquad (5)$$

In the alternative, Canada-wide, specification of ownership pattern, analysis can proceed in a similar fashion once the
appropriate changes in variable definition have been made. Ownership of a television station by a concern which owns another television station anywhere in Canada is denoted by TT. Ownership of
a radio station anywhere in Canada by the owner of a particular
television station is denoted by TR. Cross-ownership of a newspaper anywhere in Canada by a television station's owners is de-

noted TN. Competition by a television station with stations of
the above types is denoted by CTT, CTR, and CTN respectively.

CBC ownership and competition with a CBC station continue to be denoted as CBC and CCBC respectively. Ownership of a
television station by a conglomerate (i.e., a firm with important
non-broadcasting assets) can be denoted CON; while competition
with such a station is denoted CCON.

The estimating equation in the case of a Canada-wide
specification of the ownership pattern remain in the same form as
equations (4) and (5) with the appropriate re-specification of
ownership structure variables.

Note to Appendix 5.1

1. Regulatory constraints cause this to be an empty set in nearly
all markets.

Appendix 5.2

THE PRICING OF TELEVISION COMMERCIAL TIME: THE DATA

Estimates of the determinants of television advertising rates were based on data for a sample of 34 stations. Twenty-one of the original 56 stations used in the estimation of audience size were omitted in the estimation of advertising rates because they were located outside the markets being studied. One had no quoted ad rate. Ownership pattern and other market structure characteristics of the local market cannot plausibly be used to examine the determinants of the advertising rates of non-local stations.

The advertising rates used were obtained from the April 1975 issue of Canadian Advertising Rates and Data, a monthly trade publication prepared for the use of advertisers.[1] It contains data on station facilities, contract terms, and advertising rates for commercials at various times as well as some program rates. The advertising rates used in this chapter are those for 30 second commercials during prime time. Prime time varies slightly among stations, but typically it is the four evening hours between 7 p.m. to 11 p.m.

The use of quoted price may be open to some criticism in that it is not clear what proportion of transactions take place at quoted prices. Since information on actual transaction prices is unavailable, data on quoted prices - which would serve as a point of departure in any negotiation - provide the best available measure of the prices at which commercial time sales take place. It time sales take place. It is assumed that deviations between actual and quoted prices for a given station are small relative to price variations amongst stations and that the deviations are uncorrelated with any explanatory variables.

Two audience measures were used for each station. Both were obtained from BBM Coverage and Circulation Report: Television.[2] The station's audience within the CMA was measured, as explained in section 5.2 in the text, by the seven day average of total hours tuned by all persons two years of age and over living in the station's CMA. The station's total audience in all markets was measured by the corresponding seven day average of total hours tuned by all persons two years of age and over living in all areas served by the station.

Income data for each local market CMA was obtained from the Financial Post Survey of Markets 1974/75.[3]

The Herfindahl index of market concentration and the market share measure of firm dominance were developed on the basis of both revenue and audience measures. The construction of these measures was examined in detail in Chapter 4. Herfindahl indices on a revenue basis for each market were supplied by the Department

of Communications. Use of revenue share data for regression purposes was permitted on an in-house basis under the supervision of
the federal Department of Communications' staff. Alternative Herfindahl index and market share calculations based on audience data
were prepared using each station's audience in its local CMA.

A detailed description of the pattern of ownership of television and radio stations in Canada, as at September 1975, is contained in the appendices of Volume II of the Report of the CRTC
Ownership Study Group.[4] Supplementary information on newspaper
cross-ownership was supplied by the Ownership Study Group. Identification of the ownership of CBC stations was made from the
CRTC's List of Broadcasting Stations in Canada.[5]

Notes to Appendix 5.2

1. Canadian Advertising Rates and Data (Toronto: Maclean Hunter,
   April 1975).

2. Bureau of Broadcast Measurement, BBM Coverage and Circulation
   Report: Television, October 28-November 10, 1974 (Toronto:
   BBM, 1974).

3. Financial Post Survey of Markets 1974/75 (Toronto: Maclean
   Hunter, 1974).

4. Canadian Radio-Television and Telecommunications Commission,
   The Contemporary Status of Ownership and the Level of Concen-
   tration in the Canadian Broadcasting Industry, Background
   Study II to the Report of the Ownership Study Group (Ottawa:
   CRTC, 1978).

5. Canadian Radio-Television Commission, List of Broadcasting
   Stations in Canada (Ottawa: Information Canada, 1975).

Chapter 6

Radio Station Audience Size

The similarities in the fundamental economics of the television and radio industries permit the adoption of a common analy-
tical approach. Firms in the radio industry engage in both competition for audience and price competition. The effect of radio
industry market structure on these dimensions of market conduct as
well as the influence of both market structure and market conduct
on the economic performance of the industry can be analyzed using
the basic methodology developed in the examination of the television industry.

In this chapter we examine the influence of market structure
on the size of audience obtained by a radio station. These audience size results are then used in subsequent chapters to analyze
the pricing of 30 second prime time radio commercials and radio
station profits and price-cost margins.

One of the prime determinants of the audience size of a particular radio station is the number of potential listeners or the
population, in the station's market. For a given standard of programming, the larger the potential audience of a station, the
larger the actual audience size that can be expected. Audience
size is not a direct function of population, however, for as the
market grows additional radio stations can be expected to start
up. Additional choice may somewhat expand the total audience to
all radio stations, but the principal effect of new entrants can
be expected to be a fragmentation of the audience of existing
stations.

This type of audience fragmentation analysis is based on the
premise that, other things being equal, the audience of a particular radio station is a function of the population in the station's
market divided by the number of stations. But all stations do not
compete on equal terms. The principal differences relate to non-
local location, whether AM or FM, and the type of programming.

The first of these, non-local stations, may place an important limit on the ability of a station to reach audiences. Radio
stations strive for local identification, and this can be expected

to hamper them in competing for audience in areas outside their prime market. Signal reception may also be impaired in such areas. Analysis of the role of non-local stations is complicated by two factors: exactly which non-local stations should be considered to be competitors in the local market; and how the competitive weakness of non-local stations influences the audience size of their stronger local competitors.

In Chapter 3 we decided that a radio station located outside the local CMA should be considered to be a competitor for audience so long as it was a Canadian station and over 50 percent of its total hours tuned were from the local CMA, or if between 20 and 50 percent, that the local CMA be the station's largest market. The benefit which local stations reap as a result of the out-of-market location of competitors is examined by including an out-of-market "recapture" variable in the analysis. This variable is formulated on the hypothesis that some portion of the "handicap" is recaptured and that the amount recaptured is allocated equally amongst all other radio stations in the local market. Estimation of the coefficient of this recapture variable permits measurement of the extent to which the audience losses of non-local radio stations are recaptured by other stations. This, coupled with the direct estimation of the audience losses involved, provides a more complete analysis of the role of non-local stations as competitors for audience share in the local market.

The second major difference in a radio station's ability to compete for audience share relates to whether it broadcasts on the AM or FM band. In most markets, stations which broadcast on the FM band are at a competitive disadvantage as compared to AM stations because of the historically lower levels of listener acceptability of FM broadcasting (not technical quality) and the restriction of some receiving sets to AM only.

The third difference between stations relates to the nature of their programming. Program formats that are investigated include minority language, classical music, jazz, progressive, news, adult, multi-format (variety of music), contemporary, pop music, middle-of-the-road, country and western, easy listening, and hit music (including top 40 and gold music). But it should be noted at the outset that analysis of the influence of program format on radio station audience size is not a straightforward task. Certain formats such as minority language (i.e., English language in Montreal or Quebec City; language other than English elsewhere) may be of limited overall appeal, but may draw strongly from certain market sub-segments. Also the audience of stations broadcast in popular formats may be split by competition from other stations offering the same format. Finally, the various formats may have quite different impacts depending upon whether the station involved broadcasts on the AM or FM band.

6.1 MODEL SPECIFICATION

All the principal elements of the above discussion are re-flected in the model developed in Appendix 6.1 to estimate the determinants of radio station audience size.

6.2 THE DATA

The nature and sources of the data used to test this model are described in Appendix 6.2

6.3 EMPIRICAL RESULTS

The determinants of radio station audience size were esti-mated in three different ways. In the first, data for all sta-tions competing in our 16 sample markets were included in the analysis. In the second, data for only AM stations located in the local CMA were included. In the third, only FM stations located in the local CMA were included. This procedure provides a general picture as well as permitting attention to be paid to the pro-gramming differences between AM and FM stations. The results for these approaches are shown in equations 1, 2, and 3 respectively of Table 6.1

In the discussion of results that follows all co-efficients are significant at the 95 percent level unless otherwise indi-cated.

6.3.1 Audience Size: All Stations

The inclusion of all stations competing in the 16 markets yields a sample of 160 stations with an average market audience of 953,451. Radio audience data, it should be noted, is based on "total hours tuned, Monday through Sunday by all persons age 2 and over," i.e., a weekly total of hours tuned rather than a daily average as in the case of television. Again, if we consider for example CFRN-AM in Edmonton, a market audience of 603,400 in a city with a population of 523,480, implies that each person lis-tens to approximately 1.2 hours each week to this station.

The estimated equation 1 accounts for 66 percent of the var-iation in size of local market audience achieved by all stations. The constant term is -338,181. On top of this flat amount each station can be expected to attract, additional weekly hours amounting to 22.94 times its share of potential audience. In the ten-station Edmonton market this would account for additional audience of 22.94 times (523,480/10) or approximately 1,200,000.

Out-of-market location is estimated to cost a station 13.99 times potential audience. As in Besen's work, the coefficient on the "recapture" variable is larger than that of the associated "handicap" variable.[1] Here, the recapture of the audience loss of out-of-market stations is estimated at 24.59 times potential audience. Again, in the Edmonton market these coefficients would imply an audience handicap of 730,000 for each non-local station with a recapture associated with each amounting to 1,290,000. This recapture would be shared equally by all 10 competing stations.

These estimates for all stations confirm the well-known FM handicap and estimate its importance at 7.79 times potential audience (for Edmonton this would amount to 410,000 weekly hours tuned). In the case of program formats, both middle-of-the-road and classical were associated with increases in weekly hours tuned of 11.91 and 11.04 times potential audience respectively. Country and western and jazz were associated with decreases of 9.12 and 7.98 times potential audience respectively. In the Edmonton market, these estimates indicate an advantage of 623,465 and 577,922 weekly audience hours for middle-of-the-road and classical music respectively. Country and western and jazz handicaps for such a market would be 477,414 and 417,737 weekly audience hours respectively.

In an equally interesting finding, all other formats including minority language, progressive, news, adult, multi-format (variety of music[2]), contemporary, pop, easy listening, and hit music (including top 40 and gold music) had no statistically significant association with radio station audience size when all 160 stations were considered. This last should not be interpreted as an evaluation of the relative popularity of these formats, but rather, we would suggest, as an indicator of the extent to which the overall pattern of format choices by various stations has been adapted to provide compatability with the wishes of consumers. Stations directed at minority audience segments (such as minority language, adult, and news stations) achieve satisfactory audiences, popular formats appear to be sufficiently duplicated that they confer no competitive advantage.

6.3.2 Audience Size: AM Stations

Equation 2 of Table 6.1 was estimated using data for the 56 AM stations physically located in the 16 markets covered by this study. It is able to explain 64 percent of the variation in AM radio station audience size. Average weekly hours for all 56 AM stations was 1,722,920. The constant term of is not statistically significant. The basic audience share of each station amounts to 28.60 times potential audience.

The out-of-market "handicap" cannot be estimated for this sample since it excludes such stations. There is no evidence of a statistically significant recapture of the out-of-market stations' lost audience.

The strong positive influence of middle-of-the-road format and the negative influence of country and western format, 11.41 times potential audience and -13.21 times potential audience re-

Table 6.1

REGRESSION RESULTS: RADIO STATION AUDIENCE SIZE[1]

Dependent Variable		Eqn. 1 Market Audience For All Stations	Eqn. 2 Market Audience For AM Stations	Eqn. 3 Market Audience For FM Stations
Independent Variables:				
Constant		-338,181(2.52)**	-395,086(1.36)	-335,020(2.05)**
(POP/N)	Potential Audience	22.94(10.91)**	28.60(6.80)**	13.40(7.56)**
(POP/N)J	Out-of market	-13.99(2.92)**		
(POP/N) $\frac{NJ-J}{N-1}$	Out-of-market recapture	24.59(2.70)**		70.70(6.55)**
(POP/N)FM	FM station	-7.79(4.07)**		
(POP/N)MOR	Middle of the road	11.91(4.94)**	11.41(2.90)**	-13.90(2.30)**
(POP/N)C&W	Country and Western	-9.12(3.14)**	-13.21(2.03)**	
(POP/N)MIN	Minority language		-10.93(2.18)**	6.57(3.46)**
(POP/N)CL	Classical	11.04(2.40)**		13.42(4.72)**
(POP/N)PR	Progressive			-7.32(4.07)**
(POP/N)JZ	Jazz	-7.98(3.89)**		-20.03(3.71)**
Mean Value of Dependent Variable		953,451	1,722,920	1,134,650
R^2		.66	.64	.92
n = no. of stations[2]		160	56	26

[1] The figures in parentheses are t-statistics; all others are regression coefficients.
[2] The sample of AM stations used to estimate equation 2, and of FM stations used to estimate equation 3, was restricted to those stations which were physically located in the sixteen major markets covered by this study. These are the same samples as those used in Chapter 7.

* Significant at the 90 percent level.
** Significant at the 95 percent level.

spectively, are found again here. In addition, there is evidence that, although minority language broadcasting may have no detrimental effect when all stations are considered, that it strongly detracts from the audience of an AM station, i.e., to the extent of 10.93 times potential audience. Other formats have no statistically significant influence.

In the Edmonton market where potential audience is (523,480/10) these estimates would translate into a basic audience share per station of 1,497,153, a middle-of-the-road format advantage of 597,291, and country and western and minority language handicaps of 691,517 and 572,164 weekly hours respectively.

6.3.3 Audience Size: FM Stations

Equation 3 of Table 6.1 presents the results of an estimation of the audience model for the sample of 26 FM stations physically located in the 16 sample markets. This equation has a much better fit than the estimates for all stations and for AM stations only; it is able to account for 92 percent of the variation in the audience size of FM radio stations. Mean audience size for all FM stations is 1,134,650 weekly hours.

The constant for each FM station is estimated at -355,020 weekly hours. To this is added an increment equal to 13.40 times potential audience. There is a recapture from out-of-market stations amounting to an estimated 70.70 times potential audience.

In contrast to the results for AM stations, middle-of-the-road format decreased audiences by 13.90 while minority language broadcasting increased them by 6.57 times potential audience respectively. The results for classical and jazz formats accord with results noted in the all-stations analysis. Classical music is associated with an increase in weekly hours tuned of 13.42 times potential audience and jazz with a decrease of 20.02 times potential audience. The progressive format is associated with an audience loss of 7.32 times potential audience. Other formats have no statistically significant impact.

For the Edmonton market, as in the previous sections, these estimates can be translated to a weekly audience hours basis by multiplying each coefficient by 52,348.

6.4 CONCLUSIONS

In the radio industry, as in the television industry, audience is a significant economic variable since what is sold is an audience for commercial messages. The ability of radio stations to attract listeners can be expected to play an important role in determining the prices they are able to charge advertisers as well as total revenues and profits.

The audience model developed in Appendix 6.1 was able to satisfactorily account for about two-thirds of the variation in audience size for samples including all 160 stations competing in the 16 sample markets and all locally located AM stations. The model provided the best fit in the case of locally located FM stations, accounting for 92 percent of the variation in audience size of such stations.

In both the all-station and FM sample the constant term accounted for a large number of weekly hours tuned (-338,000 and -355,000 respectively). Additional audience hours as a function of potential audience (CMA population divided by the number of radio stations) is largest for AM stations (28.60 times) and smallest for FM stations (13.40 times) with all station value at an intermediate level (22.94).

Out-of-market stations suffer substantial audience handicap (estimated at 13.99 times potential audience). It is estimated that losses of out-of-market stations are more than fully recaptured by local stations.

The all-station sample reveals FM stations to suffer an audience handicap of 7.79 times potential audience. This finding is supported by the data on average weekly hours tuned of the 56 local AM stations at 1,723,000 as compared to an average of 1,135,000 weekly hours for the 26 local FM stations.

Comparison of the three estimated equations reveals that the results for the all-station sample conceal some interesting differences between AM and FM stations. For example, while middle-of-the-road format is associated in the all-station sample with a large audience increment of 11.91 times potential audience, it seems that this results solely from the experience of AM stations with a similar 11.41 times potential audience figure. For FM stations a middle-of-the-road format is associated with a sharp decrease in audience size of 13.90 times potential. Minority language is associated with a 10.93 times potential audience drop in weekly hours tuned if an AM station, but if the station broadcasts on the FM band the associated change is an increase of 6.57 times potential audience. The results for the all-station sample appear to net out these effects for a statistically insignificant result.

In other cases comparison of the three estimates serves to identify the type of station involved in a particular finding in the all station sample. Most of these are very predictable however. For example the country and western -9.12 times potential audience effect observed in the all-station sample can be traced to AM stations (with a -13.21 times potential estimate). The positive influence of a classical music format on audience size for all stations (11.04 times potential) derives from the 13.42 times potential estimate for FM stations. Similarly, the negative influence of a jazz format in the all station sample (-7.98 times

potential) can be traced to the -20.02 times potential estimate
for FM stations.

Notes to Chapter 6

1.   Stanley M. Beson, The Value of Television Time and the Pros-
     pects for New Stations, (Santa Monica, Cal.:   RAND, 1973).

2.   Gold music consists of records (singles or albums) that have
     sold one million or 100,000 copies respectively.

Appendix 6.1

RADIO STATION AUDIENCE SIZE: MODEL SPECIFICATION

The model used to estimate the determinants of radio station
audience size attempts to reflect all the principal elements of
the discussion in the text. First, the model makes a station's
audience size depend on a number of potential listeners in its
market and on the total number (including major stations in neigh-
bouring cities) of competing signals it faces. It distinguishes
between AM stations and FM stations and treats stations deriving
major portions of their revenue in the local market differently
from stations based in distant markets. Finally, the model allows
for differences in the programming format of all stations.

For a given standard of programming, the audience size
achieved by a radio station can be expected to vary in direct
proportion to the potential audience available. If all stations
in a market have the same transmission and reception characteristics, and have access to the same program materials, they should
achieve the same audience size. If AUD is the total audience, in
terms of hours tuned achieved by the station in the local CMA, N
the number of stations in the market, and POP the population in
the market,

$$AUD = a_0 + a_1(POP/N) \qquad\qquad (1)$$

Certain stations received in the local market may be based in
another city. Such stations may be handicapped in attracting com-
mence either because of the strong identification of their programming with the distant local market, or by simple reception
difficulties. If the reduction in audience station experiences as
a result of this distance handicap does not affect the audience of
its competitors,

$$AUD = a_0 + a_1(POP/N) + a_2(POP/N)J \qquad\qquad (2)$$

where J is a variable taking on the value 1 if a station is located outside the local CMA but inside Canada and either (a) over
50 percent of the total hours turned for all persons two years of
age and over to the station are from the local CMA, or (b) 20 percent to 50 percent of the total hours tuned to the station are
from the local CMA and the local CMA is the single largest market
for this station. In the case of local stations, J takes on the
value zero. Non-local stations which are unable to satisfy either
criterion (a) or criterion (b) are excluded from the market.

According to equation (2), the effect of non-local location
varies according to the audience a station would have attained had
it had no handicap. Alternatively, local radio stations may benefit from the distance handicap of their competitors. The simplest
hypothesis is that some portion of the handicap is captured and

that the amount captured is allocated equally amongst local radio stations. For example, if there were three stations in a market, one of them being a non-local station, and c_1 is the proportion of the distant station handicap captured by the local stations, then each of the two local radio stations would achieve an increase in audience equal to one-half $c_1 a_2 (POP/N)$. On the other hand, if there is one local station and two non-local stations the total available for capture would be $2c_1 a_2 (POP/N)$ which would be split $\frac{1}{2}$ $c_1 a_2 (POP/N)$ to the local station and $\frac{1}{4}c_1 a_2 (POP/N)$ to each of the non-local stations since each obtains half of the handicap loss of the other. The general estimating equation which results is

$$AUD = a_0 + a_1 (POP/N) + a_2 (POP/N)J + a_3 (POP/N) \left\{ \frac{NJ - J}{N - 1} \right\}^2 \tag{3}$$

where NJ is the number of non-local radio stations available in the market and c_1 is greater than zero.[1] The gain to a station resulting from a competitor's non-local location handicap is its share of the captured loss. With equal sharing, a station gains $1/(N-1)$ times the total amount captured from each non-local competitor. Each local radio station competes with NJ such competitors while each distant station competes with NJ-1.

The handicap a station faces as a result of broadcasting on the FM band can be treated using a variable FM which takes the value 1 if a station broadcasts on the FM band and a value zero if it broadcasts on the AM band. Inclusion of such a variable results in a model of the form

$$AUD = a_0 + a_1 (POP/N) + a_2 (POP/N)J + a_3 (POP/N) \left\{ \frac{NJ - J}{N - 1} \right\}^2 + a_4 (POP/N)FM \tag{4}$$

Stations offer different types of programming which have various degrees of attractiveness to potential listeners. Since each station's programming is much more individualized than is the case of television stations, analysis along this dimension is much richer in detail. Fortunately, program formats are not so individualized as to render statistical analysis impossible. Formats of all stations are categorized in broadcasting trade publications. Incorporation of the effect of format variables in the audience model requires definition of appropriate format handicap dummy variables. The format variables included and their coding are: contemporary (COT), pop (PO), middle-of-the-road (MOR), country and western (CW), easy listening (EL), hit music, top 40, gold music (HM), minority language (MIN), classical music (CL), jazz (JZ), progressive (PR), talk, information and news (NE), adult (AD), and multi format or variety of music (MU). When these variables are included the model takes the form

$$AUD = a_0 + a_1 (POP/N) + a_2 (POP/N)J + a_3 (POP/N) \left\{ \frac{NJ - J}{N - 1} \right\}^2 + a_4 (POP/N)FM$$

$$+ a_5(POP/N)COT + a_6(POP/N)PO + a_7(POP/N)MOR$$
$$+ a_8(POP/N)CW + a_9(POP/N)EL + a_{10}(POP/N)HM$$
$$+ a_{11}(POP/N)MIN + a_{12}(POP/N)CL + a_{13}(POP/N)JZ$$
$$+ a_{14}(POP/N)PR + a_{15}(POP/N)NE + a_{16}(POP/N)AD$$
$$+ a_{17}(POP/N)MU \tag{5}$$

The programming format of each station can be described using a variable taking on the value of 1 if it is in the category described and zero otherwise.

Note to Appendix 6.1

1. Beson in his estimation of the determinants of television program rates coupled recapture variables of this type with each of his recapture variables. He encountered difficulties, however, in developing reasonable coefficients for the recapture variables. Early specifications of our audience equations included recapture variables associated with each handicap variable but this proved to be a very poor specification since all recapture variables, with the exception of non-local location, were statistically insignificant and greatly reduced explanatory power of the overall mode. See Stanley M. Beson, The Value of Television Time and the Prospects for New Stations (Santa Monica, Cal.:   RAND, 1973).

Appendix 6.2

RADIO STATION AUDIENCE SIZE: DATA SPECIFICATION

Having defined the relevant market and determined market population, the principal data problems remaining arise in determining which station should be considered as competitors for audience
share. All stations must then be classified as to whether they
are local or out of market, AM or FM, minority language or not,
and CBC owned or affiliated or not. Finally, the programming format of all stations must be determined.

The Census Metropolitan Area as defined by Statistics Canada
was used to define each market area. The 1974 population of each
CMA was obtained from the BBM Coverage and Circulation Report:
Radio.[1]

Number of stations to be included in the market as competitors for audience share was determined by including all radio stations with one percent or more of the total CMA audience. Local
audience for each station was measured by total hours tuned, Monday through Sunday, in the market CMA by all persons two years of
age and over.[2] Total audience in all areas for each station was
measured by total hours tuned, Monday through Sunday, in all areas
by all persons two years and older. Audience information was obtained from the BBM Coverage and Circulation Report: Radio.[3]

CBC ownership and affiliation of radio stations was established using List of Broadcasting Stations in Canada.[4] Whether
a station broadcasts on the AM or FM band and whether it broadcasts a language other than that used by the majority of persons
living in the CMA, were both determined from Broadcaster, "Fall
'74 Directory: Radio Stations."[5] The same source also provided
information on the programming format of each of the radio stations.

Notes to Appendix 6.2

1. Bureau of Broadcast Measurement, BBM Coverage and Circulation
    Report: Radio, October 28-November 10, 1974 (Toronto: BBM,
    1974).

2. Data on prime time audience was available for stations based
    in the local market but not for other non-local stations.
    Since the latter compete for audience share it was necessary
    to use a measure, total hours tuned, which was available for
    both types.

3. Bureau of Broadcast Measurement, op. cit.

4. Canadian Radio Television Commission, List of Broadcasting Stations in Canada (Ottawa: Information Canada, 1975), pp. 1-3.

5. Broadcaster, "Fall '74 Directory: Radio Stations," November 1974.

Chapter 7

The Pricing of Radio Commercial Time

According to the structure-conduct-performance paradigm, the conduct of the firms in an industry is largerly dependent on the market structure, including the ownership structure, of the industry. In this chapter, we examine pricing conduct in the radio industry with a view to identifying, and measuring the impact of the various factors, including elements of ownership structure, affecting the pricing of 30 second prime-time radio commercials.

7.1 RADIO ADVERTISING RATES

Radio commercials lack the visual element of television commercials. Also, radio prime time is in the morning and afternoon commuting hours, while television prime time is the mid-evening hours. Nevertheless, the basic product which a radio station, like a television station, produces and sells is the exposure of an audience to commercial messages. Again, two viewpoints on pricing are possible depending upon whether the advertiser is considered to be buying 30 seconds of air-time on a radio station or a certain number of exposures to his commercial message. Since analysis of both alternatives promises to yield useful insights, this chapter examines the determinants of both the dollar price attached to the 30 second commercial as well as the price per 100,000 weekly hours of market audience.

The relationship between ownership structure and pricing behaviour is of primary importance in this study, but ownership structure in the radio industry cannot be treated in isolation. The interrelationships between audience size and advertising rates must be properly treated. The impact of local market characteristics such as market concentration, population, and income levels need to be considered. Finally, ownership structure, from both the local market and national viewpoints should be included.

7.1.1 The Competitive Position of the Firm

A firm's competitive position in the markets in which it operates can clearly be expected to influence its pricing behaviour. A radio station's audience, both in its local CMA and elsewhere,

as well as its share of total market revenues, all provide indications of this competitive position.

Since advertisers are concerned with the purchase of audience
exposures to their messages, increases in audience size can be expected to exert an important influence in raising the price of
radio commercial time. This follows, however, only so long as the
variable to be explained is the price of a 30 second commercial.
When the price variable is redefined on a price per 100,000 audience exposure basis, audience must be eliminated as an explanatory
variable.

Another factor complicating the role of audience size is the
possibility that all audience exposures may not be of equal value
to advertisers. Examination of the role of audience drawn from
within the station's local CMA as opposed to audience drawn from
other areas provides some insight into the nature of the demand
function firms face in the radio industry. Specifically, it provides information in regard to the importance advertisers place
on targeting their advertising to a station's local CMA.

A radio station's share of total market revenue provides another indication of its competitive position. Whether a large
revenue share should be expected to be associated with higher or
lower prices is not entirely clear however. One possibility is
that stations with large shares of total market revenue should be
considered to be in a strong market position on that account and
therefore be able to extract higher prices. Alternatively, at-
taining and maintaining a large market share may call for strong
competitive tactics, amongst them the offering of cut rates.

7.1.2 Local Market Characteristics

Certain local market characteristics such as market population, average income levels, and the degree of seller concentration are elements of market structure common to all competitors in
that market. Population in a station's market area provides one
measure of potential audience or total market size. Since commercial time must be sold prior to the time of broadcast, advertising
rates may be influenced by such a measure of potential audience.

The income level of a station's audience is also of concern
to advertisers. Increases in the income level of the audience increases buying power. If radio advertising is a normal good produced under condition of increasing cost, then higher incomes can
be expected to increase the rates which can be charged for commercial time.

In the analysis of market concentration, the traditional industrial organization theory should apply. Markets characterized
by a small number of firms and a high concentration of radio advertising sales revenue would be expected to exhibit prices higher
than the competitive norm because of the market power wielded by

each of the sellers. Even if there is no formal collusion in the
setting of advertising rates, when radio advertising revenues are
concentrated in a few hands firms become much more interdependent.
They become much more unwilling to cut prices or otherwise compete
vigorously for advertising customers because of their recognition
that such actions harm their rivals and may stimulate retaliatory
competitive responses.

7.1.3 Ownership Structure

When the analysis of the setting of advertising rates is conducted on a market-by-market basis, there are two ways of looking
at ownership structure. The first is to consider only the pattern
of ownership within the local market, i.e., whether two radio stations in the market are owned by a group owner or whether a local
radio station is cross-owned by the owners of a local newspaper or
television station. The second is to examine the implications for
the local market of the pattern of ownership of the broadcasting
industry across Canada, i.e., whether a radio station in the market is owned by a group owner with another radio station anywhere
in Canada or whether a local radio station is cross-owned by the
owners of a newspaper or television station anywhere in Canada.

Consider first group ownership (radio/radio) using a local
market (CMA) definition of ownership structure. Multiple holdings
of radio stations in a single market reduce the number of competitors for the radio advertising dollar in that market. This can be
expected to increase the interdependence of the remaining stations
and to produce a tendency toward higher advertising rates. In
contrast to the situation in television, group holdings at the local market level are common in the radio industry. Most of these
take the form of AM/FM "twins," a policy originally fostered by
the CRTC to ensure the economic viability of fledgling FM operations. The continued existence of these group holdings can be
expected to have an important influence on the pricing policies of
the radio industry.

Group ownership at the national level, where it does not affect the level of market concentration, can be expected to be a
much less important influence on pricing policy. It may, however,
reduce the cost of collusion and hence increase its likelihood or
it may be viewed as limiting potential competition offered by stations in alternative cities where important groups of advertisers
consider listeners in different cities to be close substitutes for
one another.

The analysis of cross-ownership arrangements between newspapers, television stations, and radio stations developed for the
case of television applies with equal force to the radio industry.
In the case where one firm owns both a newspaper and a radio station in the same market if significant interdependencies of demand
exist they will cause the firm to alter the price of both newspaper space and radio commercial time from the price which would

have been obtained had they been priced independently. The same reasoning applies to groups owning both radio and TV stations in the same market.

If radio, television, and newspapers all compete for the advertising dollar, cross-ownership amongst media may increase seller interdependence and facilitate collusive pricing arrangements. The gains from conscious parallel action or collusion are determined by the nature and extent of the demand and cost interrelationships. The empirical work in this chapter seeks to quantify the importance of these effects.

The influence of cross-ownership defined on a nation-wide basis must also be examined. Where advertising buyers consider audiences in one city to be a close substitute for those in another, and coverage in one medium to be a close substitute for coverage in another, cross-owned holdings in television, radio and newspapers located in different markets may influence the setting of advertising rates.

Some consideration should be given to the role of the publicly owned CBC radio network, Canada's largest. Prior to 1975 the CBC had been a full-fledged competitor for the radio advertising dollar but during 1975, the year that is analyzed, the CBC was implementing a policy decision to phase out commercial advertisements. Accordingly, CBC-owned stations were included in the analysis of the pricing of radio commercial time only as competitors for audience, not as competitors for advertising revenues.

7.2 MODEL SPECIFICATION

In order to allow for interdependency between radio advertising rates and audience size a two-stage least squares model is used. It acknowledges joint dependency, but is able to produce an unbiased estimate of the audience-advertising rate relationship. First, audience estimates are prepared using the methodology developed to analyze radio station audience size, but allowing for the possible influence on audience size of various additional determinants of advertising rates. Then, these fitted audience values are used as one of the independent variables in the estimation of advertising rates. A detailed explanation of the development of the radio advertising rate model is contained in Appendix 7.1.

7.3 THE DATA

The nature of the data used to test the models developed in Appendix 7.1, and the sources of this data are described in Appendix 7.2.

7.4 EMPIRICAL EVIDENCE

The use of local market ownership variables and nationally-defined ownership variables provide two completely different approaches to the question of ownership structure. Therefore, the empirical evidence on the determinants of radio station advertising rates is presented separately for each.

7.4.1 Empirical Evidence Using Market Defined Ownership Variables

The results of the estimation of radio station advertising rates using local market ownership variables are shown in Table 7.1. Separate AM (equations 1 and 3) and FM (equations 2 and 4) samples are used since there appear to be significant differences between the two types; for example, the average ad rate for a 30 second spot for all AM stations was $41.43 but for FM stations it was only $18.77.

The tables in this chapter do not present estimated coefficients for all variables included on an a priori basis in the models developed in Appendix 7.1. Variables found to be both statistically insignificant and lacking in explanatory power in preliminary estimates for these models have been excluded. Results presented in all cases report the estimation of a functional form reflecting the elimination of such variables one after another on a step-by-step basis. All estimated co-efficients are significant at the 95 percent level unless otherwise noted.

Equations 1 and 2 in Table 7.1 report estimates of the determinants of the price of a 30 second prime time radio commercial for AM stations and FM stations respectively. Equation 1 accounts for 84 percent of the variation in AM station advertising rates. The constant term of $43.34 is significant at the 90 percent level. Equation 2 accounts for 72 percent of the variation in FM station advertising rates. The constant term it is not statistically significant.

Equations 3 and 4 report on the determinants of advertising rates per unit of audience for AM stations and FM stations respectively. To provide a dependent variable of convenient magnitude the precise dependent variable used is advertising rate per 100,000 weekly hours of market audience. Thus, for example, in the case of CFRN-AM in Edmonton with an audience in the Edmonton CMA of 603,400 weekly hours and a 30 second ad rate of $34 the rate per 100,000 hours of market audience would be 34/6.034 or approximately $5.67. The average rate per 100,000 hours of market audience is $3.73 for all 56 AM stations and $2.57 for all 26 FM stations. Equation 3, is able to account for only 28 percent of the variation in AM ad rates per 100,000 hours market audience. This is a surprising result in view of the strong explanatory power in the case of the AM rate itself (equation 1). Clearly, in the case of AM radio stations, the approach developed here is much better at explaining the pricing of a unit of time than of an audience exposure. This is not the case for FM stations. Equation 4 is able to account for 73 percent of the variation in FM rates per 100,000 hours of market audience. The constant terms, 14.69

Table 7.1

REGRESSION RESULTS: RADIO STATION ADVERTISING RATE ESTIMATES
USING MARKET DEFINED OWNERSHIP VARIABLES

Dependent Variable	Eqn. 1 AM Rate [1]	Eqn. 2 FM Rate [1]	Eqn. 3 AM Rate per 100,000 weekly hours in a market audience	Eqn. 4 FM Rate per 100,000 weekly hours in a market audience
Independent Variables:				
Constant	43.34(1.77)*	9.51(1.65)	14.69(2.36)**	7.40(1.88)*
Fitted market audience	.000015(9.18)**	.000011(6.01)**		
SHR (revenue share)		-39.38(3.30)**	-5.30(1.64)	-8.96(4.99)**
HRF (revenue Herfindahl)	39.28(1.79)*	41.66(2.08)**	13.88(3.15)**	18.25(7.09)**
POP (population)	.0000055(1.47)			
INC (income)	-.012(2.06)**		-.0034(2.40)**	-.0018(2.01)*
RRM (radio/radio in market)	7.02(2.09)**		.87(.96)	
RNM (radio/news in market)	9.67(1.51)		1.22(.82)	1.69(1.82)*
CRTM (competes with radio/television in market)		-9.45(2.48)**		
CRNM (competes with radio/newspaper in market)	5.99(1.14)		1.08(1.01)	1.48(2.65)**
Mean Value of Dependent Variable	41.43	18.77	3.73	2.57
R^2	.84	.72	.28	.73
n[2]	56	26	56	26

[1] Per 30 second prime time commercial.
[2] Number of stations.

* Significant at the 90 percent level.
** Significant at the 95 percent level.

in equation 3 and 7.40 in equation 4, are statistically significant in both equations at the 95 and 90 percent levels respectively.

7.4.1.1 The Competitive Position of the Firm

The size of a radio station's audience in its local CMA is an
important influence on the advertising rates of both AM and FM
stations. Equation 1 in Table 7.1 shows an increase of 100,000
weekly hours of market audience to be associated with a $1.50 in-
crease in the AM ad rate. In equation 2 the corresponding effect
for FM stations is an increase of $1.10. Again, since advertising
rates per 100,000 hours of audience are based on market audience,
the latter cannot, of course, be used as an explanatory variable
in equations 3 and 4.

Results in all four equations provide strong support for a
target audience approach to the pricing of radio commercial time.
A radio station's audience drawn from outside its local CMA was
not found to be a significant factor in 30 second spot rates or
rates per 100,000 hours for either AM or FM stations.

There is no evidence that an AM station's share of total market revenue influences its pricing of advertising. In the case of
FM stations, increases in share of total market revenue are associated with large decreases in both 30 second ad rates (down $3.94
for a .10 increase in revenue share) and ad rates per 100,000
hours of market audience (down 90¢ for a similar 10 percent increase in revenue share). Rather than reflecting the results of a
struggle for market share these findings may result from cost
pressures on FM stations in very weak market positions. FM stations with very small shares of total market revenue may well be
at or below the break-even point and thereby be induced to charge
higher prices for commercial time than would otherwise be justified.

7.4.1.2 Local Market Characteristics

There is no evidence that the population of a station's local
CMA has any statistically significant influence on the advertising
rates of either AM or FM stations.

The influence of the level of market income is the reverse of
that postulated for a normal good; increased levels of market income are associated with decreases in radio advertising rates.
These effects are most pronounced in the case of AM radio where a
$1000 increase in income levels is associated with decreases of
$12.00 in the 30 second spot rate and $3.40 in the rate per
100,000 weekly hours of market audience. In FM, although there is
no evidence of an influence on the 30 second rate, a reduction of
$1.80 in rate per 100,000 weekly hours of market audience is in-
dicated. (This result is significant at the 90 percent level.)
These results indicate that radio time is considered to be worth

more in cities where income levels are low which is consistent
with radio advertising's being an inferior good. Possibly radio
is the most cost-effective method of reaching lower income audiences because of low newspaper readership rates and the high costs
of television advertising. If so, despite the lower purchasing
power of the audience involved, this type of comparative advantage
could put a premium on the price of radio commercial time in low
income areas.

All estimates in Table 7.1 point to the level of market concentration as the single most important influence on the pricing
of radio station commercial time. An increase of .10 in the revenue Herfindahl index for a market is associated with a $3.93 (90
percent confidence level) increase in the advertising rate of all
AM stations and a $4.17 increase in the advertising rate of all FM
stations based in that market. Compared to average ad rates of
$41.43 and $18.77 for AM and FM respectively, these are very
strong influences. The corresponding effect on advertising rates
per 100,000 weekly hours of market audience are $1.39 and $1.83.
Again compared to a mean AM value of $3.73 and a mean FM value of
$2.57 these are very large changes associated with increased
concentration.

7.4.1.3 Ownership Structure

While ownership of both a radio station and a television station was found to have exerted a significant upward influence on
television ad rates, there is no evidence that firms of this type
charge more for radio time. To the contrary, the evidence suggests that they are formidable competitors. FM stations that compete with local market radio/television group owned stations were
found to suffer a $9.45 reduction in their 30 second prime time ad
rate.

The postulated influence of radio/radio group ownership is
clearly evident in equation 1 where it results in an estimated
$7.02 increase in AM 30 second ad rates. Elsewhere, no statis-
tically significant impact is evident.

Radio/newspaper cross-ownership within the local market is
associated with a $1.69 increase in the FM rate per 100,000 hours
market audience (significant at the 90 percent level). Competition with a local market radio/newspaper cross-holding is associated with a $1.48 increase in FM rates per 100,000 hours market
audience. Taken together these findings suggest that cross-ownership between newspapers and FM radio stations reduces competition
in the sale of advertising and results in higher rates.

7.4.2 Empirical Evidence Using Nationally-Defined Ownership Variables

Redefinition of the ownership variables to reflect group and
cross-ownership patterns for Canada as a whole focuses the analy-

sis on the pricing implications of national ownership patterns. The results of the estimation of 30 second advertising rates using nationally defined ownership variables are shown in equations 1 and 2 in Table 7.2. The results for rates on a per 100,000 hours weekly market audience basis are shown in equations 3 and 4. It should be noted that the mean values of the dependent variables are unchanged from those appearing in Table 7.1.

Equation 1 is able to account for 86 percent of the variation in the 30 second AM commercial rate but the constant term is not statistically significant. Equation 2 accounts for 80 percent of the variation in 30 second FM rates with a statistically signi- ficant constant term of $-27.62. The constant terms in both equa- tion 3 ($13.21) and equation 4 ($3.40) are both statistically sig- nificant. While equation 4 explained 74 percent of the variation in the price of commercials, equation 3 can account for only 27 percent of the variation in AM rate per 100,000 hours market au- dience.

7.4.2.1 The Competitive Position of the Firm

The size of an AM station's audience in its local CMA con- tinues to be a significant determinant of 30 second ad rate with a 100,000 increment in weekly audience hours associated with a $2.10 rate increase. Local market audience size is not, however, sta- tistically significant for FM stations.

One of the more interesting results of the re- specification of ownership variables is the enhanced importance of audience drawn from areas outside a station's local CMA. Results for AM stations provide further support for the target audience hypoth- esis. An increase of 100,000 hours in audience outside the sta- tion's local CMA is actually associated with a $1.10 decrease in 30 second advertising rates. A similar increase in external audience is associated with a $2.50 ad rate increase for FM stations. This result suggests that buyers of advertising on FM stations may not target their advertising as tightly to the local market.

A .10 increase in an FM station's share of total market reve- nue was found to be associated with a $.94 decrease in rate per 100,000 hours market audience. A decrease of this magnitude is large in relation to the mean value of 2.57. Again it suggests an elastic demand for FM advertising - a lower ad rate resulting in higher revenues.

7.4.2.2 Local Market Characteristics

As in the local market ownership variables specification, the powerful influence of market concentration on the pricing of radio commercial time is evident. A .10 increase in the revenue Herfin- dahl index is associated with increases of $4.28 (AM) and $6.66 (FM) in 30 second ad rates and increases of $1.02 (AM) and $1.29

Table 7.2

REGRESSION RESULTS: RADIO STATION ADVERTISING RATE ESTIMATES
USING NATIONALLY DEFINED OWNERSHIP VARIABLES

	Eqn. 1	Eqn. 2	Eqn. 3	Eqn. 4
Dependent Variable	AM Rate [1]	FM Rate [1]	AM Rate per 100,000 weekly hours in a market audience	FM Rate per 100,000 weekly hours in a market audience
Independent Variables:				
Constant	33.38(1.56)	-27.62(2.43)**	13.21(2.28)**	3.40(2.46)**
Fitted market audience	.000021(8.94)**	.0000018(.68)		
AUDE (audience outside CMA)	-.000011(2.25)**	.000025(2.29)**		-.00019(1.61)
SHR (revenue share)				-9.36(5.23)**
HRF (revenue Herfindahl)	42.82(2.51)**	66.61(3.32)**	10.23(2.79)**	12.88(4.32)**
POP (population)		.000011(2.97)**		-.00000069(1.57)
INC (income)	-.0094(2.00)**		-.0035(2.64)**	
RR (national radio/ radio)	6.12(1.38)			
RT (national radio/TV)		-8.03(2.54)**	1.31(1.51)	
RN (national radio/news)	10.17(2.07)**	12.96(1.95)*		
CRT (competes with national radio/TV)			1.94(1.44)	
CRN (competes with national radio/news)		18.21(3.31)**		-.87(1.37)
Mean Value of Dependent Variable	41.43	18.77	3.73	2.57
R^2	.86	.80	.27	.74
n[2]	56	26	56	26

[1] Per 30 second prime time commercial.
[2] Number of stations.

 * Significant at the 90 percent level.
** Significant at the 95 percent level.

(FM) in ad rates for 100,000 weekly hours of local market audience. Comparison with the respective average values of $41.43 and $18.77 for 30 second rates and $3.73 and $2.57 for rates per 100,000 hours market audience confirms the quantitative impact of this influence.

A 100,000 increase in market population is associated with a $1.10 increase in the 30 second ad rate of FM stations, but is not statistically elsewhere. While there is no evidence that market income levels are a factor in the pricing of commercials by FM radio stations, a $1000 income increment is associated with decreases of $9.40 in the 30 second ad rate and $3.50 in the ad rate per 100,000 hours of market audience for AM stations.

7.4.2.3 Ownership Structure

When ownership is analyzed on a nation-wide basis cross-ownership between the radio industry and the newspaper industry has the greatest impact on the pricing of radio commercial time. Membership in a nationally-defined radio/newspaper cross-holding is associated with increases of $10.17 and $12.96 in the 30 second ad rates of AM and FM stations respectively. (The FM result being significant at the 90 percent level). Possibly even more important, the results show FM stations that compete with others belonging to national radio/ newspaper groups to have 30 second rates $18.21 higher than would otherwise be the case.

Membership in a national radio/television group, although not found to influence AM ad rates, was associated with an $8.03 decrease in the rates of FM stations.

The national ownership structure variables in equations 3 and 4, dealing with ad rates on a per 100,000 hours weekly market audience basis, are all statistically insignificant, i.e., they fail to be significant at the 90 percent level of confidence.

7.5 CONCLUSIONS

Evidence as to the influence of the level of market concentration on the level of radio advertising rates is unequivocal. When market revenue is concentrated in a few hands the resultant market power is the single most important factor in driving up the price of commercial air time. When the price of 30 second spot commercials is considered, a .10 increase in the Herfindahl index of market concentration is estimated to result in rate increases ranging from $3.93 to $4.28 for AM stations (mean equals $41.43) and from $4.17 to $6.66 for FM stations (mean equals $18.77). On a rate per 100,000 weekly audience hours basis the corresponding increases range from $1.02 to $1.39 for AM stations (mean equals $3.73) and from $1.29 to $1.83 for FM stations (mean equals $2.57). Compared to their respective mean values, these are very powerful effects indices. Remember that the Herfindahl indices for our sample markets range from .13 for Montreal to .85 for

Regina.   This is a spread of .72 and it implies that on a conservative estimate the price of a 30 second AM radio commercial can
be expected to be ($3.93 x 7.2) = $24.70 higher in Regina than in
Montreal solely on account of the greater market power of Regina
firms.   The corresponding increase in Regina FM rates is (4.17 x
7.2) = $30.02.

The level of average income in the local CMA is an important
factor in the pricing of commercial time on AM radio stations.
Surprisingly, the estimated relationship is the converse of that
hypothesized.   Consumers in high income areas may have greater
spending power, but they are not thereby valued more highly by AM
radio advertisers.   The evidence seems clear that AM radio commercials are worth more in lower income areas.   A $1000 decrease in
average income levels is associated with an increase of between
$9.40 and $12.00 in 30 second ad rates or between $3.40 and $3.50
on a rate per 100,000 weekly audience hours basis.   This effect
does not carry through to FM stations however.   There is no evidence that the level of average market income affects their rates
at all.

The results of the ownership structure analysis conform
closely to our theoretical predictions.   Ownership of more than
one radio station in the same CMA, which could be expected to increase a firm's market power, was found to be associated with a
$7.02 increase in 30 second AM advertising rates, sizeable in re-
lation to the $41.43 mean.   Nearly all of these radio/radio groups
are AM/FM twins but there was no evidence that the FM twin involved was able to charge higher rates on account of group ownership.   Examination of radio/radio group ownership on a national
basis yielded weaker results.   This was as expected since market
power is little affected when group stations are located in different markets.

Appendix 7.1

THE PRICING OF RADIO COMMERCIAL TIME: MODEL SPECIFICATION

The determinants of radio station advertising rates were estimated using a two-stage least squares regression model which allows for interdependency between radio advertising rates and audience size, but is able to produce an unbiased estimate of the audience-advertising rate relationship. First, audience estimates were prepared using the approach developed for the analysis of radio station audience size. Then these fitted values were used as one of the independent variables in the estimation of advertising rates. When ownership variables were defined on a market-by-market basis the model used to estimate these fitted audience values takes the form

$$
\begin{aligned}
FAUD = {}& a_0 + a_1(POP/N) + a_2(POP/N)J \\
& + a_3(POP/N)\left\{\frac{NJ - J}{N - 1}\right\} + a_4(POP/N)FM \\[4pt]
& + a_5(POP/N)COT + a_6(POP/N)PO + a_7(POP/N)MOR \\
& + a_8(POP/N)CW + a_9(POP/N)EL + a_{10}(POP/N)HM \\
& + a_{11}(POP/N)MIN + a_{12}(POP/N)CL \\
& + a_{13}(POP/N)JZ + a_{14}(POP/N)PR + a_{15}(POP/N)NE \\
& + a_{16}(POP/N)AD + a_{17}(POP/N)MU + a_{18}AUDE \\
& + a_{19}SHR + a_{20}INC + a_{21}HRF + a_{22}POP \\
& + a_{23}RRM + a_{24}RTM + a_{25}RNM + a_{26}CRRM \\
& + a_{27}CRTM + a_{28}CRNM
\end{aligned}
\tag{1}
$$

basis the appropriate changes in the group and cross-ownership variables in equation (1) must be made. The additional variables are defined below.

This approach allows for interdependency between advertising rates and audience size. It also permits consideration, in the audience equation, of the audience competition effects of non-local Canadian stations while permitting the exclusion of such stations, where they are not competitors for advertising revenue in the local market, from measures of competitive conditions and ownership structure in the local market. Since such stations are not based in the markets under consideration data on them in also excluded in the estimation of advertising rates, revenues, and profits. CBC-owned radio stations are treated in a similar fashion.

A7.1 COMPETITIVE POSITION OF THE FIRM

In general, the analysis of other variables parallels that adopted in the television advertising analysis. First additional descriptions of a station's competitive position in the local market are considered. A firm's share (SHR) of aggregate radio station revenues (or audience) provides one of them.

Using only local market audience implies a target-audience approach by buyers of commercial time. Many radio stations have large numbers of listeners outside their local CMA. The role these extra listeners play in rate setting can be examined by including in the model a variable AUDE representing the excess of total viewing audience of a station over its audience in the local CMA.

radio commercial, FAUD is the fitted value of weekly local market audience achieved by the station, AUDE is the station's audience drawn outside its local CMA, and SHR is its share of aggregate radio advertising revenues in the market, then

$$RATE = a_0 + a_1 FAUD + a_2 AUDE + a_3 SHR \qquad (2)$$

A7.2 LOCAL MARKET CHARACTERISTICS

Among the principal economic characteristics of the local market are POP, the population of the market area in which the station operates, and INC the average income in this area.

Competitive conditions of the local market can be considered using the Herfindahl index of market concentration HRF and the firm's share SHR of aggregate radio station revenues or audience for the market. Incorporating the influence of these overall market structure variables results in

$$RATE = a_0 + a_1 FAUD + a_2 AUDE + a_3 SHR$$
$$+ a_4 POP + a_5 INC + a_6 HRF \qquad (3)$$

Ownership structure must be considered at two different levels. For the first, ownership structure in terms of the individual local market, variables must be added to represent multiple ownership of radio stations in a given local market RRM, ownership of a radio station by the owner of a television station in the same market TRM, and ownership of a radio station by the owners of a newspaper in the same market RNM. In addition, wherever a radio station competes with a station in any one of these three categories this can be denoted by variables CRRM, CTRM, and CRNM respectively.

A7.3 OWNERSHIP STRUCTURE

Analysis of ownership structure on this market- by-market basis results in an estimating equation of the form

$$RATE = a_0 + a_1 FAUD + a_2 AUDE + a_3 SHR$$
$$+ a_4 POP + a_5 INC + a_6 HRF + a_7 RRM$$
$$+ a_8 TRM + a_9 RNM + a_{10} CRRM + a_{11} CTRM$$
$$+ a_{12} CRNM \qquad (4)$$

Each of the ownership structure characteristics is described by a dummy variable taking the value 1 when the characteristic applies in the case of the firm at hand, 0 otherwise.

When the dependent variable is re-defined as advertising rate per 100,000 hours of weekly market audience ADPM the estimating equation becomes

$$\begin{aligned}
ADPM = a_0 &+ a_1 FAUD + a_2 AUDE + a_3 SHR \\
&+ a_4 POP + a_5 INC + a_6 HRF + a_7 RRM \\
&+ a_8 TRM + a_9 RNM + a_{10} CRRM + a_{11} CTRM \\
&+ a_{12} CRNM
\end{aligned}$$

(5)

In the alternative, Canada-wide specification of ownership pattern, analysis can proceed in a similar fashion once the appropriate changes in variable definition have been made. Ownership inition have been made. Ownership of a radio station by a concern which owns another radio station anywhere in Canada is denoted by RR. Ownership of a television station anywhere in Canada by the owner of a local radio station is denoted by TR. Cross-ownership of a newspaper anywhere in Canada by a local radio station's owners is denoted by RN. Competition by a radio station with stations of the above type is denoted by CRR, CTR, and CRN respectively. The estimating equation in the case of a Canada-wide specification of the ownership pattern remains in the same form as equations (4) and (5) with the appropriate re-specification of the ownership structure variables.

Appendix 7.2

THE PRICING OF RADIO COMMERCIAL TIME: THE DATA

The advertising rates used were obtained from the April 1975 issue of Canadian Advertising Rates and Data, a monthly trade publication.[1]   The advertising rates used in this chapter are those for 30 second prime time commercials.   Prime time varies slightly among stations.   As in the case of television, deviations of actual transaction prices from quoted prices may present problems. It is assumed that such deviations for any given station are small relative to price variations amongst stations and that the deviations are uncorrelated with any explanatory variables.

Audience data was obtained from BBM Coverage and Circulation Report: Radio; format information from Broadcaster, "Fall '74 Directory;   Radio Stations."[2]   Income data for each local market CMA was obtained from the Financial Post Survey of Markets 1974/ 75.[3]

The Herfindahl index of market concentration and the market share measures were developed on the basis of both revenue and audience measures.   The construction of these measures was examined in detail in Chapter 3.   Herfindahl indices on a revenue basis for each market were supplied by the federal Department of Communications.   Use of revenue share data for regression purposes was permitted on an in-house basis under the supervision of the Department of Communications' staff.   Herfindahl index and market share calculations were based on audience data for each stations audience.

The ownership structure of the radio industry, on both a local market and on a national definition, is based on information contained in the appendices of Volume II of the report of the CRTC Ownership Study Group.[4]   Supplementary information on newspaper cross-ownership was supplied by the Ownership Study Group.

Notes to Appendix 7.2

1.   Canadian Advertising Rates and Data (Toronto: Maclean-Hunter, April 1975).

2.   For details see Appendix 6.2.

3.   Financial Post Survey of Markets 1974/75 (Toronto: Maclean-Hunter, 1974).

4. Canadian Radio-television and Telecommunications Commission, <u>The Contemporary Status of Ownership and the Level of Concentration in the Canadian Broadcasting Industry</u>, Background Study II to the Report of the Ownership Study Group (Ottawa: CRTC, 1978).

Chapter 8

Profitability and Risk

Aggregate data on revenues, expenses and operating profits in the television, radio, and cable television industries were presented in Chapter 2. The most significant of these indicators of industry performance is profits. But data on aggregate dollar profits are relatively meaningless without some benchmark.

This chapter presents two approaches to the measurement of industry profit performance. In sections 8.1 and 8.2 weighted average rate of return measures are developed for the television and radio industries respectively. These rates of return are then compared to corresponding measures for other non-broadcasting firms. Because of the large number of cable television concerns it was not possible with the available resources to prepare a similar analysis of the cable television industry.

Section 8.3 introduces risk. A high return does not necessarily indicate superior economic performance from the viewpoint of a risk averse investor. The crucial question is whether the return of a company is higher or lower than appropriate for its level of risk. In section 8.3 we attempt to answer this question for six publicly-quoted communications companies to see if profitability is unusually high when allowance is made for the risk element.

8.1 RATES OF RETURN IN THE TELEVISION INDUSTRY

Various measures of rate of return are available and the choice of measure must be determined by the use to which it is being put. The measure of profits can be either before, or after, income taxes. Interest, a payment for services of debt capital, must be taken into account. And the base over which rate of return is to be calculated must be specified. Should only shareholder's equity be considered or should long-term debt also be taken into account as part of the base upon which a return is being earned?

In the analysis of television in this section, and radio in the next, the methodology employed is as follows. First, in gen-

Table 8.1

TELEVISION CORPORATIONS, 1975 WEIGHTED AVERAGE RATE OF RETURN[1]

Revenue Size Class ($ millions)	No. of Corps.	Total Rev. ($000s)	Weighted Average Rate of Return
4.5 & over	13	134,861	39.6%
1.8 - 4.5	14	41,519	13.3
1.0 - 1.8	18	24,423	15.7
Under 1.0	14	8,076	19.0
Overall	59	208,879	32.2

1. Profits after tax plus interest divided by long term debt plus shareholders equity.

Source: Statistical Information Services, Department of Communications, Ottawa.

Table 8.2

TELEVISION GROUPS, 1975 WEIGHTED AVERAGE RATE OF RETURN[1]
(groups classified by revenue size)

Revenue Size Class ($ millions)	No. of Corps.	Total Rev. ($000s)	Weighted Average Rate of Return
4.5 & over	14	159,749	35.0%
1.8 - 4.5	10	30,642	10.5
1.0 - 1.8	9	11,737	12.9
Under 1.0	12	6,751	19.0
Overall	45	208,879	30.1

1. Profits after tax plus interest divided by long term debt plus shareholders equity.

Source: Statistical Information Services, Department of Communications, Ottawa.

eral, the investment capital base upon which a return is being earned has been defined as the total of long term debt plus share-holder's equity. This total of invested capital should roughly equal the total of long term assets on which the business must earn an economic return, i.e., current assets roughly equal to current liabilities. In certain cases, such as conglomerates, it was necessary to adjust the measured capital base to properly reflect only the broadcasting assets of a corporation since it would be clearly invalid to compute returns from broadcasting as a percentage of an overall asset base including significant non-broadcasting assets. The presence of negative shareholders equity in the case of 12 radio corporations, for which data on broad-casting assets was lacking, required their elimination from all calculations.[1] A rate of return on a negative capital base is meaningless.

The measure of return chosen for use in calculating the re-sults shown in Tables 8.1 to 8.6 was the total of interest expense plus profits after tax. This measure, although of little value in assessing precisely the profitability of the industry, does show the magnitude of the return provided to all those supplying capi-tal to television (or radio) corporations regardless of whether this capital is extended on an ownership (equity) or debt basis. The rate of return of each corporation (or group, as the case may be) is weighted by the total of long term debt plus equity, or broadcasting assets, according to whichever was used in the calcu-lation of rate of return.

Evaluation of rates of return calculated in this fashion re-quires the reader to compare the calculated rate with correspond-ing rates of return in competitive industries. Such a rate would correspond to a "pure" rate of return adjusted to reflect the riskiness of the investment plus an inflation premium. A study by Ibbotson and Sinquefield[2] for the U.S. shows that common stocks in the Standard & Poor's Composite Index earned an inflation-ad-justed return of 6.4 percent between 1926 and 1978. As this sam-ple includes firms in uncompetitive industries, this return should be a little greater than the "pure" return plus the risk premium for a competitive industry. The annual rate of inflation in the Canadian Consumer Price Index for 1970-1975 was just over 7 per-cent.[3] This gives us a competitive benchmark rate of return of approximately 13 percent. Overall returns on capital investments in excess of this rate would be indicative of super-normal profits attributable to positions of market power.

Table 8.1 presents the weighted average rates of return on an after tax profits plus interest divided by shareholders equity plus long term debt basis for television corporations in 1975. The groupings, by television revenue size class, show highest rates of return, 39.6 percent, to be earned by the corporations with the largest broadcasting asset base. The smallest corpor-ations earned 19.0 percent with intermediate sizes lower still. The overall average weighted rate of return for all 59 television

Table 8.3

TELEVISION GROUPS, 1975 WEIGHTED AVERAGE RATE OF RETURN[1]
(Groups classified by type of cross-ownership)

Type of Cross-Ownership	No. of Groups	Total Rev. ($000s)	Weighted Average Rate of Return
Television-television	15	122,361	45.2%
Television-radio	19	112,376	19.6

1. Profits after tax plus interest divided by long term debt plus shareholders equity.

Source: Statistical Information Services, Department of Communications, Ottawa.

Table 8.4

RADIO CORPORATIONS, 1975 WEIGHTED AVERAGE RATE OF RETURN[1]

Revenue Size Class ($000s)	No. of Corps.	Total Rev. ($000s)	Weighted Average Rate of Return
1.700 & over	31	104,353	21.9%
1.000 - 1.700	20	25,187	14.5
0.700 - 1.000	24	19,870	13.4
580 - 700	23	14,620	15.2
434 - 580	25	12,213	16.2
349 - 434	26	9,889	9.9
273 - 349	24	7,365	14.6
184 - 272	20	4,414	18.1
107 - 184	14	2,051	0.4
Under 107	9	382	31.8
Overall	216	200,344	18.1

1. Profits after tax plus interest divided by long term debt plus shareholders equity.

Source: Statistical Information Services, Department of Communications, Ottawa.

corporations was 32.2 percent. This is far in excess of the rate of return required to attract investment capital to the industry under competitive conditions in capital markets.

Bain has argued that measurement of an industry's profit "on the average and in the long run" is necessary in order to elim- inate temporary fluctuations.[4] Examination of broadcasting pro- fits for more than a year was not possible with the resources available. However, evidence of continued high levels of broad- casting profits has been presented in The Financial Post in 1979.

> Over the past five years, for the communications and me- dia group has achieved a 20-25 percent return on equity vs. 12-13 percent for industry as a whole.[5]

Certain group owners, for accounting convenience or other reasons, segregate individual broadcast undertakings in separate corporations. Using the information developed by the CRTC Owner- ship Study Group,[6] it is possible to aggregate the results of these various entities and produce profit measures on a group basis.

The results of this procedure in the case of television are shown in Table 8.2 where it will be observed that the rate of re- turn for television groups is lower than that of the corresponding television corporations. On the surface, this result appears ano- malous since one normally thinks of the groups as being larger, economically stronger, and more profitable entities. What appears to be happening is that the very act of aggregating a group's broadcasting assets serves to bring into the picture other lower- yielding broadcasting assets that are excluded in the television corporation analysis. The only exception to this general finding is the increase in the television-radio group rate of return to 19.6 percent from the corresponding 18.6 percent figure for tele- vision corporations.

It is possible to identify corporations owning more than one television station (television-television group ownership) and corporations owning at least one radio station in addition to their television holdings (television-radio cross-ownership). It should be borne in mind, or course, that such classifications are not mutually exclusive. Certain group owners may fall in both ca- tegories. However, when television groups are classified in this way, the results as shown in Table 8.3 reveal television-televi- sion groups to be earning (in 1975) an overall weighted average rate of return of 45.2 percent on total capital investment (long term debt plus shareholders equity). The corresponding figure for groups with television-radio cross-holdings is 19.5 percent.

8.2 RATES OF RETURN IN THE RADIO INDUSTRY

Table 8.4 shows the rates of return for radio corporations classified by Statistics Canada revenue size classes. The overall

Table 8.5

RADIO GROUPS, 1975 WEIGHTED AVERAGE RATE OF RETURN[1]
(groups classified by revenue size)

Revenue Size Class ($000s)	No. of Corps.	Total Rev. ($000s)	Weighted Average Rate of Return
1.700 & over	27	137,789	19.6%
1.000 - 1.700	13	16,147	22.2
0.700 - 1.000	17	13,915	12.6
580 - 700	15	9,518	18.1
434 - 580	13	6,354	21.0
349 - 434	21	8,033	13.3
273 - 349	15	4,577	15.2
184 - 272	15	3,371	18.7
107 - 184	11	1,613	2.3
Under 107	6	181	35.6
Overall	153	201,498	18.8

1. Profits after tax plus interest divided by long term debt plus shareholders equity.

Source: Statistical Information Services, Department of Communications, Ottawa.

Table 8.6

RADIO GROUPS, 1975 WEIGHTED AVERAGE RATE OF RETURN[1]
(Groups classified by type of cross-ownership)

Type of Cross-Ownership	No. of Groups	Total Rev. ($000s)	Weighted Average Rate of Return
Radio-Radio (including AM-FMs)	75	147,705	19.6%
Radio-radio (excluding AM-FMs)	52	141,273	19.3
Radio-newspaper	6	16,696	27.6
Radio-television	19	66,408	19.6

1. Profits after tax plus interest divided by long term debt plus shareholders equity.

Source: Statistical Information Services, Department of Communications, Ottawa.

rate of return for all 216 radio corporations is 18.1 percent. The highest rates of return occur in the case of the smallest (31.9 percent) and the largest (21.9 percent) corporations with no discernible trend evident in between - save for the second small- est size class ($107,000 - $184,000 of radio revenue) which earned zero profits on average.

When we turn to rates of return for radio groups, in Table 8.5, we observe the converse of the situation noted in television. When the other, higher return, television holdings of radio group owners are brought into the picture, the weighted average rate of return for radio groups exceeds that for radio corporations - the overall rate rising from 18.1 percent to 18.8 percent. The pat- tern of rates over size classes is unaffected.

Examination of rates of return after classification by cross- ownership holdings of groups, see Table 8.6, reveals some inter- esting differences from the television case. The radio-television group rate, of course, remains constant and equal to that of the identically defined television-radio group at 19.6 percent. But, whereas television-television groups achieved rates of interest plus profits return on total capital of 45.2 percent, radio-radio groups whether defined to include or exclude AM-FM combinations earned a rate of return identical to that of radio-television groups. The only significant variation occurred in the case of radio-newspaper chains which earned an average rate of return of 27.6 percent on total capital investment.

8.3 RISK AND RETURN

The analysis in sections 8.1 and 8.2 did not consider risk. It is generally accepted, however, that most investors are risk averse. Hence, if there are two companies, one with a higher re- turn and greater risk than the other, it is possible that inves- tors will prefer the performance of the lower return/less risk company. An entire industry, the insurance industry, is indeed based on many people choosing lower expected return/lower risk options. A high return, therefore, does not necessarily indicate superior economic performance from the viewpoint of investors. The crucial issue is whether the return of a company is higher or lower than appropriate for its level of risk. In this section we attempt to obtain some insight on this matter for six publicly- quoted communications companies to see if our earlier contention, that profitability is unusually high, is still supportable when we allow for the risk element. Section 8.3.1 describes a theory re- lating the return expected from a stock to its risk and examines measurement of risk and of return-risk performance. In section 8.3.2 we present and analyze the results for the six companies.

8.3.1 Model Specification

Companies in the private sector are assumed to operate in the interests of shareholders. Shareholders of a broadcasting com-

Figure 8.1

THE SECURITY MARKET RETURN-RISK LINE

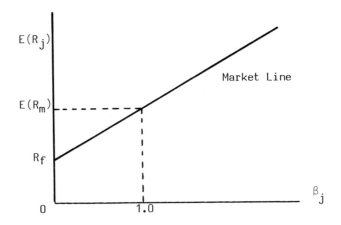

Figure 8.2

THE CHARACTERISTIC LINE FOR SECURITY j

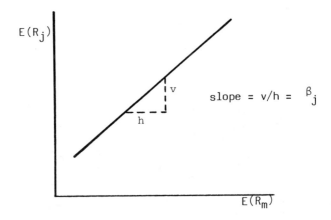

pany, or any other company, should expect a rate of return equal
to that available from other investments with the same risk. If
that return is not forthcoming, investors will sell shares causing
a decrease in stock price and an increase in the return to the
level appropriate for the risk. The Capital Asset Pricing Model
(CAPM) demonstrates that, for diversified investors, the relevant
risk associated with a security is the systematic risk, beta (β),
attributable to factors which simultaneously affect the prices of
all marketable securities. Diversification virtually eliminates
the unsystematic (non-market related) risk and hence this type of
risk should not command a risk premium. A risk premium will be
demanded, however, for the systematic risk because this cannot be
reduced by diversification. Hence, assuming efficient capital
markets, trade off between return and systematic risk is established by the market. Where $E(R_j)$ is the return on security j or
portfolio j, R_f is the risk-free rate of return, and β_j is the
systematic risk of security j or portfolio j, the return-risk
trade-off is illustrated in Figure 8.1.

The market portfolio, with expected return $E(R_m)$, by definition
has a beta value of 1.00 and will lie on this Market Line. In
equilibrium the return - risk combination of individual stocks and
individual portfolios would also be expected to lie on this line.
Therefore, $E(R_j)$ is given by:

$$E(R_j) = R_f + [E(R_m) - R_f]\ \beta_j$$

The predicted β_j, the systematic risk of security j, measures
the volatility of the expected return of security j to changes in
the market rate of return and is the slope of the security's char-
ateristic line. This is illustrated in Figure 8.2.

Assuming that relevant predictions do not change from year to
year, past outcomes of security and market returns can be used as
surrogates for ex ante expectations and an estimate of predicted
beta for security j, b_j, is given by the slope of the regression
line based on actual returns of stock j and the actual returns of
a market index. The data manipulation used to estimate β_j are described in Appendix 8.2. Of interest to us is whether the communications companies are aggressive securities with $\beta > 1$. If they
are, then the high profits reported in Section 8.1 and 8.2 may be
explainable in terms of compensation for above average risk. If
there is no general evidence that $\beta > 1$ then no such explanation
exists.

Using past outcomes as surrogates for ex ante expectations,
we can also examine the performance of a security j by comparing
the actual realized average rate of return on stock j, R_j, with
the equilibrium expected return predicted by the Capital Asset
Pricing Model (CAPM), $E(R_j)$, where the latter is given by:

$$E(R_j) = \overline{R}_f + (\overline{R}_m - \overline{R}_f)b_j$$

where $\overline{R}_m$ is the actual realized average rate of return on the market index, and R_f is the actual realized average rate of return on a proxy for the risk-free asset. The concept of $E(R_j)$ as the return that should be expected by shareholders, has been advocated and used in some public utility rate regulation cases.[7] If $\overline{R}_j > E(R_j)$ then the actual return-risk combination of security j is above the Market Line and superior to that predicted by the CAPM.

Another method of determining whether the return-risk combination for a broadcasting company is above or below the Market Line is to calculate Treynor's reward-to-volatility or reward-per-unit of risk ratio[8] and compare it to the ratio for the market portfolio. The Treynor Ratio, T_j for company j, is calculated as the ratio of the mean excess return to estimated beta[9]:

$$T_j = (\overline{R}_j - \overline{R}_f)/b_j$$

The Treynor Ratio not only indicates whether a stock has outperformed the market but also allows us to rank the performance of different stocks. This is demonstrated in Appendix 8.1. As a result, the Treynor Ratio has been employed extensively in the academic literature to evaluate performance, usually of mutual funds, and indirectly as a test of capital market theory.[10]

It should be noted that a return-risk combination above the Market Line is a disequilibrium situation. If capital markets are perfect the benefits will be capitalized in the form of a once-and-for-all stock price increase. Thus continuing stock undervaluation (indicated by continuing $\overline{R}_j > E(R_j)$ and T_j greater than the Treynor Ratio for the market index) will exist only if there are market imperfections[11] or if broadcast companies discover a continuing supply of unforeseen opportunities.

8.3.2   The Results

In this section we evaluate the b_j for the broadcasting stocks, compare the Treynor Ratios of the stocks with the Ratio for the Market Index, and compare the actual realized average rate of return on each stock with that expected. Appendix 8.2 describes the data manipulations undertaken. Data availability restricts us to a choice of three overlapping six-year periods (1967-72, 1968-73, and 1969-74) and limits our analysis to six broadcasting companies, namely Canadian Cablesystems, IWC Communications, Maclean-Hunter, Selkirk Holdings, Standard Broadcasting and Western Broadcasting, that were publicly quoted throughout this period. The nature and interests of these companies were described in Chapter 3. Some of the companies are not confined to broadcasting operations and it is not possible to separate the performance of their broadcasting operations from their total activities. Even for a company like Maclean-Hunter with substantial non-broadcasting operations, however, The Financial Post[12] indi-

Table 8.7

ESTIMATED SYSTEMATIC RISK, b$_j$, OF CANADIAN
BROADCASTING STOCKS, 1967-72, 1968-73, 1969-74

Stock Name	1967-72	1968-73	1969-74
Canadian Cablesystems Ltd.	0.74	0.85	1.01
IWC Communications Ltd.	1.68	1.65	1.48
Maclean-Hunter Ltd. 'A'	1.18	1.08	1.07
Selkirk Holdings Ltd. 'A'	0.84	0.88	0.84
Standard Broadcasting Corp.	0.76	0.77	0.85
Western Broadcasting Co. 'ACV'	0.81	0.95	1.08

Source: Appendix 8.2

Table 8.8

PERFORMANCE OF CANADIAN BROADCASTING STOCKS, 1967-72

Code	Stock Name	b	R	E(R)	T
1	Canadian Cablesystems Ltd.	0.74	0.016	0.0059	0.0159
2	IWC Communications Ltd.	1.68	0.009	0.0080	0.0029
3	Maclean-Hunter Ltd. 'A'	1.18	0.024	0.0068	0.0164
4	Selkirk Holdings Ltd. 'A'	0.84	0.021	0.0061	0.0197
5	Standard Broadcasting Corp.	0.76	0.020	0.0059	0.0206
6	Western Broadcasting Co. 'ACV'	0.81	0.034	0.0060	0.0363
7	Toronto Stock Exchange 300	1.00	0.006	0.0065	0.0022

Source: Appendix 8.2

cates that broadcasting operations contribute more than 50 percent of their profits.

Table 8.7 shows the value of b_j for each broadcast company for the periods 1967-72, 1968-73, and 1969-74. As the periods overlap the estimates of beta are not independent. Two of the stocks, IWC Communications and Maclean-Hunter are aggressive stocks, the former being substantially more aggressive than the latter, with $b_j > 1.00$ in all three periods. Thus only on these stocks would the expected return be greater than the market return and could a higher than average return be justified on the grounds of compensation for above average risk. Two stocks, Selkirk Holdings and Standard Broadcasting are defensive stocks with $b_j > 1.00$ for all three periods and the CAPM would predict a return less than that of the market. Canadian Cablesystems and Western Broadcasting exhibit $b_j > 1.00$ for two periods and $b_j > 1.00$ for one period.

In this sample of companies there is obviously no general tendency for above average systematic risk. Firmer conclusions would have been possible if there had been more publicly quoted companies during this period. But if this sample is at all representative of broadcasting stocks as a whole, then unusually high returns to the industry are not explainable in terms of compensation for risk.

Although the evaluation of b_j did not suggest above average systematic risk, it is still useful to compare the Treynor Ratios of each stock with the ratio for the Market Index and compare the actual realized average rate of return for each stock with that expected. Table 8.8 shows the value of b_j, R_j, $E(R_j)$ and T_j for each company and for the TSE 300, the proxy for the market portfolio, for the period 1967-72. R_j and $E(R_j)$, in this and subsequent tables, are expressed as monthly rates of return. The monthly Canadian Treasury yield, the proxy for the risk-free rate, for this period was .0042 and this value was used in the calculation of $E(R_j)$ and T_j.

It can be seen that for each stock $\overline{R}_j > E(R_j)$ and $T_j > .0022$, the value of the Treynor Ratio for the Toronto Stock Exchange 300. Although it is not possible to test for significance, these results are consistent with a return-risk performance superior to that of the market. The stock with the best performance in the period, indicated by the highest Treynor Ratio, was Western Broadcasting. The results are illustrated in Figure 8.3. The return-risk combination of the stock is shown using the stock number coding given in Table 8.8. The slopes of the lines drawn from R through these numbers are the Treynor Ratios. Although not shown, to avoid cluttering the graph, the value of E(R) is the vertical distance at b between the horizontal axis and the Market Line.

Table 8.9 shows the results for the period 1968-73 during which $\overline{R}_f$ = .0043. Five companies have $\overline{R}_j > E(R_j)$ and $T_j > .0004$,

Figure 8.3

ILLUSTRATION OF RISK-RETURN PERFORMANCE OF
BROADCASTING COMPANIES, 1967-1972[1]

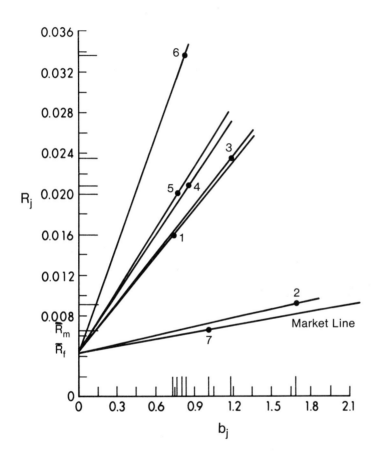

1.   Names of the companies are given in Table 8.8.

Table 8.9

PERFORMANCE OF CANADIAN BROADCASTING STOCKS, 1968-73

Stock j	b	R	E(R)	T
- Canadian Cablesystems Ltd.	0.85	0.010	0.0046	0.0066
- IWC Communications Ltd.	1.65	0.000	0.0049	-0.0029
- Maclean-Hunter Ltd. 'A'	1.08	0.006	0.0047	0.0014
- Selkirk Holdings Ltd. 'A'	0.88	0.009	0.0047	0.0052
- Standard Broadcasting Corp.	0.77	0.008	0.0046	0.0044
- Western Broadcasting				
Co. 'ACV'	0.95	0.017	0.0047	0.0132
- Toronto Stock Exchange 300	1.00	0.005	0.0047	0.0004

Source: Appendix 8.2

Table 8.10

PERFORMANCE OF CANADIAN BROADCASTING STOCKS, 1969-74

Stock j	b	R	E(R)	T
- Canadian Cablesystems Ltd.	1.01	-0.002	-0.0016	-0.0066
- IWC Communications Ltd.	1.48	-0.009	-0.0044	-0.0091
- Maclean-Hunter Ltd. 'A'	1.07	-0.001	-0.0019	-0.0047
- Selkirk Holdings Ltd. 'A'	0.84	0.008	-0.0006	0.0040
- Standard Broadcasting Corp.	0.85	0.000	-0.0006	0.0050
- Western Broadcasting				
Co. 'ACV'	1.08	0.007	-0.0020	0.0025
- Toronto Stock Exchange 300	1.00	-0.002	-0.0020	-0.0061

Source: Appendix 8.2

the Treynor Ratio for the Toronto Stock Exchange (TSE) 300. IWC Communications is the exception.

For the period 1969-1974, during which $\bar{R}_f = .0046$, the results in Table 8.10 show that for four companies $\bar{R}_j > E(R_j)$ and T_j greater than that of the Toronto Stock Exchange 300. IWC Communications again turned in an inferior performance as did, in this period only, Canadian Cablesystems.

In summary, the beta values for the six stocks indicate that they are not, on average, riskier than the market. Although it is not possible to test for significance, the estimated Treynor Ratios, indicating the reward-per-unit of risk, were on balance greater than that for the market. Maclean-Hunter, Selkirk Holdings, Standard Broadcasting, and Western Broadcasting had higher ratios, in many cases substantially higher, in each of the three overlapping periods. Canadian Cablesystems had a higher Treynor Ratio than the market in two periods and lower in one period, while IWC Communications had a higher Ratio than the market in one period and lower in two.

8.4 SUMMARY AND CONCLUSION

This chapter presented two approaches to the measurement of industry profit performance. Firstly, the weighted average rate of return was calculated for television in Section 8.1 and radio in Section 8.2. This rate of return was defined as the total of interest expense plus after-tax profits divided by long-term debt plus shareholders equity. For the 59 television corporations this return was found to be 32.2 percent whereas for the 216 radio corporations the return was 18.1 percent. These returns were both well above a competitive benchmark estimated to be about 13 percent. The second approach, presented in Section 8.3, explicitly recognized that most investors are risk averse and considered whether unusually high returns can be explained in terms of compensation for high risk. On the basis of our sample, we found no evidence to suggest that broadcasting is of above average risk and hence no support for such an explanation. This section also included an alternative approach to measuring performance, Treynor's reward-per-unit of risk ratio. Although no test of significance is possible, the estimated Treynor Ratios were on balance greater than the Ratio for the market.

Notes to Chapter 8

1. Data on broadcasting assets of these firms was not available. The twelve accounted for approximately $1 million in negative shareholder's equity, $270,000 in interest expense, and zero profits.

2. R.G. Ibbotson and R.A. Sinquefield, "Stocks, Bonds, Bills &
    Inflation: Updates," Financial Analysts Journal, July-August,
    Vol. 35, 9179, pp. 40-44. See also R. Mirus, "Opportunities
    for Portfolio Diversification," Canadian Public Policy, Febru-
    ary 1980, Vol. VI, Supplement, pp. 236-244.

3. Statistics Canada (Cat. No. 62-002) Prices and Price Indexes
    (Ottawa, monthly).

4. Joe S. Bain, Industrial Organization, 2nd ed. (New York:
    Wiley, 1968), p. 395.

5. The Financial Post, Special Report on the Media, September 22,
    1979, p. S15.

6. Canadian Radio-television and Telecommunications Commission,
    The Contemporary Status of Ownership and the Level of Concen-
    tration in the Canadian Broadcasting Industry, Background
    Study II to the Report of the Ownership Study Group (Ottawa:
    CRTC, 1978).

7. The relevance of the CAPM to rate regulation has been dis-
    cussed by S.C. Myers, "The Application of Finance Theory to
    Public Utility Rate Cases," The Bell Journal of Economics and
    Management Science, Spring 1972, pp. 52-97; D.A. West and A.A.
    Ewbank, "An Automatic Cost Adjustment Model for Regulating
    Public Utilities," Financial Management, Vol. 5, No. 1, Spring
    1976, pp. 23-31; R.L. Hagerman, "Finance Theory in Rate Hear-
    ings," Financial Management, Vol. 5, No. 1, Spring 1976, pp.
    18-22; and E.F. Brigham and R.L. Crum, "On the Use of the CAPM
    in Public Utility Rate Cases, Financial Management, Vol. 6,
    No. 2, Summer 1977, pp. 7-15.

8. J.L. Treynor, "How to Rate Management of Investment Funds,"
    Harvard Business Review, January-February, 1965, pp. 63-75.

9. The Treynor Ratio is a relevant measure of stock performance
    for diversified shareholders because they are subject only to
    systematic risk. Shareholders who do not hold a diversified
    portfolio, however, will also be concerned with unsystematic
    risk and the relevant risk of a stock for such a shareholder
    is the total risk measured by the standard deviation of re-
    turns, σ. A measure of the performance of stock j, that is
    appropriate for non-diversified shareholders, is the Sharpe
    Ratio, S_j:

$$S_j = \frac{R_j - R_f}{\sigma_j}$$

There is evidence, however, that the Sharpe Ratio gives very
similar rankings to the Treynor Ratio. For example, W.F.
Sharpe ("Mutual Fund Performance," Journal of Business, Sup-
plement, Vol. 39, January 1966, p. 129) found a rank correla-

tion coefficient of .97 for the two rankings of 34 portfolios. As a consequence we do not consider it necessary, in this section, to calculate σ_j and S_j.

10. See, for example, J.G. McDonald, "Objectives and Performance of Mutual Funds," Journal of Finance and Quantitative Analysis, Vol. 9, June 1974, pp. 311-333; and W.F. Sharpe and O.M. Cooper, "Risk - Return Classes of New York Stock Exchange Common Stocks, 1931-67," Financial Analysis Journal, Vol. 28, March-April 1972, p. 46.

11. See M.C. Findlay and A.A. Danan, "A Free Lunch on the Toronto Stock Exchange," Journal of Business Administration, Vol. 6, No. 2, Spring 1978, pp. 31-40, for evidence that suggests the Toronto Stock Exchange is not as efficient as the New York Stock Exchange.

12. The Financial Post, "Special Report on the Media," November 19, 1977.

Appendix 8.1

THE TREYNOR RATIO AND RANKING THE PERFORMANCE OF STOCKS

The Treynor Ratio permits us to rank the performance of different stocks whereas a comparison of $\bar{R}_j$ and $E(R_j)$ does not. This is illustrated in Figure A8.1

Figure A8.1

MEASUREMENTS OF PERFORMANCE

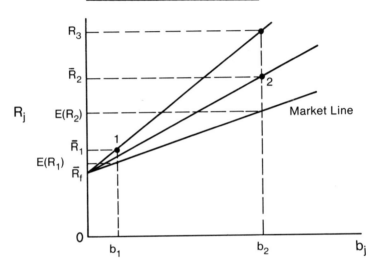

In Figure A8.1 we have stocks 1 and 2 with related returns of $\bar{R}_1$ and $\bar{R}_2$ respectively and estimated systematic risk of b_1 and b_2 respectively. The Treynor Ratio for stock 1, T_1, is the slope of the line drawn from R_f through the return-risk combination of stock 1. $T_1 > T_2$ although $\bar{R}_1 - E(R_1) < \bar{R}_2 - E(R_2)$. The Treynor Ratio thus indicates that the performance of stock 1 is superior. This assessment is correct because by borrowing at $\bar{R}_f$ and investing the additional money in stock 1, it would be possible to achieve return $\bar{R}_3$, where $R_3 > R_2$, for systematic risk b_2.

Appendix 8.2

THE ESTIMATION OF SYSTEMATIC RISK (B_j) AND
CALCULATION OF THE TREYNOR RATIO: DATA MANIPULATION

The value of b_j, necessary to calculate the Treynor Ratio and calculate the expected return on the stock of company j, was obtained using the regression equation for the characteristic line:

$$R_{jt} = a_j + b_j R_{mt} + e_{jt}$$

where R_{mt} is the return on the market in period t, e_{jt} is the error term attributable to unsystematic risk, and R_{jt} is the return on stock j in period t. R_{jt} equals the ratio of the capital gain plus the dividend in the period to the stock price in the previous period:

$$R_{jt} = (P_{jt} - P_{jt-1} + D_{jt})/P_{jt-1}$$

where P_{jt} is the price of stock j in period t, P_{jt-1} is the price of stock j in period t - 1, and D_{jt} is the cash dividend per share during period t. D_{jt} was extracted by hand from the Financial Post Cards. Weekly closing stock prices were converted by hand to monthly, ex-dividend, closing prices. Where necessary the prices were adjusted for stock splits. The Toronto Stock Exchange 300 was chosen as the proxy for the market portfolio.

To estimate the systematic risk, b_j, from the regression of the characteristic line, it was decided to use monthly data for three overlapping six year periods between 1967 and 1974, the latter being the last year for which the stock price data is available on tape. A six year period was chosen as a good compromise between conflicting estimating problems; the longer the period the greater the possibility of shifts in the b value over time whereas the shorter the period the greater the influence of random fluctuations. The companies for which estimates could be made were thus restricted to those broadcasting companies with publicly traded share for which stock price data was available on tape from 1967 to 1974. Such data was available for Canadian Cablesystems, IWC Communications, Maclean-Hunter, Selkirk Holdings, Standard Broadcasting, and Western Broadcasting.

The regression results showed that the returns for each broadcasting company, for each six year overlapping period, were significantly related to the Toronto Stock Exchange 300's return with all estimates of b_j being more than two-and-a-half times greater than their standard errors. In each case the F-test indicated the relationship to be significant at the 95 percent level. The R^2 values indicated that about 20 percent of the variation in returns on stocks was explained by the Toronto Stock Exchange 300 return.

144 Canadian Broadcasting

To calculate the Treynor Ratio and the expected return on the stock of company j it was also necessary to obtain a value for $\bar{R}_f$, the actual realized average risk-free rate of return. Treasury Bill yields were used as a proxy with the annual yields being converted to monthly rates and then weighted, by frequency of occurrence, to obtain the average monthly risk-free rate for the three six-year periods.

Chapter 9

Television Station Price-Cost Margins, Revenues and Expenses

Developing an understanding of the factors affecting industry performance is one of the principle objectives of a study of an industry such as television broadcasting. Such an understanding permits the development of policies designed to alter these factors so as to improve industry performance. In a market economy profits are one of the most important indicators of economic performance. Therefore, this section focuses on an examination of the factors affecting profits in television broadcasting.

As we have argued above, the owners of television stations are not in the business of producing programs but rather of producing and selling audience exposures to commercial messages. They engage in this business for the purpose of earning profits (although other goals may also be involved). Television stations may be interested in increasing audience size in order to justify higher advertising rates but they do not seek to maximize either audience size or advertising rate. As Owen, Beebe, and Manning have argued:

> First, advertisers are interested not merely in the size of an audience, but in its characteristics. In the trade these audience characteristics are called "demographics", and refer to the age, sex, and income composition of the audience. Thus, some audiences of given size are more valuable than others. Second, a TV station may be able to maximize its audience only at prohibitive program cost. If TV station managers are rational businessmen, as their stockholders have every right to expect them to be, they will be interested in maximizing the difference between advertising revenue and costs, and this difference is of course profit. Thus, while it is certainly true that TV stations are interested in achieving as large an audience as possible for any given program expenditure, we should not expect to find stations seeking to obtain an indefinitely large audience regardless of the cost.

They continue,

To the extent that there is competition among stations and between TV stations and other media, individual TV stations have little choice but to attempt to maximize long-run profits. This does not mean that they are not good citizens interested in public-interest objectives. But they are engaged in a business, and have responsibilities to stockholders that cannot be disregarded.[1]

The question of whether or not privately-owned profit-seeking concerns should be permitted to participate in the television industry is not at issue here. Rather, the existence of these firms is acknowledged and their economic behaviour is analyzed. It is assumed that firms attempt to maximize long-run profits taking due account of basic market limitations, behaviour of competitors, regulation, etc. CBC television stations, since they are publicly owned, play a mixed role. They compete for audience and advertising revenues with private stations but are not motivated by considerations of profit-maximization. Accordingly, the competitive effect of these stations must be taken into account in estimating the revenue and profitability of private stations. But revenues and profits of CBC stations themselves cannot properly be analyzed on the basis of the profit maximization assumption.

9.1 PRICE-COST MARGIN, REVENUES AND EXPENSES

Our evaluation of economic performance in the broadcasting industry has already included an examination of rates of return achieved by investors in broadcasting corporations and of rates of return on the assets of the broadcasting corporations themselves (see Chapter 8). Why turn to yet another measure of profitability? Since we know the rate of return earned on the broadcasting corporation's assets why not look directly to the various ownership structure and other market characteristics of each broadcasting corporation as major influences on these profit levels?

This is logical, but difficult to carry out in practice, because of the multiple ownership of broadcast undertakings by single corporations and the commingling of broadcasting and non-broadcasting assets within a single corporation. The problems arise it should be noted, not in the measurement of profits themselves, but in the definition of an appropriate investment capital base upon which to calculate a rate of return. While the rate of return for a broadcasting corporation as a whole may be known the rate of return of the various corporate components, such as individual television and radio stations, remains unknown because there is no objective method of properly allocating total invested capital to the various components.

It is this difficulty which has led to the development of a two part evaluation of profit performance. In the first part, in Chapter 8, the existence of super-normal rates of return was established. In this chapter the factors that influence the level of television station profits (not rate of return on capital) must be identified. No direct linkage can be established between the two parts of this analysis, but so long as corresponding changes in the investment base do not occur those factors increasing television station profits will also increase the rate of return.

While balance sheet information on individual television stations is not generally available, data are available on their revenues, expenses, and net income. Using this information it is possible to construct a profitability measure on an individual station basis. This measure can then be examined in light of the appropriate ownership structure and market characteristic variables. The profitability measure adopted here is the price-cost margin (PCM) defined as the ratio of operating income to total revenue.

Total revenue (R) includes revenue from sale of air time and network payments to stations as well as production and syndication revenue. Operating income is the excess of total revenue over total expenses (E) where the latter includes remuneration to employees, program acquisition, technical, sales, and administrative expenses, but excludes depreciation and interest. Therefore, price-cost margin can be defined as PCM = $(R-E)/R$.

The price-cost margin can never exceed one, the value it takes on when expenses are zero, but it can take on negative values, when expenses exceed revenue. A high price-cost margin is evidence that a television station is highly profitable and an indication (but not a demonstration) that its owners are earning a high rate of return on their investment in television assets.

When we turn to an examination of the factors influencing the size of the price-cost margin it seems appropriate to build on the approach used above for the pricing of commercial time. As defined above, price-cost margin is a function of only revenues and expenses. Revenue is primarily advertising revenue which depends on the advertising rate and the number of commercial minutes sold. Since the number of commercial minutes is limited by regulation, advertising revenue may in turn be largely a function of advertising rates per unit of time. Therefore, to the extent that movements in expenses are insignificant, the two-stage least squares approach developed in the case of pricing television advertising time may usefully be adopted for the analysis of price-cost margins. The determinants of revenues alone, and of expenses, can then be examined subsequently.

When advertising rates were analyzed, market structure was considered in terms of (i) the competitive position of the firm in the local market, (ii) the characteristics of that market, and (iii) ownership structure. In the case of price-cost margins, revenues and expenses, it seems useful to add a fourth category, programming competition, to introduce product differentiation and production considerations.

9.1.1 The Competitive Position of the Firm

When nationally-defined ownership variables were used, television stations with larger total audiences were found to be charging higher prices for commercial time (Chapter 5). In the local market ownership specification only audience outside the station's own Census Metropolitan Area appeared to influence advertising rates. It is to be expected that these relationships should be reflected in an examination of the determinants of television station revenues. Increases in audience outside a station's home CMA, however, may involve substantial outlays on transmitter facilities and programming.[2] Therefore, on balance, increases in audience size need not necessarily be associated with improvements in a station's price-cost margin.

9.1.2 Local Market Characteristics

The level of seller concentration can be expected to be an important determinant of television station profitability. Where market concentration, as measured by the Herfindahl index, is high, prices and profits can be expected to be high since even if there is no collusion between firms they come to recognize their interdependence. Higher levels of profitability can be expected because of the resultant unwillingness to compete vigorously.

Market population might be expected to exert some influence on revenues as a rough proxy for potential audience. (There was limited support for this in the previous chapter.) Offsetting influences on the expense side appear, however, to be potentially more important. A larger population may imply a larger geographic area of coverage requiring more expensive transmission facilities. More importantly, cities with larger populations may necessitate increased programming expenditures as, for example, increased costs of local news coverage. If increases in population have greater impact on television station expenses than they do on station revenues then each population increment should lead, other things being equal, to a decrease in the pricecost margin of local television stations.

The direct relationship between the level of market income and advertising rates should be reflected in television station revenues. The influence of average market income on television station expenses should be minor but there may be some effect through wage rates paid technical, sales, and administrative personnel. Overall, higher levels of market income should be associated with higher price-cost margins.

9.1.3 Programming Competition

Our audience analysis focused on competition at the network level. But individual stations have considerable scope for varying their program offerings in order to meet the desires of consumers. These variations will be examined along two dimensions here, first the news versus entertainment balance, and second the extent of commitment to local and Canadian programming.

The hypothesis on news versus entertainment programming is a simple one. If television is principally an entertainment medium expenditures on entertainment programming should be expected to increase revenues and profitability whereas the converse should be expected in the case of expenditures on news programming.

The strong audience results for the CBC, presented in Chapter 4, provide evidence that high Canadian content need not detract from a station's audience size. It is therefore unlikely that minutes of prime time Canadian broadcasting will significantly influence television station revenues. However, since such programming is much more expensive than comparable purchased American material, stations with higher levels of Canadian content can be expected to suffer higher costs and reduced levels of profitability.

Local programming can be expected to be cheaper than network programming. If it were also able to attract greater station revenues, increases in the number of minutes of local programming could be expected to be associated with higher price-cost margins.

9.1.4 Ownership Structure

As in the ad rate analysis it is both feasible and desirable to consider the implications of ownership structure from the viewpoint of both the local market and the nation as a whole. Since the local marketplace is the focus of competitive forces it is to be expected that an analysis from that viewpoint would be more fruitful in revealing the determinants of television station revenues and price-cost margins. Economies of the multi-plant firm and other expense factors may however show up more strongly in analysis from a national perspective.

Multiple holdings of television stations (television/television groups) occur primarily at the national level. Since such holdings have little effect on a firm's market power in any of the local markets in which it has stations, there is no reason to expect important revenue effects for these stations. While cost savings resulting from the ability to spread managerial and program production costs may well exist it is unlikely that they would be important enough to result in significant increases in profitability.

A television/radio cross-holding at the local market level enhances a firm's market power in the overall local market for advertising. Accordingly, such an ownership arrangement can be expected to be associated with higher levels of station revenues and profitability. Television/radio cross-ownership (either at the local or national level) should permit cost savings from the sharing of management and production overheads and from co-production (such as the supplying of TV sound tracks to associated radio stations).

A priori, a corresponding argument can be developed that television/newspaper cross-ownership increases market power in the advertising market and leads to enhanced revenues and profitability. But our examination of the pricing of commercial time has already provided evidence that television/newspaper cross-ownership tends to depress rather than elevate a firm's ad rate (Chapter 5). This influence should be expected to carry through to lower station revenues. Unless off-set by cost savings such revenue reductions would in turn lead to lower price-cost margins. The existence of offsetting savings in managerial and production costs could, however, lead to television station price-cost margins being unaffected by television/newspaper cross-ownership.

Since publicly owned (CBC) television stations are not operated on a profit-oriented basis, and since financial data on individual CBC stations was not available, no analysis of the influence of public ownership on the profitability, revenues, and expenses of individual CBC stations was attempted.

Economic theory provides us with little solid guidance as to how the existence of particular cross- ownership arrangements might be expected to affect the profitability of competing firms. On the one hand, television/radio cross-ownership that enables a firm to increase its ad rate, revenues, and price-cost margin may provide a pricing umbrella which permits similar increases to its competitors. On the other hand, the existence of such a strong competitor may reduce the profitability of all other stations operating in the same market. As will be seen the results below support the latter hypothesis.

If the presence of a strong competitor (television/radio cross-holding in the local market) cuts the profitability of all other stations in its market, then the presence of a weak competitor (television/newspaper cross-holding in the local market) can be expected to enhance the profitability of competing stations.

9.2 MODEL SPECIFICATION

The econometric models used to analyze the determinants of television station price-cost margins, revenues, and expenses are developed in Appendix 9.1.

9.3 THE DATA

The nature of the data used to test the econometric models in Appendix 9.1, and the sources of this data, are described in Appendix 9.2.

9.4 EMPIRICAL EVIDENCE: TELEVISION STATION PRICE-COST MARGINS

The results of the analysis of the determinants of television station price-cost margins are shown in Table 9.1. Equation 1 gives the results for a specification using market-defined ownership variables; equation 2 for nationally-defined ownership variables. Equation 1 has nine degrees of freedom and equation 2 has seven (degrees of freedom equal sample size less the number of independent variables). Standard statistical tests are based on large samples of data which can be assumed to follow a normal distribution; as sample size falls it becomes more likely that the data will not correspond to this distribution.

One of the most important findings is the difference in explanatory power of the two specifications. Equation 1 is able to account for 94 percent of the variation in price-cost margin whereas equation 2 is only able to account for 77 percent the variation. This highlights the importance of local market factors and suggests that public policy analysis of the economic performance of the television industry might well be better directed to problems at the local market level rather than the national level.

In evaluating the relative importance of the various determinants of price-cost margin, it might be well to bear in mind that in equation 1 the constant term is -1.18 and in equation 2 it is -.93 (both significant at the 95 percent level of confidence). The mean value of the price-cost margin for all twenty stations was .18. A value of 1 would mean that a station had revenue but no expenses. A value of zero that station revenues exactly equalled station expenses.

The level of statistical significance of all coefficients is shown in the tables. In the text all coefficients discussed are significant at the 95 percent level unless otherwise stated.

9.4.1 The Competitive Position of the Firm

The size of fitted values of audience in the local CMA has no significant influence on price-cost margin when ownership is analyzed from the local market perspective. From a national ownership perspective it has a statistically significant, but small effect, with an increase of 100,000 in average daily hours market audience (roughly a third for the average station) associated with a .03 increase in price-cost margin (mean = .18).

There is no evidence that a station's audience outside its local CMA has any influence on its price-cost margin. Share of market revenue was not included in the analysis.

9.4.2 Local Market Characteristics

The theoretical predictions that increase in market concentration and in average income levels would lead to increased pro-

Table 9.1

REGRESSION RESULTS: TELEVISION STATION PRICE-COST MARGINS[1]

Dependent Variable	Eqn. 1 PCM	Eqn. 2 PCM
Independent Variables:		
Constant	-1.18 (2.57)**	-.93 (2.09)**
Fitted market audience		.00000030 (3.68)**
HRF (revenue Herfindahl)	.37 (2.59)**	
POP (population)	-.000000093 (2.02)*	
INC (income)	.00033 (4.18)**	.00025 (2.46)**
NEWS (cost of news)	-.00000049 (5.07)**	-.00000055 (3.95)**
ENT (cost of entertainment)	.00000013 (6.52)**	
MLP (minutes of local programming)	.0000038 (4.71)**	.0000023 (2.25)**
MCB (minutes of Canadian programming)	-.000010 (1.95)*	
TRM (TV/radio in market)	.60 (9.16)**	
CTRM (competes with TV/radio in market)	-.16 (2.38)**	
CTNM (competes with TV/news in market)	.32 (2.94)**	
CCBC (competes with CBC)	-.20 (1.72)	-.32 (3.04)**
TR (national TV/radio)		.46 (5.13)**
CTR (competes with national TV/radio)		-.15 (1.98)*
Mean value of dependent variable	.18	.18
R^2	.94	.77
n = no. of stations	20	20

1. Figures in parentheses are t-statistics, others are regression coefficients.

* Significant at the 90 percent level of confidence.
** Significant at the 95 percent level of confidence.

fitability were supported by the results in equation 1. There an increase of .10 in the Herfindahl index is associated with a .037 increase in the price-cost margin while a $1000 increase in average income is associated with a .33 increase in price-cost margin, a very substantial increase when we recall that the average price-cost margin is only .18. Equation 2, with nationally-defined ownership variables, showed a .25 increase in price-cost margin for each $1000 increase in average income.

The population of the local CMA was found to have only a small and statistically weak (significant only in equation 1 and there only at the 90 percent level of confidence) effect on profitability.

9.4.3 Programming Competition

The results support the hypothesis that, from an economic point of view, television is basically an entertainment medium. An increase of $100,000 in entertainment programming is associated with an increase of .013 in a television station's price-cost margin in equation 1 (not significant in equation 2). A similar increase in news programming expenditures, however, is associated with a reduction in price-cost margin of .049 in equation 1 (.055 in equation 2).

Over a full year, the 20 television stations in the sample average approximately 45,000 minutes of local programming (on a full day basis) and 67,000 minutes of prime time Canadian programming. An increase of 10,000 minutes in local programming was found to be associated with a .038 increase in price-cost margin in equation 1 (.023 in equation 2). A similar increase in prime time Canadian content was associated with a very large (since the mean is only .18) .10 decrease in price-cost margin, significant at the 90 percent level.

An extra hour per day of local programming therefore adds .050 to .083 to the price-cost margin while an extra hour per day of prime time Canadian programming reduces the price-cost margin by .219. When we recall that the average station's price-cost margin is only .18 the depressing effect of Canadian programming on profits is apparent.

9.4.4 Ownership Structure

Television/radio cross-ownership is the single most important element of ownership structure insofar as the determination of television station price-cost margins is concerned. Where the owners of a television station also own a radio station in the same market this alone accounts for an extremely large .60 increase in the station's price-cost margin. Ownership of a radio station located elsewhere in Canada is associated with a .46 increase in price-cost margin. Moreover, these stations appear to be such strong competitors that their presence in the market reduces the

Table 9.2

REGRESSION RESULTS: TELEVISION STATION REVENUE[1]

Dependent Variable	Eqn. 1 Revenue	Eqn. 2 Revenue
Independent Variables:		
Constant	-16,990,000 (2.77)**	1,420,000 (2.21)**
Fitted market audience		4.50 (3.38)**
HRF (revenue Herfindahl) INC (income)	5,840,000 (3.88)** 2375.24 (2.07)*	
NEWS (cost of news) ENT (cost of entertainment) MLP (minutes of local programming)	-3.59 (2.23)** 3.24 (12.91)** 29.68 (3.04)**	-2.73 (1.74)* 2.07 (5.55)**
TRM (TV/radio in market) TNM (TV/news in market)	5,600,000 (5.32)** -2,630,000 (2.70)**	
TT (national TV/TV group) CTR (competes with national TV/radio group)		1,140,000 (1.34) -2,180,000 (2.26)**
Mean Value of Dependent Variable	7,300,000	7,300,000
R^2	.96	.94
n = no. of stations	20	20

1. Figures in parentheses are t-statistics, others are regression
    coefficients.

 * Significant at the 90 percent level of confidence.
** Significant at the 95 percent level of confidence.

profitability of all stations forced to compete against them. The presence of a firm with a local market television radio cross-holding is associated with a reduction of .16 in the price-cost margin of all other stations in that market. When ownership is analyzed from a national perspective television/radio cross-owner-ship is associated with a similar .15 reduction in the price-cost margin of competitors (significant at the 90 percent level).

On the other hand, stations which find themselves fortunate enough to compete against a firm owning both a television station and a local newspaper can expect to find their price-cost margin enhanced by .32 on this account alone. Those stations which com-pete against CBC stations can be expected to experience reduced price-cost margins, by .32 in the national ownership variable analysis.

9.5 EMPIRICAL EVIDENCE: TELEVISION STATION REVENUE

The results of the analysis of the determinants of television station revenues are shown in Table 9.2. Equation 1 reports the results for a specification using market-defined ownership vari-ables; equation 2 for nationally-defined ownership variables. Equation 1 is able to account for 96 percent of the variation in television station revenues; equation 2 for 94 percent.

Station revenues varied over a wide range with the average revenue of all twenty stations in the sample being $7.3 million. In the discussion of the factors influencing the size of station revenue statistical significance levels will be noted only when they differ from 95 percent.

9.5.1 The Competitive Position of the Firm

As in the analysis of advertising rates, audience size is statistically significant only when the ownership variables are defined from a national perspective. Then, an increase of 100,000 daily hours in a station's local market audience (roughly a third for the average station) is associated with a modest $450,000 in-crease in annual revenues.

Regardless of the specification employed, there is no evi-dence that the size of a station's audience outside its local CMA has any affect on its revenues. Share of market revenue was not included in the analysis.

9.5.2 Local Market Characteristics

The extremely important role which the level of market con-centration played in the pricing of commercial time is reflected in the revenue results. Every .10 increase in the Herfindahl index of market concentration is associated with an increment of $584,000 in the total revenue of the typical station (in equation 1; statistically insignificant in equation 2).

Equation 1 also shows that stations located in higher income markets can expect to generate greater revenues with every $1,000 increase in average income being associated with a $2,375,000 revenue increment (significant at the 90 percent level; insignificant in equation 2).

9.5.3 Programming Competition

Both equations provide strong evidence that the relationship between programming expenditures and price-cost margins revealed earlier is rooted in revenue effects. Every additional $1 of expenditure on news programming is associated with a $3.59 drop in revenues in equation 1 ($2.73 drop in equation 2 significant at the 90 percent level). At the same time an increase of $1 in entertainment programming expenditures is associated with a $3.24 rise in station total revenue in equation 1 (a $2.07 rise in equation 2).

Equation 1 provides evidence of the predicted association between minutes of local programming and station revenues. The magnitude of the relationship is, however, unexpectedly large with every additional minute of local programming being associated with $29.68 in additional revenues. To put this in perspective, this means that an additional hour per day of local programming would generate additional revenue of $650,000 per year, quite a substantial increase when compared to average station revenue of $7.3 million. As hypothesized, the number of minutes of prime time Canadian programming does not appear to be a significant determinant of television station revenues.

9.5.4 Ownership Structure

The influence which ownership structure, defined for the local market, had on the determination of advertising rates is reflected in the revenue analysis. A television/radio cross-holding in the local market is associated with an increment of $5.6 million in station revenues while a television/newspaper cross-holding is associated with a $2.6 million decrease in revenues.

As we have argued in Chapter 5, both types of cross-ownership would be expected to decrease competition in the sale of advertising and increase television advertising rates, revenues and price-cost margins. Our results for television/radio cross-holdings are consistent with this expectation. There is no obvious economic explanation why corporations that own both a television station and a newspaper in the same market should have lower prices for advertising, and earn lower revenues and profits, but the evidence is clear that in Canada this is the case.

In the national ownership variable specification the parallel television/radio and television/newspaper influence on ad rates is surprisingly not reflected in station revenues. The only statistically significant result is that pointing to a $2.18 million

drop in the revenue of any station competing with a station belonging to a national television/radio group.

9.6 EMPIRICAL EVIDENCE: TELEVISION STATION EXPENSES

The results of the analysis of the determinants of television
station expenses are shown in Table 9.3. Equation 1 reports on a
specification using market-defined ownership variables; equation 2
nationally-defined ownership variables. Both specifications are
able to account for 98 percent of the variation in television station total expenses. The average level of these expenses over all
twenty stations is $5.6 million.

In equation 2 the constant term of -$16.9 million is signifi-
cant at the 95 percent level (insignificant in equation 1). This
value reflects the influence of variables excluded from the regression model. In the following discussion all coefficients are
significant at the 95 percent level unless otherwise stated.

9.6.1 The Competitive Position of the Firm

No statistically significant relationship exists between a
television station's expenses and the size of its audience in its
local CMA. On the other hand, the size of audience outside the
local CMA proved to be a significant determinant of total station
expenses with each increment of 100,000 daily viewer hours (roughly a third for the average station) being associated with a
$499,000 increase in expenses in equation 1 ($1,037,000 in equation 2).

A television station's share of total market revenue was
found to be strongly related to total expenses with each 10 percentage points of total revenue being associated with roughly a
$1 million increase in total expenses ($999,000 in equation 1;
$874,000 in equation 2). Compared to average station expenses of
$5.6 million this is an increase of from 16 to 18 percent.

9.6.2 Local Market Characteristics

Leibenstein and others have argued that reduced competition
permits and typically leads to inefficiency and increased
costs.[3] A surprising and important result is the finding of the
strong relationship between the level of market concentration and
total expenses. Thus it appears that a lessening of competitive
pressure in a local market leads not only to higher prices, and
revenues, but it also reduces station expenses, all other things
being equal. Each increase of 10 percentage points in the Herfindahl index of concentration of market revenue is associated
with a reduction of over $1 million in total expenses ($1,323,000
in equation 1; $1,157,000 in equation 2). What may be happening
here is that television stations in concentrated markets may be
able to get away with lower program expenditures because of the
reduced competition for audience.

Table 9.3

REGRESSION RESULTS: TELEVISION STATION EXPENSES[1]

	Eqn. 1	Eqn. 2
Dependent Variable	Expenses	Expenses
Independent Variables:		
Constant	-1,850,000 (.55)	-16,900,000 (4.29)**
AUDE (audience outside CMA)	4.99 (5.05)**	10.37 (10.03)**
SHR (revenue share)	9,990,000 (5.28)**	8,740,000 (4.33)**
HRF (revenue Herfindahl)	-13,230,000 (6.58)**	-11,570,000 (4.62)**
POP (population)	2.76 (8.89)**	
INC (income)	-1,295.51 (1.98)*	
MLP (minutes of local programming)	-30.43 (4.52)**	-31.00 (4.31)**
MCB (minutes of Canadian broadcasting)	200.77 (5.24)**	308.64 (6.83)**
TRM (TV/radio in market)	-2,650,000 (5.45)**	
TR (national TV/radio)		-3,130,000 (6.11)**
CTT (competes with national TV/TV group)		6,580,000 (9.82)**
CTN (competes with national TV/news)		-7,480,000 (6.32)**
CCBC (competes with CBC)		2,710,000 (2.43)**
Mean Value of Dependent Variable	5,620,000	5,620,000
R^2	.98	.98
n = no. of stations	20	20

1. Figures in parentheses are t-statistics, others are regression
    coefficients.

*   Significant at the 90 percent level of confidence.
** Significant at the 95 percent level of confidence.

As predicted on the basis of transmission and programming costs, a direct relationship exists between the population of a station's CMA and its total expenses. Each increase of 1,000 in CMA population is associated with a $2,760 rise in expenses in equation 1 (insignificant in equation 2).

The situation in relation to market income is not so satisfactory. Whereas it was expected that increases in average incomes would be reflected in higher station expenses (as a result of influences on station wage rates) the results in equation 1 indicate that, in fact, an increase of $1000 in market income is association with a decrease of $1,295,000 in station expenses. This finding is significant at the 90 percent level of confidence. There is no apparent reason why television station expenses should be inversely related to the level of market income.

9.6.3 Programming Competition

Since expenditures on news and entertainment programming constitute part of total expenses it is of course not possible to examine their influence as independent determinants of total expense. Minutes of Canadian and local programming, because of differences in production costs, had their expected effect on total expenses. Local programming proved to be cheaper than network programming, with each additional minute being associated with an expense reduction of about $30. Each additional minute of prime-time Canadian programming, on the other hand, was associated with an expense increment of between $201 in equation 1 and $309 in equation 2.

To put these results in perspective, an extra hour a day of prime-time Canadian programming adds $4.4 million to $6.8 million to a television station's expenses. As their expenses, on average, are $5.6 million a year this represents about a doubling of their expenses. It is scarcely surprising that Canadian television broadcasters are reluctant to invest in Canadian programming.

9.6.4 Ownership Structure

In contrast to the price-cost margin and revenue results, ownership structure as viewed from a national perspective appears to have a much more important influence on television station expenses than does the ownership structure of the local market. Four such national ownership structure variables are statistically significant at the 95 percent level. Only one of these, however, relates to the ownership structure of the station itself. The other three relate to the ownership structure characteristics of the stations against which it must compete in the local market.

Insofar as the ownership structure of the station itself is concerned, only television/radio cross-ownership has a significant effect on the level of television station expenses. Membership in a national television/radio group is associated with a $3.1 mil-

lion reduction in the television station's expenses while ownership of a radio station located in the same market is associated
with a reduction of $2.6 million in a television station's ex-
penses.

Results for the remaining national ownership structure variables provide strong evidence that cross-ownership patterns at the
national level have an important influence on the competitive potential of a particular station. Stations in the strongest competitive position appear to be those belonging to ownership groups
holding more than one Canadian television station. In equation 2
it is estimated that any station forced to compete against a station belonging to such a television/television group can be expected to incur $6.6 million additional expenses. Competition
against a CBC station is associated with an increment of $2.7 mil-
lion in total expenses. Stations belonging to national televi-
sion/newspaper groups appear to be the weakest competitors as
competition with such a station is associated with a $7.5 million
reduction in the total expenses of each competing station.

9.7   CONCLUSIONS

Because of the difficulties in measuring the invested capital
base of an individual television station embedded in a large corporation, the price-cost margin has been adopted in this chapter
as an indicator of television station profitability. The analysis
has been directed to an estimation of the relative influence of
various elements of market structure on station profitability
measured in this fashion. In order to provide an in-depth examination of the role played by various determinants of price-cost
margins an examination of the determinants of the underlying station revenues and expenses was also carried out. A common group
of structural factors was considered in all three cases with ownership structure being analyzed from both the national and local
market viewpoints.[4]

9.7.1   The Competitive Position of the Firm

Although it is true that what television stations sell is
audience exposures to commercial messages, our results indicate
that it is overly simplistic to view audience size as the driving
economic force in a station's operations. Total expenses, for example, were found to be unrelated to market audience size. Also,
while size of market audience had a statistically significant influence on station revenues and price-cost margins in a national
ownership specification, this influence was very small. It was
estimated that it would take a massive 100,000 increase in a television station's daily hours of local market audience to increase
its revenues by $450,000 and its price-cost margin by .03.

Audience attracted from outside a station's local CMA proved
to have a significant influence on total expenses ranging from
raising them by an estimated $5,000 (local market ownership speci-

fication to $10,000 (national ownership specification) for each
1000 daily hour increment in such audience. There was no evidence
of any relationship between the size of audience achieved outside
the local market and either station revenues or price-cost margin.
Taken together these findings suggest that, not only is it expensive to build up audience size outside a station's local CMA
(presumably because of incremental programming and transmission
costs), but also such audiences contribute litle to station revenues and profitability. A notable lack of market incentives to
service fringe viewers appears to exist.

The relationship between a station's share of total market
revenue and its price-cost margin and revenue was not examined. A
strong relationship was, however, established between revenue
share and station expenses with each .10 increment in share found
to be associated with between $900,000 (national ownership speci-
fication) and $1 million (local market ownership specification) in
additional expenses. It is possible to interpret this finding as
an indication that stations with large market shares tend to dis-
sipate corporate resources in unduly large expense outlays, but
this seems unlikely. More plausibly, what is at hand is evidence
of the high cost of gaining, and maintaining a large market share.

9.7.2 Local Market Characteristics

On the basis of the results of the ad rate analysis it had
not been expected that population size would exert any important
influence on television station revenues. Expense increases, on
the basis of increased transmission and programming expenses, and
resultant price-cost margin reductions were, however, expected.
The results provided evidence of the hypothesized relationships
but indicated that all effects were minor.

No statistically significant relationship was found between
the size of a television station's revenues and the population of
the market in which it is based. If television stations in large
cities have large revenues these can be attributed fully to factors other than the population of the market in which they are
based. On the other hand, while increases in market population
were found to be associated with expense increases and price-cost
margin reductions the effects were minor. A population increase
of 100,000 was associated with a rise in expenses of only $275,000
and a reduction in the price-cost margin of only .0093. This is
worth noting, but not worthy of much concern.

It had been expected that the positive relationship between
the level of market income and advertising rates would be reflected in station revenues, but that income increases would also
raise wage costs and possibly programming costs leading to higher
expenses. Since revenue effects were expected to outweigh expense
effects on an overall basis it was hypothesized that increases in
the level of market income would be associated with price-cost
margin increases.

Although a statistically significant relationship was only identified in the local market ownership variable specification, and then significance was only at the 90 percent level, it is estimated that a $1,000 increase in the average income level in a station's home market is associated with a $2.4 million rise in revenues and a $1.3 million drop in expenses. Thus both revenue and expense considerations become mutually reinforcing, leading to price-cost margin increases of between .25 and .33 for each $1,000 increase in the level of average income in the market.

Because of the wide variations that exist in per capita income, these results provide evidence of a very important role for market income levels as a determinant of the economic fortunes of a television station. St. John's at $3,180 and Ottawa/Hull at $4,970 provide the extreme values of per capita income over the 14 markets included in this study. Even using the more conservative estimate (.25 national ownership specification) of the effect of market income on price-cost margins would suggest that a television station located in Ottawa/Hull could be expected to have a price-cost margin .45 greater than that of an otherwise comparable St. John's station on account of the difference in per capita income levels alone. The comparable result using the coefficient estimated in the local market ownership variable specification would be .60. Since the average price-cost margin over all twenty stations in the sample is only .18, the level of per capita income in a station's home market is clearly a crucial factor in determining its profitability.

The most interesting finding here has been the identification of the important influence of market concentration on television station expenses, revenues, and price-cost margins in an analysis using local market defined ownership variables. A .10 increase in the Herfindahl index is associated with an expense reduction of $1.3 million, a revenue increase of $.6 million and a price-cost margin increase of .037.

Since revenue based Herfindahl indices vary from .272 in the case of Toronto to 1.0 in cities such as London, the effects involved are clearly very large. While the average level of television station expenses is only $5.6 million, the expenses of a station in London could be expected to be over $9 million lower than those of a comparable Toronto station on account of lack of competition alone. In the case of revenues, where the average for all 20 stations is $7.3 million, the monopoly position of a station in London could be expected to be associated with additional revenues of over $4 million. Since market power is associated with expense reductions and revenue increases the combined influence on price-cost margins is even more powerful. The average price-cost margin for all 20 stations in the sample is only .18, but the single Canadian station in London could be expected to generate a pricecost margin higher by .26 than a comparable Toronto station solely on account of differences in levels of seller concentration.

These are powerful findings and they indicate severe limitations to previous examinations of the Canadian television industry
which have ignored competitive conditions at the local market level. Seller concentration at the local market level plays a key
role in determining the economic success or failure of a television station.

9.7.3 Programming Competition

The evidence of this study supports the idea that from an
economic point of view television is basically an entertainment
rather than a news medium. In the local ownership specification
each additional $1 spent on entertainment programming was asso-
ciated with a $3.25 increase in revenues while $1 spent on news
programming was associated with a $3.60 decrease in revenues.
(The corresponding figures in the national ownership specification
were $2.10 and $2.75.) These influences were also evident in the
price-cost margin analysis where a $100,000 increment in enter-
tainment programming was associated with a .013 increase in price-
cost margin while the same increment in news programming was associated with a decrease of between .049 (local ownership specification) and .055 (national ownership specification). The behavioural implications are clear. Private, profit-oriented owners of
television stations, are faced with strong economic incentives to
expand entertainment programming expenditures and reduce those for
news programming. Such economic incentives may not always accord
with wider public objectives.

It is well established that it is more expensive to produce
Canadian programming than to purchase comparable programming from
American sources.[5] The analysis of television station expenses
reflects the influence of the harsh realities of Canadian television program production. An extra hour a day of prime-time Canadian programming adds $4.4 million to $6.8 million a year to a
television station's expenses. As their expenses, on average, are
$5.6 million a year this represents a doubling of their expenses.

In a result that may seem surprising to some, no statistical
relationship was found between the volume of prime time Canadian
programming and television station revenues. Nevertheless, expense side considerations were sufficiently prominent to show
through in the econometric results: an additional 1,000 minutes
of Canadian programming was associated with a .010 reduction in
price-cost margin. While the economic disadvantages of increased
Canadian content may show up only on the production cost side,
this offers but cold comfort to television station owners. Even
if Canadian programming is able to attract advertisers its production cost disadvantage provides an unambiguous market incentive
for station owners to reduce their Canadian programming to the
legally constrained minima. It should also be noted that these
results also provide an estimate of the impact on television station expenses, and price-cost margins of changes in government-
mandated Canadian content requirements.

The hypothesized relationship between the number of minutes of local programming and television station expenses, revenues, and price-cost margins was supported by the evidence. The results indicated local programming was cheaper to produce, with each additional minute associated with a $31 reduction in expenses (both specifications). At the same time, the local ownership specification showed that local programming is attractive to advertisers with each additional minute associated with a $30 increase in revenues. Naturally, in these circumstances, increased local programming could be expected to lead to higher profitability. We found that an increase of 1,000 minutes was associated with an increase of from .0038 (local ownership specification) to .0023 (national ownership specification) in a television station's price-cost margin. This means that for the average station an additional hour per day of local programming would add $666,000 annually to expenses; generate additional annual revenues of $650,000; and result in an increase of between .05 and .08 in the price-cost margin (mean = .18).

These results seem to constitute the only "good news" on programming competition. While economic incentives favour entertainment over news, and foreign programming over Canadian programming, at least they do point television station owners in the direction of increased local programming.

9.7.4 Ownership Structure

There was no evidence that the price-cost margins of television/television group owned stations are higher than those of other stations. This is consistent with the work of Levin who found in the United States that groups had only slight differences in profit margins suggesting little cost advantage and that group stations earned profits comparable to those of single-owned stations.[6]

Television/radio cross-ownership is the single most important element of ownership structure insofar as the determination of television station price-cost margins is concerned. Where the owners of a television station also own a radio station in the same market this alone accounts for a .60 increase in the station's price-cost margin. Ownership of a radio station located elsewhere in Canada is associated with a .46 increase in price-cost margin. The magnitude of these effects makes them extremely important. Their relative importance is best judged by comparing them to the average price-cost margin for all 20 stations which is .18. Radio/television cross-ownership is associated with price-cost margin increases double or triple the magnitude of these average values.

These strong price-cost margin results occur as a consequence of the cumulative impact of television/radio cross-ownership on both revenues and expenses. In the case of revenues, it had been expected that since television/radio cross-ownership had been as-

sociated with higher ad rates, these higher rates would be reflected in higher station revenues. When ownership variables were
specified on a local market basis these revenue effects were evident with local market television/radio cross-ownership associated
with a $5.6 million revenue increase. At the same time estimated
expense reductions of from $2.6 million (local market ownership
specification) to $3.1 million (national ownership specification)
occurred. The impacts of these revenue increases (presumably as a
result of increased market power in the overall market for advertising) and expense savings (on managerial and production costs)
combine to produce the extremely large increases in price-cost
margins found to have been associated with television/radio cross-
ownership whether at the local market or national level.

Moreover, television/radio cross-owned stations appear to be
such strong competitors that their presence in the market reduces
the profitability of all stations forced to compete against them.
The presence of a firm with a local market television/radio cross-
holding is associated with a reduction of .16 in the price-cost
margin of all other stations in that market. When ownership is
analyzed from a national perspective television/radio cross-ownership is associated with a similar .15 reduction in the price-cost
margin of competitors (significant at the 90 percent level).

These price-cost margin effects appear to result principally
from the influence which television/radio cross-owned stations
have on the revenues of competing stations. In a national ownership specification a revenue loss for each competing station of
$2.2 million was estimated.

No evidence was found that owners of television/newspaper
cross-holdings were able to increase the price-cost margins of
their television stations on this account. In fact, following the
ad rate results, revenues of such stations were estimated to be
$2.6 million lower (local ownership specification) than other
stations.

On the other hand, stations which find themselves fortunate
enough to compete against a firm owning both a television station
and a local newspaper can expect to find their price-cost margin
enhanced by .32 on this account alone. Those stations which compete against CBC stations, however, can be expected to experience
reduced price-cost margins by .32 in the national ownership variable analysis.

These results seem to stem directly from expense side considerations. In the national ownership variable specification those
stations competing against television/newspaper cross-owned stations are able to reduce expenses by $7.5 million while those
forced to compete against a CBC station are forced to increase
outlays by $2.7 million. Competition against a television/tele-
vision group owned station is associated with an expense increment
of $6.6 million. These results suggest that ownership structure

can influence a station's competitive potential and that competing
stations may be forced to take these influences into account in
determining the levels of their expense outlays.

If the level of profits in television is excessive (evidence
on this point was presented in Chapter 8), then ownership structures contributing to increased profit levels are not in the public interest. The evidence of this chapter indicates that televi-
sion/radio cross-ownership, whether at the local market or national level, is a major offender on this score. It is associated
with large increases in the price-cost margins (profitability) of
the TV stations in such groups. These findings call into question
the regulatory stance which has permitted the existence of widespread television/radio cross-holdings.

The role of the CBC stations, in holding down the profits of
their competitors, points to a previously unsuspected economic
effect of the operations of the publicly owned corporation.

Notes to Chapter 9

1. Bruce M. Owen, Jack H. Beebe and Willard G. Manning, _Televi-
    sion Economics_ (Lexington, Mass.: Lexington Books, D.C.
    Heath, 1974), pp. 4-5.

2. It is also possible as Rosse, Owen, and Grey have argued that
    audience size, through its effect on advertising rates and
    revenues, will influence the level of program expenditures.
    The findings of this study do not support this hypothesis how-
    ever. See James N. Rosse, Bruce M. Owen and David L. Grey,
    "Economics Issues in the Joint Ownership of Newspaper and
    Television Media," Comments in response to "Further Notice of
    Proposed Rule Making," Federal Communications Commission,
    Docket 18110, Memorandum No. 97, Stanford University Research
    Center in Economic Growth, Stanford, California, May 1970.

3. Harvey Leibenstein, "Allocative Efficiency vs. 'X-Effici-
    ency'," _American Economic Review_, Vol. 56, June 1966, pp. 392-
    415.

4. Revenue share was not considered in the analysis of revenues
    and price-cost margin. News and entertainment programming
    expenditures were not included in the analysis of expenses.

5. Canadian Radio-television and Telecommunications Commission,
    "C.R.T.C. Background Paper: The Economic Realities of Cana-
    dian Television Production," _Symposium on Television Violence_
    (Ottawa, Minister of Supply and Services Canada, 1976), pp.
    156-166.

6. H.J. Levin, "Competition, Diversity, and the Television Group Ownership Rule," <u>Columbia Law Review</u>, Vol. 70, May 1971, pp. 791-835.

Appendix 9.1

TELEVISION STATION PRICE-COST MARGINS, REVENUES, AND EXPENSES: MODEL SPECIFICATION

The two-stage least squares approach to the estimation of advertising rates was adopted because of the possibility of significant interdependency between audience size and advertising rates. The concern was that not only might increases in audience size influence ad rates but that these higher ad rates might simultaneously lead to higher audiences through higher levels of programming expenditures. Clearly, the same concern applies in the case of price-cost margins, revenues, and expenses. Increases in audience size may lead to higher price-cost margins or higher revenues but either of these may in turn feed back via programming expenditure increases to further effects on audience size. In the case of television station expenses, this feedback effect (i.e., the influence of audience size on expenditures) becomes the focus of analysis, but the potential for increases in expenses to lead in turn to further increases in audience size must be considered. As in the case of the ad rate analysis these interdependencies can be dealt with using a two-stage least squares model that acknowledges joint dependency but is able to produce an unbiased estimate of the relationship between audience and price-cost margin, revenues, or expenses as the case may be. Since the same approach is used in all three instances discussion will be confined to the case of price-cost margins.

First, audience estimates were prepared using the methodology developed in the audience size analysis but allowing for the possible influence on audience size of various additional determinants of price-cost margin. Format variables were included for only CBC network (affiliated stations only), CTV network, and independents, since no CBC owned, U.S., or cable-only stations are included in the price-cost margin data analyzed. These fitted audience values were then used as one of the independent variables in the estimation of price-cost margins. When ownership variables are defined on a market-by-market basis the model used to estimate these fitted audience values (FAUD) takes the form:

$$
\begin{aligned}
\text{FAUD} = \ &a_0 + a_1(\text{POP/N}) + a_2(\text{POP/N})(\text{CB}) \\
&+ a_3(\text{POP/N})(\text{CT}) + a_4(\text{POP/N})(\text{CN}) + a_5\text{AUDE} \\
&+ a_6\text{SHR} + a_7\text{HRF} + a_8\text{POP} + a_9\text{INC} \\
&+ a_{10}\text{NEWS} + a_{11}\text{ENT} + a_{12}\text{MLP} + a_{13}\text{MCB} \\
&+ a_{14}\text{TTM} + a_{15}\text{TRM} + a_{16}\text{TNM} + a_{17}\text{CBC} \\
&+ a_{18}\text{CTTM} + a_{19}\text{CTRM} + a_{20}\text{CTNM} + a_{21}\text{CCBC}
\end{aligned}
\tag{1}
$$

Where ownership is analyzed on a nation-wide basis the appropriate changes in the appropriate changes in the group and cross-ownership variables in equation (1) must be made.

The inclusion in N of all stations with one percent or more of local prime time audience permits consideration in the audience equation of the audience fragmentation effect of U.S. and non-local Canadian stations. At the same time such stations, since they are not competitors for advertising revenue in the local market, are excluded from measures of competitive conditions and ownership structure in that market.

When we turn to the second stage, the estimation of the determinants of price-cost margin itself, it is convenient for expositional purposes to group the explanatory variables in the categories set out in the text: (i) the competitive position of the firm, (ii) local market characteristics, (iii) product differentiation and production, and (iv) ownership structure.

A9.1 COMPETITIVE POSITION OF THE FIRM

Increases in audience size both within the local market FAUD, and outside that market (AUDE), may lead to increases in profitability. A firm's share (SHR) of aggregate television station revenues for the market provides an additional indication of its competitive position. Where the firm's price-cost margin (PCM), is total revenue minus total expenses all divided by total revenue, this approach leads to an estimating equation of the form

$$PCM = a_0 + a_1 FAUD + a_2 AUDE + a_3 SHR \qquad (2)$$

A9.2 LOCAL MARKET CHARACTERISTICS

Increases in the population of the local market in which a station operates (POP) may be associated with increased expenditures and decreased profitability. Higher levels of average income in the local market (INC), and of seller concentration (HRF), can be expected to lead to higher revenues and price-cost margins. Incorporation of these variables leads to

$$PCM = a_0 + a_1 FAUD + a_2 AUDE + a_3 SHR \\ + a_4 HRF + a_5 POP + a_6 INC \qquad (3)$$

A9.3 PROGRAMMING COMPETITION

Expenditure on entertainment programming (ENT) should be expected to increase revenues and profitability whereas the converse is expected in the case of news programming (NEWS). The number of minutes of prime time Canadian broadcasting (MCB) need not be a factor in station revenues but for cost reasons alone should be expected to reduce price-cost margins. If local programming is cheaper and can attract greater revenues then increases in the number of minutes of local programming on a full-day basis (MLP) can be expected to be associated with higher price-cost margins. Consideration of these factors leads to an estimating equation of the form

$$PCM = a_0 + a_1FAUD + a_2AUDE + a_3SHR$$
$$+ a_4HRF + a_5POP + a_6INC + a_7NEWS$$
$$+ a_8ENT + a_9MLP + a_{10}MCB \qquad (4)$$

A9.4 OWNERSHIP STRUCTURE

Analysis of ownership structure is again possible from both the local market and national perspectives. This involves the use of two different sets of ownership structure variables. Consider first variables defined on a local market basis.

Ownership of two television stations in a single market (TTM) could be expected to increase a firm's market power and hence the revenues and price-cost margins of the stations involved. Cross-ownership of a radio station (TRM) or newspaper (TNM) in the local market might serve to increase a firm's market power in the advertising market and hence increase the revenues and price-cost margin of the television station involved. Public-ownership need not be included since such stations are not operated according to the commercial objectives of privately-owned stations.

These variations in ownership structure influence not only the market performance of the firms characterized by multi and cross-ownership, but also the market performance of their competitors. This necessitates the inclusion of variables representing competition from a firm owning two television stations in a market (CTTM), competition from a firm owning both a radio station and a television station in the same market (CTRM), and competition from a firm owning both a television station and a newspaper in the market (CTNM). Competition with a CBC-owned station can be denoted by CCBC.

Analysis of ownership structure on this market-by-market basis results in a final estimating equation of the form

$$PCM = a_0 + a_1FAUD + a_2AUDE + a_3SHR$$
$$+ a_4HRF + a_5POP + a_6INC + a_7NEWS$$
$$+ a_8ENT + a_9MLP + a_{10}MCB + a_{11}TTM$$
$$+ a_{12}TRM + a_{13}TNM + a_{14}CTTM + a_{15}CTRM$$
$$+ a_{16}CTNM + a_{17}CCBC \qquad (5)$$

Each of the ownership structure characteristics is described by a dummy variable taking the value 1 when the characteristic applies in the case of the firm at hand, zero otherwise.

The estimating equation takes the same form when the dependent variable is television station total revenue (R):

$$R = a_0 + a_1FAUD + a_2AUDE + a_3SHR + a_4HRF$$
$$+ a_5POP + a_6INC + a_7NEWS + a_8ENT$$
$$+ a_9MLP + a_{10}MCB + a_{11}TTM + a_{12}TRM$$
$$+ a_{13}TNM + a_{14}CTTM + a_{15}CTRM + a_{16}CTNM$$
$$+ a_{17}CCBC \qquad (6)$$

and when the dependent variable is television station total expenses (E) it takes the form:

$$
\begin{aligned}
E = a_0 &+ a_1 FAUD + a_2 AUDE + a_3 SHR + a_4 HRF \\
&+ a_5 POP + a_6 INC + a_7 NEWS + a_8 ENT \\
&+ a_9 MLP + a_{10} MCB + a_{11} TTM + a_{12} TRM \\
&+ a_{13} TNM + a_{14} CTTM + a_{15} CTRM + a_{16} CTNM \\
&+ a_{17} CCBC
\end{aligned} \tag{7}
$$

In the alternative national specification of ownership patterns, the analysis proceeds in a similar way once the appropriate changes in variable definition have been made. Ownership of a television station by a concern which owns another television station anywhere in Canada is denoted by TT. Ownership of a radio station anywhere in Canada by the owner of a particular television station is denoted TR. Cross-ownership of a newspaper anywhere in Canada by a television station's owners is denoted TN. Competition by a television station with stations of the above types is denoted by CTT, CTR and CTN respectively; competition with a CBC-owned station by CCBC.

The estimating equations in the case of the Canada-wide specification of the ownership pattern remain in the same form as equations (5), (6) and (7) with the appropriate re-specification of ownership structure variables.

Appendix 9.2

TELEVISION STATION PRICE-COST MARGINS,
REVENUES, AND EXPENSES: THE DATA

The new variables introduced in Chapter 9 include minutes of local programming, minutes of Canadian broadcasting, and
the dependent variables television station expenses, revenues, and
price-cost margins. The sources of data for all other variables
is discussed in the Appendices to previous chapters.

Information on the 1975 total minutes of local programming on a full-day basis, and minutes of prime time Canadian
broadcasting, was obtained from the Economic Planning and Analysis
Branch of the CRTC. The financial data on television station expenses and revenues is based on information supplied by the stations in their Annual Return, Radio and Television filed by each
station with Statistics Canada. This information was not supplied
directly to the researchers but access to it was provided by the
federal Department of Communications for purposes of empirical
analysis.

Price-cost margin estimates were based on a sample of 20
stations. The analysis of the determinants of advertising rates
was based on a sample of 35 stations. However, 13 of these were
CBC-owned and revenue and expense data was not available for two
private stations.

Chapter 10

Radio Station Profits, Price-Cost Margins, Revenues and Expenses

Analysis of audience size and advertising rates provides insight into the workings of the radio industry, but a more complete picture requires additional analysis of economic performance. Various measures of industry performance are possible. This chapter examines the factors affecting the level of profits and pricecost margins in the industry. The next chapter contains an evaluation of the impact of ownership structure in the radio industry on programming performance.

Radio stations may be interested in increasing audience size in order to justify higher advertising rates, but they do not seek to maximize either audience size or advertising rate. It is assumed that firms attempt to maximize long run profits taking due account of basic market limitations, behaviour of competitors, regulation, etc. CBC radio stations, which by 1975 had largely discontinued paid commercials, compete for audience with private stations but are not competitors in the market for radio advertising. Accordingly, the analysis of revenues and profits is restricted to privately-owned radio stations.

10.1 PROFITS OF RADIO STATIONS

Information on the profitability of broadcasting corporations and on the rates of return achieved by the investors in broadcasting corporations was presented in Chapter 8. Direct examination of the determinants of radio industry profits encounters the same methodological difficulties that arose in the case of the television industry, namely the multiple ownership of broadcast undertakings by single corporations and the commingling of broadcasting and non-broadcasting assets within any single corporation. Fortunately, in the case of radio there are a number of corporations in the industry that operate only a single radio station and do not possess significant non-radio assets. For such stations the ownership structure and market characteristic variables applicable to the individual radio station can also be used in an analysis of the rate of return of the radio corporation. The profit measure used here is the return on investment defined as the ratio of the

total of interest plus profits before tax divided by the total of
long-term debt plus equity.

In order to analyze the factors influencing the profitability
of radio stations owned by corporations operating another radio
station or with other significant assets it is necessary to revert
to the use of price-cost margin as a proxy for rate of return.
The rationale for this was explained in Chapter 9. Subsequent
analysis of the determinants of radio station revenues and expenses provides further insights on the factors affecting profitability in this industry.

When advertising rates were analyzed, market structure was
considered in terms of (i) the competitive position of the firm in
the local market, (ii) the characteristics of that market and,
(iii) ownership structure. In the case of profit rates, price-
cost margins, revenues and expenses it seems useful to adopt a
similar approach, with programming variables incorporated where
this is appropriate.

10.1.1 Competitive Position of the Firm

The advertising rate analysis in Chapter 7 showed that radio
stations with larger audiences in their local Census Metropolitan
Area tended to charge more for commercial time. Accordingly, it
is to be expected that increased local market audience will tend
to lead to increased station profitability. At the same time
there was little evidence that audience drawn from outside a station's CMA influenced a station's ad rates. Little effect on profitability should be expected.

Rational, profit-maximizing radio station owners will not
wish to pursue increases in market share to the point of incurring
profit reductions. But long run market strategy or non-economic
motivations may cause this to occur. In any event, it is certainly to be expected that gains in market share will be achieved
at the cost of (possibly large) increases in expenditure.

10.1.2 Local Market Characteristics

The strong relationship between levels of seller concentration and advertising rates should be reflected in the profit rate
analysis. High seller concentration, even if it does not lead to
collusion, increases the interdependence amongst firms. Increased
interdependence can be expected to lead to a dampening of competitive pressures and hence increases in prices and profitability.

The approach to market population developed in the television
station price-cost margin analysis (Chapter 9) would seem to apply
with equal force in the radio industry. Market population, being
a rough proxy for potential audience, can be expected to exert
some influence on revenues. (There was support for this in the

analysis of FM radio pricing.) Offsetting influences on the expense side appear, however, to be potentially more important. A
larger population may imply a larger geographic area of coverage
requiring more expensive transmission facilities. More importantly, cities with larger populations may necessitate increased
programming expenditures, as for example, increased costs of local
news coverage. If increases in population have greater impact on
radio station expenses than they do on station revenues then each
population increment should lead, other things being equal, to
decreases in price-cost margins and profitability of local radio
stations.

10.1.3 Programming Competition

Lacking data on radio station local and Canadian programming,
analysis must be confined to the question of the balance between
news and entertainment programming. Our hypothesis is the converse of that adopted for television, namely, that expenditures on
news programming will have a greater impact on station profitability than expenditures on entertainment programming.

10.1.4 Ownership Structure

In considering radio/radio group ownership it should be noted
that only when a firm owns more than one radio station in a given
local market is seller concentration increased with consequent upward pressure on ad rates and profits. Accordingly, while radio/
radio group ownership at the local level should be expected to be
associated with higher profit rates and price-cost margins these
effects may be weaker or non-existent for national radio/radio
group ownership.

Radio/television and radio/newspaper cross-holdings at the
local market level should be expected to increase the firm's market power in the overall sale of advertising in the city (CMA)
concerned. This should be expected to lead to higher prices for
all advertising, including radio advertising, and increased radio
revenues, profits, and price-cost margins. The radio pricing analysis however produced little evidence of these effects so they
may well not be evident in the results of the profitability analysis.

For national radio/television and radio/newspaper groups the
influence of increased market power in a national market on revenues and profits can be expected to be much weaker. Savings on
management costs, news gathering costs and in the case of radio/
television groups, co-production, may take on greater importance.

As was noted in the discussion of television station profitability, economic theory provides us with little guidance as to
how the existence of particular cross-ownership arrangements might
be expected to affect the profitability of competing firms. On
the one hand, television/radio cross-ownership that enables a firm

to increase its ad rate, revenues, and price-cost margin may provide a pricing umbrella that permits similar increases to its
competitors. On the other hand, the existence of such a strong
competitor may reduce the profitability of all other stations
operating in the same market. Where only the results on the
"competes with" variables are known it is difficult to infer the
nature of the direct influence involved.

10.2 MODEL SPECIFICATION

As in the television analysis, in order to produce an unbiased estimate of the relationship between audience and profit
rates, price-cost margins, revenues, and expenses in turn, a two
stage least squares estimation technique was used. First, audience estimates were developed using the radio station audience
size methodology but allowing for the possible influence on audience size of various additional determinants of profit rates,
price-cost margins, revenues, and expenses. Then, these fitted
audience values were used as one of the independent variables in
the estimation of the various dependent variables. Exact details
of the model used for each of profits, price-cost margins, revenues and expenses are shown in Appendix 10.1.

10.3 THE DATA

The dependent variables radio station expenses, revenues,
price-cost margins and radio corporation profit rate are the only
new variables introduced here. The source of data for all other
variables is discussed in the Appendices to previous chapters.

The 1975 financial data on radio station expenses, revenues,
and rates of return are based on information supplied by the station in their Annual Return, Radio and Television filed by each
station with Statistics Canada. This information was not supplied
directly to the researchers, but access to it was provided on a
confidential basis by the federal Department of Communications for
purposes of the regression analysis.

The information required to calculate rates of return (interest plus profits before tax divided by the total long-term debt
plus equity) for the profit rate analysis was available for 13
corporations. Each of these owned a single radio station and did
not have significant non-radio assets. Information permitting the
calculation of pricecost margins was available for 51 radio stations in the CMAs examined in this study.

10.4 EMPIRICAL EVIDENCE: PROFIT RATES OF SINGLE RADIO STATION CORPORATIONS

Since the rate of return earned by firms in an industry is
one of the key dimensions of market performance, an analysis of
the determinants of radio corporation profit rates clearly offers
certain conceptual advantages. At the same time, because of data

Table 10.1

PROFIT RATES OF SINGLE STATION CORPORATIONS IN THE RADIO INDUSTRY, 1975[1]

Dependent Variable	Eqn. 1 Profit Rate	Eqn. 2 Profit Rate
Independent Variables:		
Constant	-2.30(1.13)	-.20(.11)
Fitted Market Audience SHR (revenue share)	-.00000060(2.05)* 2.43(1.97)*	
HRF (revenue Herfindahl) POP (population) INC (income)	-2.90(1.66) -.00000044(2.28)** .00090(1.83)*	-2.53(1.69) -.00000039(2.18)** .00053(1.23)
CRNM (competes with radio/ newspaper in market)	-.53(2.17)**	
CRT (competes with national TV/radio)		-.65(2.66)**
CRN (competes with national radio/newspaper)		-.42(1.54)
Mean Value of Dependent Variable	.21	.21
R^2	.64	.66
n = no. of stations	13	13

1. Figures in parentheses are t-statistics, the others are regression coeffecients.

 * Significant at the 90 percent level of confidence.
** Significant at the 95 percent level of confidence.

constraints, it also has definite drawbacks - principally in the area of ownership structure.

In order to obtain information on the invested capital base upon which rates of return, as defined above, can be calculated it is necessary to confine oneself to a sample of corporations operating a single radio station and possessing no significant non-radio assets. This restricts sample size, but sample size is not the root of the problem. Although corporations of this type could be affiliates or subsidiaries of other corporations with radio, television, or newspaper interests, those in our sample, in fact, are not. There is only a single station belonging to a national radio/television group and one belonging to a national radio/newspaper group. This makes it impossible to examine the role of radio/radio, radio/television, and radio/newspaper group and cross-ownership in the profit rate analysis. Also, because radio/radio group ownership is so common both at the local market and national levels, most of the single station corporations find themselves competing with such a station. Accordingly, the "competes with radio/radio group" ownership variables have been supressed. All of this means that the only ownership structure variables remaining in the profit rate analysis are those denoting competition with a radio/television or radio/newspaper group whether at the local market or national level.

Given the small sample size available, the estimated profit rate equations in Table 10.1 appear strong. But the tests of significance must be interpreted in light of the very small number of degrees of freedom. Standard statistical tests are based on large samples of data which can be assumed to follow a normal distribution, as sample size falls it becomes more likely that the data will not correspond to this distribution.

Equation 1, with the local market "competes with" ownership variables, is able to account for 64 percent of the variation in single station radio corporation profit rates. Equation 2, with the national "competes with" ownership variables, accounts for 66 percent of the variation in profit rates. The constant terms are not statistically significant in either equation. The coefficients in these and following sections are significant at the 95 percent level of confidence unless otherwise stated.

10.4.1 The Competitive Position of the Firm

The results in equation 1 indicate that an increase of 100,000 weekly hours of local market audience is associated with a decrease of .06 in rate of return (mean = .21). At the same time, an increase of .10 in a station's share of total market revenue is associated with a .24 increase in rate of return which would more then double the profits of the average station. Both findings are significant at the 90 percent level of confidence. They suggest that the competitive positioning of a radio single in its market is an important factor in its economic success. Stations with

sizeable local market audiences but low revenue shares (i.e., located in major markets) report lower rates of return than do stations with smaller audiences, but a larger market share (i.e.,
located in small urban centres).

Data on audience drawn from areas outside a station's CMA was
available for only 11 of the 13 stations in the sample and therefore the effect of extra-market audience on profitability could
not be analyzed.

10.4.2 Local Market Characteristics

Market concentration as measured by the Herfindahl index was
not statistically significant. Single radio station corporations
earn lower rates of return if their stations broadcast from larger
cities: an increase of 100,000 in CMA population being associated
with a decline of .44 in profit rates. This presumably reflects
the more competitive environment of the larger centres.

An increase of $1,000 in the average income level of a sta-
tion's CMA is associated with a .90 increase in rate of return (90
percent confidence level). This result, although it is in accord
with predictions based on general a priori reasoning, runs counter
to what was expected on the basis of the results of the advertising rate analysis. Single radio stations appear to be more profitable in higher income cities despite the general evidence that
radio commercials are of more value in lower income cities. Although there is no obvious explanation for this difference it is
possible that radio singles are not representative of all stations
in this regard.

10.4.3 Ownership Structure

In this analysis of profit rates we are examining not radio
stations but rather corporations owning a single radio station.
It is of course possible for such a corporation to be a subsidiary
of other corporations in a group ownership arrangement at either
the local or national level. But, in fact, among the 13 corporations in the sample, only one belongs to a national radio/tele-
vision group and one to a national radio/newspaper group. None
belonged to locally defined groups. Therefore. the influences of
these types of ownership structure on profit rates could not be
estimated. It was however possible to examine the effect of competition against radio/television and radio/newspaper group owned
stations. (Radio/radio group owned stations were so common that
almost all stations compete against one.)

The results indicate that competition against a radio station
belonging to a national radio/television group is associated with
a .65 reduction in the rate of return of a single radio station.
Competition by a radio single against a radio station owned by
those controlling the local newspaper is associated with a reduction of .53 in the rate of return of the radio single. In light

Table 10.2

RADIO STATION PRICE-COST MARGINS, 1975[1]

Dependent Variable	Eqn. 1 PCM	Eqn. 2 PCM
Independent Variables:		
Constant	-2.93(3.26)**	-1.27(3.52)**
Fitted market audience	-.0000020(5.13)*	
AUDE (audience outside CMA)	.0000014(2.33)**	
NEWS (cost of news)	.0000095(2.98)**	.0000084(2.70**
ENT (cost of entertainment)	.0000096(4.27)**	.0000058(2.99)**
RTM (radio/TV in market)	-1.81(1.93)*	
RNM (radio/newspaper in market)	-2.37(2.85)**	
CRRM (competes with radio/ radio in market)	1.83(2.03)**	
CRNM (competes with radio/ newspaper in market)	-.80(1.68)*	
RN (national radio/newspaper)		-.82(1.25)
Mean Value of Dependent Variable	-.47	-.47
R^2	.57	.46
n = no. of stations	51	51

1. Figures in parentheses are t-statistics, the others are regression coeffecients.

 * Significant at the 90 percent level of confidence.
** Significant at the 95 percent level of confidence.

of a mean rate of return of only .21 these are very large effects. We shall return to them in the conclusion.

10.5 EMPIRICAL EVIDENCE: RADIO STATION PRICE-COST MARGINS

The mean price-cost margin is -.47. The sign and size of this value may seem surprising. In fact, only 18 of the 51 stations have a negative price-cost margin with seven of these being new FM stations with large initial losses. However, the mathematics of the calculation of the price-cost margin are such that these stations have a disproportionate effect on the mean value. The reason for this is that as revenue is the denominator of the ratio, the smaller the revenue the higher the absolute value of the ratio, and also the higher the likelihood that it is exceeded by expenses and hence that the ratio is negative. To illustrate this suppose we have a station with revenue of $1 million and expenses of $3 million. The price-cost margin would be (1-3)/1 = -2.00. On the other hand, a profitable station with revenue of $3 million and expenses of $1 million would have a ratio of only (3-1)/3 = .67. One way to avoid this problem would have been to omit all stations having a negative price-cost margin. Since we did not want to restrict our examination of the determinants of profitability only to money-making stations, this route was not followed. The inclusion of such stations, however, invalidates the value of the mean price-cost margin as a measure of absolute profitability. Consequently, in the discussion that follows, we do not compare the regression coefficients with this mean.

Results, using 1975 data, of the estimation of the determinants of radio station price-cost margins, as defined earlier, are shown in Table 10.2. The results using local market ownership variables appear in equation 1; those for nationally defined ownership variables appear in equation 2. Equation 1 is able to account for 57 percent of the variation in radio station price-cost margins; the corresponding figure for equation 2 is 46 percent. The constant terms -2.93 in equation 2 and -1.27 in equation 2 are both significant at the 95 percent level. These reflect the influence of variables not included in the model.

10.5.1 The Competitive Position of the Firm

The estimated effect on radio station price-cost margins of a 100,000 hour increase in a station's local market weekly audience ranges from -.20 for the local ownership variable specification to zero for the national ownership specification. This inverse relationship is consistent with the results of the preceding profit rate analysis. Since it has been established that larger local market audience sizes are associated with higher ad rates one must look to cost side effects to explain a reduction in price-cost margins. But this must wait for the analysis of radio station expenses.

An increase of 100,000 weekly hours, an increase of about one-sixth for the average station, in a station's audience drawn from areas outside its local CMA is found to be associated with a .14 increase in radio station price-cost margin. Again, the subsequent radio station revenue analysis indicates the basis of these effects.

The station's share of total market revenue was found to be statistically insignificant in the national ownership variable specification. It was not included in the local market ownership variable specification.

10.5.2 Local Market Characteristics

There is no evidence that seller concentration, population, or income levels influence the size of the price-cost margin of stations operating there.

10.5.3 Programming Competition

As was hypothesized, the results of the analysis of programming competition contrast with those in the television industry. Expenditures on news programming are revealed to be just as important as expenditures on entertainment programming in terms of their influence on profitability. An increase of $100,000 in expenditures for news programming is associated with price-cost margin increases of from .95 (equation 1) to .84 (equation 2). A similar increase in entertainment programming expenditure is associated with price-cost margin increases ranging from .96 (equation 1) to .58 (equation 2).

10.5.4 Ownership Structure

In the estimation of equation 2 all nationally defined ownership structure variables proved to be statistically insignificant and lacking in explanatory power. Since this is in sharp contrast to the results for local market definition ownership variables it provides useful guidance as to the economic relevance of the two alternative viewpoints on ownership structure in the radio industry. The results provide strong evidence that insofar as ownership structure influences economic performance in the radio industry it is ownership structure at the local market level which is relevant. Concern over national group and cross-ownership patterns would appear to be misplaced.

In equation 1, where locally defined ownership pattern variables are used, there is no evidence that radio/radio group ownership affects price-cost margins. Since locally defined radio/radio groups increase seller concentration levels it might seem that stations belonging to such groups should achieve higher levels of profitability. This is, of course, true as a general proposition, but in the case at hand nearly all groups consist of a strong AM station paired with a weaker FM station. The grouping

of these strong and weak results in an all stations analysis probably serves to obscure the advantages of higher seller concentration for each type of station. There is some indirect confir-
mation of this in the results for those stations competing with
stations belonging to a radio/radio group. Such competition is
associated with a 1.83 increase in price-cost margin.

Radio/television cross-ownership at the local market level is
associated with a decline of 1.81 in the price-cost margin of the
radio station involved (90 percent confidence level). Radio/news-
paper cross-ownership at the local market level is associated with
a 2.37 reduction in price-cost margin. Competition against a station belonging to a local market radio/newspaper group is associated with a .80 reduction in price-cost margin (90 percent level).

10.6 EMPIRICAL EVIDENCE: RADIO STATION REVENUES

Results of the estimation of the determinants of radio station revenues are displayed in Table 10.3. Equation 1, using
local market ownership variables, accounts for 91 percent of the
variation in station revenue. The average station revenue was
$1.5 million. A second equation, was estimated using national
ownership variables but none were statistically significant therefore the results are not reported. The constant term of $374,360
is significant at the 95 percent level of confidence.

Audience drawn from areas outside a station's local CMA was
found to be a significant determinant of radio station revenue
with each additional 100,000 weekly hours of such audience adding
an estimated $54,000 to revenues. The basis for this effect is
unclear. The analysis of advertising rates provided only very
limited evidence of a direct relationship between ad rates and
size of audience from outside the station's local CMA. Possibly
stations with a large audience outside their home markets are able
to sell larger volumes of time. In any event, the findings here
provide an explanation for the earlier results showing increases
in extra-market audience to be associated with increases in its
price-cost margin. Evidently this is due to the revenue effect.

Radio station revenues were found to be directly related to
expenditures on both news and entertainment programming. Again
results in this area contrast sharply with those for television.
Rather than news programming expenditures being associated with
revenue losses here they lead to larger revenue increases than
similar increases in expenditure on entertainment programming. A
$1 increase in news programming expenditure is associated with an
increase of $5.56 in revenue while a corresponding increase in en-
tertainment programming expenditure is associated with a revenue
increase of only $2.69.

Competition against a local market defined radio/television
group, the only statistically significant ownership structure variable, is associated with a $263,819 increase in station revenue.

Table 10.3

RADIO STATION REVENUES, 1975[1]

Dependent Variable	Eqn. 1 Revenue
Independent Variables:	
Constant	-374,360(3.14)**
AUDE (audience outside CMA)	.54(5.49)**
NEWS (cost of news)	5.56(6.05)**
ENT (cost of entertainment)	2.69(5.06)**
CRTM (competes with radio/television in market)	263,819(2.05)**
Mean Value of Dependent Variable	1,519,000
R^2	.91
n = no. of stations	51

1. Figures in parentheses are t-statistics, the others are re-
   gression coeffecients.
 * Significant at the 90 percent level of confidence.
** Significant at the 95 percent level of confidence.

Table 10.4

RADIO STATION EXPENSES, 1975[1]

Dependent Variable	Eqn. 1 Expenses
Independent Variables:	
Constant	$49,338(.20)
Fitted audience	.10(1.18)
SHR (revenue share)	$1,520,000(2.09)**
POP (population)	.49(2.68)**
HRF (revenue Herfindahl)	
RRM (radio/radio in market)	$555,000(3.27)**
CRNM (competes with radio/newspaper in market)	$377,000(2.36)**
Mean Value of Dependent Variables	1,380,000
R^2	.70
n = no. of stations	51

1. Figures in parentheses are t-statistics, the others are re-
   gression coeffecients.
 * Significant at the 90 percent level of confidence.
** Significant at the 95 percent level of confidence.

10.7 EMPIRICAL EVIDENCE: RADIO STATION EXPENSES

Table 10.4 displays the results of the estimation of the determinants of radio station expenses. Equation 1, estimated using
locally defined ownership variables is able to account for 70 percent of expense variation. The average station expense was $4.1
million. The constant term in equation 1 was statistically insignificant. (A second equation using nationally defined ownership
variables was estimated but none proved to be statistically significant, therefore the results are not presented.)

The results indicate that there is a close linkage between a
station's competitive position and its expense outlays. For in-
stance each .10 share of total market revenues is associated with
expense increases of $152,000. Radio stations in larger cities
appear to have higher expenses, with a 100,000 increment in CMA
population associated with an expense increase of to $49,000.

The finding that radio/radio group ownership at the local
market level is associated with a $555,000 increase in station
expenses certainly provides no support for the notion of scale
economies for the multi-plant firm. Again, as in the case of the
price-cost margin results, the exact reasons for the radio/radio
group results may rest to an important degree on the peculiar
characteristics of the types of stations paired as AM/FM twins.

The influence of competition against a radio/radio group
owned station was not examined. Competition against a station
belonging to a locally defined radio/newspaper cross-ownership
arrangement was found to be associated with a $377,000 increase in
expenses (mean = $1.4 million). This presumably reflects the need
for additional resource outlays to compensate for the competitive
advantage in news gathering enjoyed by stations belonging to ra-
dio/newspaper cross-holdings.

10.8 CONCLUSIONS

It proved possible in this chapter to examine the determinants of the profit rates of a sample of corporations owning a
single radio station. Because of the infrequency of group and
cross-ownership arrangements for this type of station, a parallel
analysis of the determinants of price-cost margin for a larger
sample of stations was carried out. In order to permit some understanding of the nature of the forces influencing price-cost
margins and profits the determinants of the underlying station
revenues and expenses were also examined.

10.8.1 The Competitive Position of the Firm

The various aspects of the competitive position of the firm -
audience size in the local CMA and elsewhere and revenue share -
have been revealed as important influences on radio station profitability. The profit rate analysis indicated that increases in

revenue share were associated with higher profit rates (an increase of .24 in profit rate for each .10 increment in share -
large when compared with a mean of .21).

On the other hand, increased audience size alone was associated with reductions in both price-cost margins and single station profit rates (decreases of .06 and .20 respectively for each
100,000 hours increment in local market audience). This result
appears to be due to the large expense outlays required to achieve
and maintain larger audience sizes.

There was some evidence that increases in a station's audience drawn from areas outside its local CMA led to price-cost margin increases (with estimates ranging from zero to .14 for each
100,000 weekly hours). This result appears to be traceable to the
influence which extra-market audience has on station revenues.

10.8.2 Local Market Characteristics

There was no evidence that local market characteristics influenced the price-cost margins of radio stations. In the analysis of the profit rates of single station corporations, stations
in large cities were found to have lower profits with a 100,000
increment in CMA population (mean = 710,000) associated with a
decrease of between .39 and .44 in rate of return clearly large in
relation to the .21 average value. A partial explanation for this
profit reduction appears to be the higher expenses of stations in
larger cities. A 100,000 increment in CMA population was found to
be associated with an increase in station expenses of $49,000.

No statistical association was found between the level of
average income in a station's local market and its revenue, its
expenses, or its price-cost margin. In a statistically weak finding, higher income levels were found to be associated with higher
profit rates in the analysis of radio singles.

10.8.3 Programming Competition

The results of the analysis of programming competition contrast with those in the television industry. Expenditures in the
radio industry on news programming were revealed to be just as
important as, if not more important than, expenditures on entertainment programming in terms of their influence on profitability.
Increases of $100,000 in news programming expenditure (mean =
$124,821) resulted in estimated price-cost margin increases of be-
tween .84 and .95 while the corresponding increase for entertainment programming expenditures (mean = $1.5 million) were between
.58 and .96. Supplementary evidence on this point was provided by
the analysis of the determinants of radio station revenue where it
was discovered that a $1 expenditure on news programming was asso-
ciated with a revenue increase of $5.56. A dollar spent on en-
tertainment programming was, on the other hand, associated with a
revenue increase of only $2.69. Taken together, these findings

provide strong evidence of the relative importance of news programming as compared to entertainment programming in the radio
industry.

10.8.4 Ownership Structure

Since few of the radio stations (corporations) for which rate
of return data were available belonged to cross-ownership or group
holdings, examination of the implications of ownership structure
was principally confined to study of price-cost margins.

Economic theory would predict that ownership of two or more
radio stations in a local market would increase seller concentration and lead to higher ad rates and increased profits. Nearly
all local market radio/radio groups are AM/FM twins. The advertising rate analysis showed that the stronger AM stations were
able to achieve the predicted ad rate increases while the weaker
FM stations were not. The price-cost margin analysis, covering
both types of stations, provided no evidence of a link between
local market radio/radio group ownership and price-cost margins.
Possibly the grouping of strong AM station and weak FM stations
results obscure the advantages of higher concentration. Indirect
evidence of this advantage exists. Single stations competing
against local market radio/radio groups enjoy a 1.83 percentage
point increase in price-cost margin.

Economic theory would predict that radio/television cross-
holdings at the local market level would increase the firm's market power in the overall sale of advertising in the city concerned. This should lead to higher prices for all advertising,
including radio advertising, and increased radio revenues and
price-cost margins. The empirical evidence on these effects is
contradictory.

Just as the advertising rate analysis (Chapter 7) produced no
evidence of higher advertising rates, the revenue analysis provided no evidence of higher revenues. Furthermore, there was no
evidence of any change in expenses. However, in a statistically
weak result, television/radio cross-ownership at the local market
level was found to be associated with a 1.81 reduction in the
price-cost margin. We have no economic explanation for the latter. With respect to the competitors of such stations, the only
statistically significant result, and one that is consistent with
one of our hypotheses, is that competition against a local market
television/radio cross-owned station increases revenue by
$264,000. The same predictions would apply in the case of local
market radio/newspaper cross-ownership. In this case there was
evidence of increases in ad rates. This evidence was statistically weak, however. The price-cost margin results indicated that,
if these ad rate effects were indeed present, stations were unable
to build on them to produce higher price-cost margins. Local market radio/newspaper cross-ownership was associated with a 2.37
drop in price-cost margin.

None of the nationally-defined group and cross-ownership arrangements was found to have any statistically significant influence on radio station price-cost margins. This finding is of some importance since it means that national ownership structure which has long been the focus of concern at the policy level may be of limited economic significance to the operation of the radio industry.

The effects of competition against a local market radio/radio group have been dealt with above. Competition against a national radio/television group owned station is associated with a reduction of .65 in the rate of return of a radio single. In comparison to the average rate of return of .21 for the radio singles in our sample this is a very large profit reduction. Evidently, stations belonging to national radio-television groups provide stiff competition for the corporation owning a single radio station.

Competition against a local market radio/newspaper group is associated with substantial reductions in both the rate of return (by .53) and price-cost margin (by .80). Both of these appear to result from expense side considerations since competition of this type is associated with a $377,000 increase in a station's expenses (mean = value $1.4 million). It would appear that in a radio environment where news programming is so important newspaper cross-ownership provides a potent competitive advantage.

Appendix 10.1

RADIO STATION PROFIT RATES, PRICE-COST MARGINS,
REVENUES AND EXPENSES: MODEL SPECIFICATION

The models developed to estimate the determinants of radio
station profit rates, price-cost margins, revenues and expenses
closely parallel those developed for the corresponding television
variables in Appendix 9.1.   Accordingly the detailed build-up of
the model is not described.   Rather, the resulting estimating
equations are presented and the reader is referred to Appendix 9.1
for a discussion of the rationale behind them.   Here we focus on
the ways in which the radio models differ from those developed in
the television analysis.

Most modifications to the basic models arise from data constraints. For example, we have noted previously that radio/radio
group ownership is common at both the local market and national
levels.   This has severely restricted the number of stations within the sample set which do not compete with at least one local
market or national group owned station.   Accordingly in the profit
rate and expense models the variables CRRM and CRR have been excluded.   To give another example, because of the limited sample of
stations for which price-cost margin or profit data was available
only format variables identified as significant determinants of
audience size could be included in the development of fitted audience values.   The estimating procedure in each case follows the
same two stage least squares approach in order to allow for possible interdependencies between audience and profit rate, price-
cost margin, revenue, or expenses.

In the analysis of the profit rates of corporations owning a
single radio station the model used to estimate the required fitted audience values (in the case of local market ownership variables) takes the form

$$FAUD = a_0 + a_1(POP/N) + a_2 (POP/N)\left\{\frac{NJ-J}{N-1}\right\}$$
$$+ a_3MOR + a_4C\&W + a_5MU + a_6AUDE$$
$$+ a_7SHR + a_8INC + a_9HRF + a_{10}POP$$
$$+ a_{11}RRM + a_{12}RTM + a_{13}RNM + a_{14}CRTM$$
$$+ a_{15}CRNM \tag{1}$$

When ownership is defined on a national basis the appropriate
changes in the group and cross-ownership variables in equation (1)
must be made.

In the profit rate model itself further modifications of the
basic approach are required.   The principal changes involve the
ownership structure variables. Note, the basic sample is a set of
corporations owning a single radio station.   It is of course
possible for such a corporation to be a subsidiary or affiliate of

other corporations in a group ownership structure at either the local or national level. But, in point of fact, the sample of 13 stations includes none belonging to a national radio/radio group, only a single station belonging to a national radio/television group, and one belonging to a national radio/newspaper group. None belonged to locally defined groups. In these circumstances there was no choice but to exclude all ownership variables of these types from the model leaving only the "competes with radio/ television" and "competes with radio/newspaper" variables. In addition, data on audience drawn from outside the station's CMA is available for only eleven of the thirteen stations in the sample. Therefore AUDE was also surpressed in the model.

The corporation's rate of return was defined as the ratio of the total of interest plus before-tax profits divided by the total of long-term debt plus shareholders equity and is denoted by PFT. The radio corporation profit model using local market ownership variables takes the form

$$PFT = a_0 + a_1 FAUD + a_2 SHR + a_3 HRF + a_4 POP$$
$$+ a_5 INC + a_6 CRTM + a_7 CRNM \tag{2}$$

with the appropriate variable changes for a national ownership specification.

The analysis of profits rates is restricted to corporations owning a single radio station and possessing only insignificant amounts of non-radio assets. In order to broaden our examination of radio industry profitability to encompass corporations owning more than one radio station or possessing significant non-radio assets it is necessary to revert to the price-cost margin approch as used in the television analysis. The model should include significant audience determinants and programming competition variables covering dollar expenditures on news and on entertainment. Also incorporating the standard variables detailing competitive position of the firm, local market characteristics and ownership structure results in a fitted audience model of the following form (using national ownership pattern variables):

$$FAUD = a_0 + a_1 (POP/N) + a_2 (POP/N) \left\{ \frac{NJ-J}{N-1} \right\}$$
$$+ a_3 MOR + a_4 C\&W + a_5 MU + a_6 AUDE$$
$$+ a_7 SHR + a_8 HRF + a_9 POP + a_{10} INC$$
$$+ a_{11} NEWS + a_{12} ENT + a_{13} RR + a_{14} RT$$
$$+ a_{15} RN + a_{16} CRR + a_{17} CRT + a_{18} CRN \tag{3}$$

In the second stage of the estimation these fitted audience values are used as one of the independent variables in the price-cost model:

$$PCM = a_0 + a_1 FAUD + a_2 AUDE + a_3 SHR$$
$$+ a_4 HRF + a_5 POP + a_6 INC + a_7 NEWS$$
$$+ a_8 ENT + a_9 RR + a_{10} RT + a_{11} RN$$
$$+ a_{12} CRR + a_{13} CRT + a_{14} CRN \tag{4}$$

The model using local market ownership variables follows the same approach with the exception that in both equations (3) and (4) the variable SHR, the firms share of total market revenue, which was not significant in the national model, is excluded.

Analysis of the determinants of radio station revenues follows the same approach. The fitted audience values developed in the estimation of equation (3) are used as independent variables in the estimation of a revenue model of the form

$$R = a_0 + a_1 FAUD + a_2 AUDE + a_3 SHR + a_4 HRF$$
$$+ a_5 POP + a_6 INC + a_7 NEWS + a_8 ENT$$
$$+ a_9 RR + a_{10} RT + a_{11} RN + a_{12} CRR$$
$$+ a_{13} CRT + a_{14} CRN \qquad (5)$$

Again when local market ownership pattern variables are introduced the share of total market revenue variable, SHR, is excluded.

Dollar expenditures on news and on entertainment programming cannot, of course, be used as independent variables in the analysis of the determinants of radio station expenses since they are components of total expenses. Therefore the fitted audience values developed by estimating equation (1) are used as independent variables in a radio station expense model of the form (using local market ownership variables):

$$E = a_0 + a_1 FAUD + a_2 AUDE + a_3 SHR + a_4 HRF$$
$$+ a_5 POP + a_6 INC + a_7 RRM + a_8 RTM + a_9 RNM$$
$$+ a_{10} CRTM + a_{11} CRNM \qquad (6)$$

It will be noted that again, as in the case of the radio station profits equation, the "competes with radio/radio group" variable CRRM has been excluded. Examination of the influence of the national ownership pattern on radio station expenses is possible following the appropriate re-specification of the ownership structure variables.

Chapter 11

Programming Performance

This chapter examines the programming performance of television and radio in Canada in terms of program balance, diversity,
and choice. Balance concerns the mix of programming among broad
categories such as Light Entertainment, Heavy Entertainment, and
Information. Diversity also considers the programming mix but at
a more disaggregated level employing, in this study, the 14 categories used by the CRTC (see Appendix 11.2). Choice considers the
actual number of program options available to viewers in any given
market in a time period. Program performance is relevant to this
study because it is thought to be related to the structure of the
broadcasting industry. Diversity and choice in a market are expected to increase with the number of stations in a market but, if
the stations are private broadcasters dependent on advertising
revenue, it will increase only at a very slow rate. The balance
and diversity of programming by networks and other groups are
thought to depend on whether the network is private or public with
the former providing less balance and diversity because of their
concentration on popular programming.

In section 11.1 and Appendix 11.1 a model is developed which
suggests that a broadcasting industry financed by advertising will
provide inadequate balance, diversity, and choice. Inadequate is
defined in the economic welfare sense that viewers and potential
viewers could be made better-off at the same cost with a different
program mix. In section 11.2 the applicability of this model to
the Canadian broadcasting industry is examined. We consider how
the predictions of the model are affected by the presence of a
regulatory body (the CRTC), a Crown Corporation (the CBC) and some
other specific characteristics of the Canadian industry.

In section 11.3 an empirical study of performance is undertaken involving measurement of balance, diversity and choice. For
television, balance and diversity are compared at the network level. In addition, diversity and choice are examined at the market
level. Because of the unavailability of data, the analysis of
radio programming is, of necessity, less ambitious.

11.1 A MODEL RELATING PROGRAMMING PERFORMANCE TO INDUSTRY STRUCTURE

A model of the spatial competition variety similar to that employed by Steiner,[1] is developed to predict the program performance of an industry comprised of private broadcasters financed by advertising revenue. The model is equally applicable to television programming and to radio programming. A rigorous development of the model is provided in Appendix 11.1. This section presents the general assumptions of the model and uses a hypothetical numerical example to provide a simple illustration of the operation of the model and the nature of its predictions.

The private broadcasters are assumed to be profit maximizers. As we have emphasized earlier, the product being sold to advertisers by such a broadcaster is that of audiences for commercial messages. Audiences are induced to listen or watch by the program offerings. If revenue depends on audience size and if the costs of programs are equal, a broadcaster will seek to maximize advertising revenue thereby maximizing profits by choosing the program mix that maximizes audience size.

The model presumes that programs can be classified into different categories in such a way that viewers/listeners regard programs within a category to be closer substitutes than any program in another category. Obviously, such an assumption is not descriptively realistic and has been subject to criticism.[2] We believe, however, that it is a valid simplification which permits useful insights into programming behaviour. In the initial development of the model we also assume that each program costs the same to produce or buy, that each potential viewer/listener is valued equally by the advertisers and hence the broadcasters, and that programs within a category are regarded by viewers/listeners as perfect substitutes. (Hence if different broadcasters in the same market offer the same program type we would expect them to obtain an equal share of the total audience for this program type.) The implications of relaxing these simplifying assumptions are examined later.

To illustrate the operation of the model and the nature of its predictions, suppose that we have a television market where program category A is the first preference of 54 percent of viewers, program category B is the first preference of 20 percent, category C is the first preference of eight percent, and that each of the remaining program categories is the first choice of less than eight percent. Let us assume initially that if more than one program of the same type is offered the audience is shared equally, that costs of all programs are the same, and that viewers will not watch another program category if their first preference is not shown. Further, assume that no group owns more than one station in the market and that each station is allocated one channel. Given these assumptions, how many audience (and profit) maximizing stations are needed in the market before viewers receive a choice of two program categories. How many before they receive a third choice? These questions are examined in Table 11.1.

Table 11.1

PROGRAM CHOICE AND NUMBER OF STATIONS IN A MARKET:
A HYPOTHETICAL EXAMPLE

n	Program category offered by an n'th station entering the market	Audience Share for the n'th station
1	A	54 percent
2	A	27
3	B	20
4	A	18
5	A	13.5
6	A	10.8
7	B	10
8	A	9
9	C	8

We find that program B will not be offered until there are three stations in a market while C will not be provided until there are nine stations. Thus program choice increases very slowly with increases in the number of stations. Obviously, the amount of choice available with a given number of stations depends on the degree of inequality in the program preferences of viewers. If we amended the above example to indicate that 30 percent of viewers regard category A as their first preference then B would be offered if there were two stations in the market and C would be offered if there were six. Therefore, the less the inequality in preference, the greater the choice.

What is the effect of relaxing the simplifying assumptions? If we recognize the possibility of unequal audiences for programs within a category then the greater the inequality the larger the choice likely for a given number of stations. For example, a very small inequality, with one station obtaining less than eight percent of the audience when it and five other stations are offering A, would result in C being offered when there are eight stations in the market.

If we relax the assumption that all program cost the same, then if greater costs are associated with the program types which have larger audiences we would expect more choice for a given number of stations. For example, if C costs less than A, with eight stations in the market at least one might find it more profitable to produce C rather than A even though the audience and advertising revenue generated is less. Conversely, if lower costs are associated with the more popular program types we would expect less choice than indicated in Table 11.1

If some viewers/listeners are valued more than others, this can either increase or decrease choice. It will increase choice if the more valued viewers/listeners prefer minority programmes. For example, if program type C attracts highly-valued viewers/listeners, then it is likely that one station will find it profitable to show this program in an eight station market even though it could obtain a slightly larger audience duplicating A. Conversely, if the more valued viewers/listeners prefer the popular program types then there will be more duplication and less choice than predicted.

The effect of relaxing the assumption that viewers will not watch another category if their preferred category is not offered is more complex and cannot be handled adequately in terms of our simple numerical example. Readers are therefore referred to Appendix 11.1. We can say, however, that the more flexible people are in being willing to watch other categories, then the less likely their own most preferred category is to be offered. To illustrate this, assume category A will attract more viewers than any other single category, that half the viewers who regard B as their first preference will watch A if B is not offered, and, to keep the illustration simple, that none of the viewers who prefer C or any of the other categories will watch A or B when their first preference is not available. Under these assumptions, B would not be offered until four stations served the market because three or fewer stations would get more viewers offering A and sharing the 64 percent of the audience attracted by this category when B is not offered.

This illustration is for a one-period model. During a prime-time evening, however, a viewer's preferences may change and hence it may not pay a station to offer the same program category each time period. For example a viewer's first preference at 6:00 to 6:30 P.M. may be for news, but it is unlikely to remain his first preference in each succeeding half-hour until midnight. Hence, during the prime-time evening hours, more choice is likely to be offered than found in the one-period model.

11.2 IMPLICATIONS OF THE MODEL FOR PROGRAMMING IN CANADA

The model developed presumed an industry comprised of private broadcasters each of which attempts to maximize profits by pursuing a programming policy aimed at maximizing its audience. Both the television and the radio broadcasting industries in Canada differ from this scenario in important ways. There is a regulatory commission, the CRTC, and a Crown corporation, the CBC. Programs are not of equal cost. There is not a single positive relationship between audience size and revenue (see Chapter 9). The implications for programming of these and some other aspects of the Canadian industry are examined for television and radio in Sections 11.2.1 and 11.2.2 respectively.

11.2.1 The Model and Canadian Television Programming

In the initial development of the model we assumed that the cost of each program to the station is the same. As we have already noted, if the programs which attract the larger audiences are less costly then this would result in even more duplication and less diversity than predicted by the model. In Canada, the programs with the highest audiences are mainly entertainment programs of a crime drama or situation comedy variety, both of which come under CRTC program category 7 (see Appendix 11.2). These are procured at low cost from the United States. A good insight into the economics of program purchasing versus production is provided by a CRTC paper.[3]

This paper indicates that the typical program imported from the U.S. by the Canadian networks during the 1974-75 season could be purchased by them for about $2,000 per half hour episode although the cost to the U.S. producer would be about $125,000. The American producer relies on sale to a U.S. network to cover his costs and any additional sales outside the U.S. are regarded as a bonus. With a much smaller market the Canadian producer spends about $30,000 on a similar type of program. It is scarcely surprising that Canadian viewers regard a program costing $30,000 to produce as inferior to one costing $125,000. Hence fewer watch the former. The advertising rate structure reflects this with the CTV prime time 30 second spot rate in January 1975 being 22 percent less for Canadian programs than for foreign programs. The CRTC has estimated that, for the prime time schedule of January 1975, CTV was obtaining an average margin (revenue - costs) per half hour of $55 on Canadian programs compared with an averge margin per half hour of $21,000 for foreign programs.[4] Similar estimates for the CBC English prime-time schedule are -$2,050 and $20,600 respectively. When two specific programs of the same type are compared, we find examples such as "Excuse My French," a Canadian situation comedy, with an estimated revenue of $16,000 and production cost of $30,000 per episode while "M*A*S*H" brought in an estimated revenue of $24,000 for a purchase cost per episode of about $2,000.

Our results in Chapter 9 also bear on this question. We found that an extra hour per day of prime time Canadian programming reduces a station's price-cost margin by .219, a very substantial reduction when we recall that the average price-cost margin is only .18.

The economics of program production and purchase are thus such that Canadian private broadcasters, if left to their own devices, would purchase the overwhelming majority of their programs from abroad. The primary influence of the CRTC has been to prevent this by the use of Canadian content regulations. For 1974-75, the year in question, the regulations required that for the 12 month period beginning October 1st, 60 percent of a television station's total broadcast time between 6 A.M. and midnight, and 50 percent between 6 P.M. and midnight, be Canadian content. Co-productions with Commonwealth or French language countries qualify as Canadian content if 30 percent or more is spent in Canada on Canadian participation. Co-production with other countries quali-fies if the figure is 50 percent or more.[5]

Possible reactions of private broadcasters to such regula-tions include evasion and attempts to obtain exemption. There is evidence of both. In its Decision 75-594, the CRTC discussed "Global's difficulties in meeting the Canadian content regula-tions."[6] This suggests that the Global network was not achiev-ing the required percentages. An attempt to obtain exemption from the regulations, or at least an amendment to ease the requirement, for all independents, was made by Global in 1975. The request was refused by the CRTC.[7]

Profit maximizing behaviour, subject to satisfying the regu-latory constraint, would seem to entail either production of low-cost Canadian programs in order to minimize possible losses or co-production with foreign producers in order to spread the cost of production and provide an expectation of selling abroad. Both routes seem to have been followed with "Police Surgeon" and "Swiss Family Robinson" being examples of the latter. Another reaction to be expected is that the Canadian content requirement in prime time will be satisfied as far as possible by scheduling Canadian programs at the less popular times when the opportunity cost in terms of revenues foregone is smallest. Thus one would expect Ca-nadian programs to be scheduled for early and late in the evening with the most popular mid-evening time slots reserved for foreign (primarily American-produced) programs. The following statement by the CRTC provides evidence that this has indeed happened:

In three major metropolitan centres, important commer-cial Canadian English language stations have seen the percentage of Canadian programming hours per week, in the prime time 8:00 P.M. to 9:30 P.M. time period, fall from an average of 33% in 1966 to 19% in 1976, and at one station to 14%.[8]

It appears that the trend to decreasing Canadian content in the peak period has continued to the present. The CRTC states that in 1978-79 less than six percent of the programming offered by CTV between 8 P.M. and 10:30 P.M. is Canadian.[9] Similarly, at the 1978 CRTC hearings into the CBC licence renewal, Mr. Al Johnson, President of the CBC (and a strong advocate of Canadian cultural nationalism), suggested that private broadcasters satisfied Cana-dian programs in prime time in the off-season, i.e., the summer.

The CRTC has power to grant and renew licences. In such de-cisions the Commission has frequently stressed the need to provide local programming and the opportunity for local input.[10] This concern has extended into decisions concerning changes in owner-ship. In licencing second and third Canadian television services the CRTC has adopted the priciple that new "broadcasters should complement and extend available programming and avoid unnecessary duplication of service."[11] Our model has suggested that audience maximizing and profit maximizing programming will often involve duplication. Once they have been granted a licence, we would expect new stations to avoid extension of available programming and provision of diversity when this is at the expense of audience and profits. This is confirmed by Robert Babe's analysis.[12]

The Canadian television broadcasting industry also differs from that envisaged in the model because of the presence of a Crown Corporation. The CBC does not rely exclusively on advertising revenue. Only about 20 percent (26 percent in 1974, 23 percent in 1975, 20 percent in 1976, 19 percent in 1977) of its revenue is from advertising with the major source of its income being annual Parliamentary appropriations. As Richwood has noted[13], however, the uncertainty associated with the size of the annual appropriations makes the CBC more reliant on the relatively stable source of advertising revenue than its share of the total might suggest. Although the CBC would not be expected to act like the pure audience maximizer of our model, its partial reliance on advertising revenue would be sufficient reason for it not behaving like an "Ideal Public Broadcasting Corporation" (IPBC). This is Steiner's term for a public broadcaster with the role of promoting a socially optimal pattern of program offerings which would maximize the utility of television set owners. He has suggested that this would entail complementary programming whereby the IPBC would offer the otherwise unproduced program with the largest audience. Such a policy is approximated in Britain where BBC 2 provides a complementary service to BBC 1. There is no general agreement, however, that complementary programming is likely to maximize utility. Blank, for example, argues that what people really want is more choice within the most popular categories.[14]

Section 3 of the Broadcasting Act (1968) provides the CBC with a mandate to:

(i)   be a balanced service of information, enlightenment and entertainment for people of different ages, interests and tastes covering the whole range of programming in fair proportion;

(ii) be extended to all parts of Canada, as public funds become available;

(iii) be in English and French, serving the special needs of geographic regions, and actively contributing to the flow and exchange of cultural and regional information and entertainment; and

(iv) contribute to the development of national unity and provide for a continuing expression of Canadian identity.

The mandate is thus to contribute to national goals and to provide balanced rather than complementary programming. One would expect CBC to offer a smaller proportion of otherwise unproduced programs than an IPBC but more than private broadcasters. Unless the stipulation to provide balanced programming is meaningless, the implication is that CBC, to a greater extent than private stations constrained by Canadian content requirements and licence renewal considerations, is obliged in some time periods to offer program categories that do not further profit maximization. If indeed, CBC offers a higher proportion of otherwise unproduced programs, then more program diversity can be expected from CBC stations than from private stations.

11.2.2 The Model and Canadian Radio Programming

The policies, and probably influence, of the CRTC with respect to radio programming have been similar to those already discussed in the context of television programming. The Canadian content regulations for AM radio that came into effect in January 1973, were that 30 percent of the music played between 6 A.M. and midnight must be Canadian on the basis of at least two of the following criteria; performer, lyrics, music, or production.[15]

In granting and renewing licences, particularly FM licences, the CRTC has stressed the need to provide diversity and complementarity in programming. Thus, on May 28, 1968, the CRTC denied applications for four new FM stations because the "applicants did not undertake to provide significantly new or different programming opportunities to the communities concerned."[16] The announcement went on to say that the Commission would ensure that FM radio "be developed in such a way as to contribute to a more varied program service which will complement and enrich services already available from existing stations." The CRTC does not want FM stations offering the "Rolling Format" employed by many AM stations. This format involves musical recordings interspersed with time, weather, traffic and similar announcements. It is inexpensive to produce and is entirely consistent with our multi-period model prediction of repetitive programming. On September 6, 1976, regulations came into effect to try and prevent this on FM. The regulations require, between 7 A.M. and midnight, 25 percent "Foreground Format" for FM stations within an AM/FM group and 16 percent for independently-owned FM stations. The "Foreground Format" involves at least 15 minutes uninterrupted presentation of a particular theme, subject, or personality.[17] As this specific requirement came into effect after the 1974-75 period, for which we have programming data, it would not be a factor in this period.

In 1974-75 the CBC was phasing out advertising on radio. Accordingly, there was no revenue incentive for CBC to attempt to maximize its audience size and no financial reason why it should not produce different programming. The CRTC has always stressed that CBC should provide the latter. Thus a CBC proposal for "Radio One" and "Radio Two" was rejected by the CRTC because the

"Radio One" proposal would "shift CBC AM programming away from what is unique and bring it much too close to the programming already available on many of the privately owned stations."[18]

11.3 MEASUREMENT AND ANALYSIS OF PROGRAMMING PERFORMANCE

For television networks, or similar groupings, we are concerned with whether the balance and diversity of programs offered differ. This is examined in section 11.3.1. At the market level we are interested in the diversity of television programs and the extent of choice offered to viewers in each market. This is studied in section 11.3.2. Section 11.3.3 spotlights some of the results of the television programming analysis. In section 11.3.4 a limited analysis of radio programming is undertaken.

The Canadian data used in this section were provided to us by the CRTC and the CBC and is in the form of number of time units allotted by stations to each of the 14 Program Categories defined by the CRTC. Descriptions of these Program Categories appear in Appendix 11.2. Programming for U.S. stations was obtained from TV Guide and classified by the authors.

11.3.1 Balance and Diversity of Television Programming by Network

In order to measure the balance of programs offered, three broad categories of program are distinguished: Light Entertainment, Heavy Entertainment, and Information. Light Entertainment includes the program categories designated by CRTC as being of this variety plus the sports and outdoors category (CRTC categories 6, 7, 8, 9, and 14). This last category was included on the basis that it makes few demands on viewers and fits under the heading of "escapism." Information includes the categories CRTC describes as being of an "Information and Orientation" nature plus science and critical evaluation (categories 1, 2, 3, 4, 5, 12, and 13). It is thought that these two categories fit more naturally under the information label than the CRTC grouping that includes them with exceptionally distinguished performances in music, dance, drama, and poetry. This allows us to restrict Heavy Entertainment to the actual performances of music, dance, drama, and poetry (categories 10 and 11).

The aggregate proportion of each of these three broad program categories is shown in Table 11.2 for the eight networks or other station groupings indicated. All of the stations in the network or group are included; the stations are not restricted to our 14 markets. The Aggregate Proportion of, for example, Light Entertainment is defined as the number of minutes of Light Entertainment programs in the year divided by the total number of minutes of programming in the year. The Aggregate Proportions are shown for All Programs (Prime Time: 6 P.M. to midnight) and Canadian Programs (Prime Time) and apply for the year of September 29, 1974, to September 27, 1975.

Table 11.2

PROGRAM BALANCE AND DIVERSITY BY NETWORK, 1974/75

Network or Station Grouping	Number of Stations	All Programs (Prime Time) Aggregate Proportions					Canadian Programs (Prime Time) Aggregate Proportions				
		Heavy Enter- tainment	Light Enter- tainment	Infor- mation	L.I.	C.I.	Heavy Enter- tainment	Light Enter- tainment	Infor- mation	L.I.	C.I.
CBC Owned English	16	.0140	.6537	.3323	3.08	.81	.0147	.4984	.4869	3.45	.84
CBC Owned French	9	.0499	.6291	.3190	3.21	.81	.0273	.5539	.4201	3.57	.85
CBC English Affiliates	28	.0137	.7174	.2690	2.91	.76	.0173	.5136	.4691	3.60	.84
CBC French Affiliates	7	.0489	.7215	.2296	3.02	.79	.0276	.6467	.3258	3.54	.85
CTV Affil- iates	19	.0020	.7343	.2637	2.49	.65	.0023	.4712	.5264	3.07	.81
TVA Affil- iates	5	.0008	.8166	.1826	2.42	.70	.0150	.6571	.3413	3.03	.80
Global	1	.0002	.6774	.3263	2.03	.63	.0005	.3016	.6979	2.40	.74
Indepen- dents	4	.0005	.7280	.2715	2.82	.75	.0011	.4524	.5465	3.32	.83

L.I. = A diversity index (defined in text); min. = 1.00; max. = 7.50.
C.I. = A diversity index (defined in text); min. = 0; max. = .929.

Source: Data provided by the CRTC and the CBC.

The Aggregate Proportions for All Programs reveal that CBC-owned English stations, CBC-owned French, and Global have substantially less Light Entertainment and more Information than the others. TVA (French language) affiliates have substantially more Light Entertainment and less Information than the other groups. CBC English affiliates, CBC French affiliates, CTV affiliates, and Independents have very similar proportions between these extremes. For all groups the Aggregate Proportion of Heavy Entertainment is small. Nevertheless, the CBC-owned French stations and the CBC French affiliates have much more programming of this type than the other groups. The CBC-owned English stations and CBC English affiliates, while lagging their French counterparts, also have substantially more than the miniscule proportions offered by the others. In summary, the CBC-owned French and CBC-owned English stations do provide the best overall balance. Global provides as good a balance between Light Entertainment and Information but substantially less Heavy Entertainment, CBC French affiliates score well on the provision of Heavy Entertainment but not on the balance between Light Entertainment and Information.

When we examine the Aggregate Proportions for Canadian Programs, the interesting aspect to note is that CTV affiliates, Global, and the Independents all show a higher proportion of Information programs than Light Entertainment, although the All Program split is about 30 percent to 70 percent. Presumably the strategy of these groups is to use Information programs, that, irrespective of their source, are unlikely to be substantial money earners, to fill a good portion of their Canadian content requirements. This permits a very high percentage of their foreign programs to be of the lucrative Light Entertainment type.

Coding into the very broad categories of Information and Entertainment does provide insight into the overall balance of program offering but indicates nothing about the balance within each broad category. To examine this, an analysis using the 14 categories defined by the CRTC (see Appendix 11.2) has also been undertaken and measurements of diversity made. A measure of diversity, which we denote by L.I., employed by Land[19] is defined as:

$$L.I. = \sum_{j=1}^{n} m_j R_j \Big/ \sum_{j=1}^{n} m_j$$

Where m_j is the number of minutes of programming of category j, R_j is the rank order (1 to 14) of the category according to the number of minutes of broadcasting, and n is the number of program categories. Hence, the larger the value of the Index the greater the diversity. Maximum diversity, with an equal number of minutes devoted to each of the 14 categories, would give an L.I. = 7.50. Minimum diversity, with all broadcast minutes devoted to one program category, would give an L.I. = 1.00. The L.I. for each network or station grouping is shown in Table 11.2 for the year beginning September 29, 1974.

A good measure of diversity should reflect both the number and the size distribution of minutes allocated to the different program categories. In a different context we saw, in Chapter 3, that the Herfindahl Index has these characteristics. We thus propose to calculate a diversity index based on the Herfindahl Index. We denote this diversity index as C.I. and defined it as:

$$C.I. = 1 - \sum_{j=1}^{n} P_j^2 ,$$

where P_j is the proportion of programming allotted to program j and n is the number of categories. If all programs supplied have equal proportions, C.I. varies directly with the number of program categories offered, while an increase in the inequality of program proportions would result in a decrease in C.I. The maximum diversity, for 14 categories, would give C.I. = .929, whereas the minimum diversity would give C.I. = 0. To our knowledge, no one has used this index as a measure of program diversity although Caves has measured product diversity in this way.[20]

Table 11.2 reveals that L.I. and C.I. provide largely consistent rankings of network, or station grouping, programming performance. CBC-owned English and CBC-owned French stations provide the most diversity with a L.I. > 3.00 and C.I. > 0.800. Next in performance are CBC English affiliates and CBC French affiliates followed by the Independents. The least diversity is found in the programming of Global.

We conclude, consistent with our expectations in Section 11.2, that CBC-owned English and CBC-owned French stations do provide the best balance of programming and the most diversity.

11.3.2 Television Program Diversity by Market

Table 11.3 provides the L.I. and the C.I. for the 14 markets for All Programs (Prime Time: 6 P.M. to midnight) for the year beginning September 29, 1974. The stations included in the markets, for purposes of calculating the L.I. and the C.I., are the Canadian stations identified as audience competitors in Chapter 3.

Table 11.3

DIVERSITY BY MARKET, 1974/75

Market CMA	Number of Canadian Audience Competitors	L.I.	C.I.
St. John's	2	2.86	.75
Halifax	2	2.87	.75
Quebec	5	2.92	.77
Montreal	4	2.91	.74
Ottawa-Hull	8	2.79	.75
Toronto	6⌊1⌋	2.79	.75
Kitchener	6	2.63	.74
London	4	2.52	.72
Windsor	2	2.52	.72
Winnipeg	2	2.79	.77
Regina	2	3.05	.77
Edmonton	3	2.87	.76
Calgary	2	2.75	.72
Vancouver	3	2.68	.75

1. Excludes station CICA for which no programming data was supplied by the CRTC.

Source: Computed by the authors from data supplied by the CRTC and the CBC.

In the calculation of the L.I. for each market, the number of minutes devoted to each program type by station are summed before the rank order is determined. Hence the L.I. for the market is not simply the mean of the L.I. for the stations comprising the market. Unless the number of minutes devoted to different program categories by each station in the market is identical, the programming will to some extent be complementary and the L.I. for the market will be greater than that of the average of the stations in the market. For example, in a two station market, if one station devoted all its broadcasting time to one program type, while the other station devoted all its broadcasting time to another program type then the Index for the market would be 1.50 whereas the L.I. for each station would be 1.00. Similarly, in the calculation of the C.I., the aggregate number of minutes devoted by all stations in the market to a given program type is expressed as a proportion of the total number of minutes of prime time programming by all the stations in the market before squaring (see the definition of the formulae given above).

According to both the L.I. and the C.I., the least diversity is offered in London and Windsor CMAs. As these are two of the three markets without either a CBC-owned French or English station, lack of such a station would seem to be a possible explanation. The other market without a CBC-owned station, Calgary, has a similar C.I. although not the next lowest L.I. The most diversity is found in the Regina CMA.

To test the effect of different types of stations on diversity of program offerings in a market, an ordinary least squares
regression was run with the following variables:

X_0 = L.I. for All Programs (Prime Time: 6 P.M. to midnight) for
the year beginning September 29, 1974.

Independent Variables:

X_2 = number of CBC-owned English stations in the market.
X_3 = number of CBC-owned French stations in the market.
X_4 = number of CBC English affiliates stations in the market.
X_5 = number of CTV affiliate staitons in the market.
X_6 = number of Global stations in the market.
X_7 = number of Canadian Independent stations in the market.

Two other independent variables were considered but omitted. CBC
French affiliates were omitted because there is only one such station in our markets. TVA affiliates were omitted because of a
very high correlation with X_3. The results are shown in Table
11.4

Table 11.4

MULTIPLE REGRESSION ON L.I. DIVERSITY IN 14 MARKETS

Constant	X_2	X_3	X_4	
2.780	0.084	0.145	-0.063	
	(0.93)	(1.93)*	(0.92)	
	X_5	X_6	X_7	R^2
	-0.009	-0.173	0.059	.73
	(0.10)	(1.81)*	(.94)	

Number of observations = 14.
Mean of dependent variable = 2.78.
* Significant at 90 percent level in a two-tail test.
- Figures in parentheses are t-statistics.

The results partially support the suggestion that CBC-owned
stations provide complementary programming which increases diversity in a market. A significant finding is that the presence of a
CBC-owned French station in a market adds 0.145 to the L.I. measure of diversity. Although the coefficient for CBC-owned English
stations is of the expected sign it is not, however, statistically
significant. The only other significant result is the negative
impact of the presence of a Global station on the L.I. of a market. A regression was similarly run with the same independent
variables but with the C.I. measure of market diversity as the
dependent variable. This regression equation did not provide any
significant results.

11.3.3 Television Viewer Choice by Market

Over time the degree of choice is influenced not only by the diversity of program offerings, but also by each station's scheduling. For example, if in a two-station market both stations provide five half-hour programs of one program type and five of another in an evening, then the average number of program options for the evening can vary from one, if both stations match their offerings so that the same type of program is offered on both channels during the same half hours, to two if the offerings are staggered so that there is no duplication in any half hour.

Viewer choice is analyzed for Canadian markets for prime time (6:30 P.M. to 11:30 P.M.) for the week of November 3 - 9, 1974. Two indicators of choice are calculated, the Average Number of Options and the Proportion of Options. These are defined as follows:

Average No. of Options =

$$\frac{\text{Summation of the No. of Options Each } \frac{1}{2} \text{ Hr. Time Period}}{\text{No. of } \frac{1}{2} \text{ Hr. Time Periods}}$$

Proportion of Options =

$$\frac{\text{Summation of the No. of Options Each } \frac{1}{2} \text{ Hr. Time Period}}{(\text{Number of } \frac{1}{2} \text{ Hr. Time Periods}) \ (\text{Number of Stations})}$$

The denominator in the definition of Proportion of Options gives the maximum possible number of options. These measures of choice performance are calculated twice for each market, once for Canadian audience competitors and once for all audience competitors. The latter will show the effect on choice of the availability of American stations. The stations included as Canadian and U.S. audience competitors are listed by market in the tables in Chapter 3. The criterion used to identify an audience competitor was that the station must account for one percent or more of the Total Hours Tuned in the market. As we noted in Chapter 3, this criterion excludes the PBS station in every market except Vancouver. This seems unfortunate because PBS provides additional choice even if few people watch it. Hence it was decided, for the markets where PBS is available, to also examine the choice provided by all audience competitors plus PBS. The only other significant effect of the one percent rule is to eliminate CBC-owned French stations in Toronto, Winnipeg, and Edmonton. Although a very significant choice for a small linguistic minority, these stations do not provide a relevant choice for the vast majority of people in these markets, hence no attempt is made to analyze their effect on choice.

Data on the CRTC program category offered by each Canadian station in each half-hour time period in the week was supplied, on computer tape, by the CRTC. Equivalent data for American stations

Table 11.5

VIEWER CHOICE BY MARKET, NOVEMBER 3 - 9, 1974

Market	Canadian Audience Competitors			All Audience Competitors			All Audience Competitors Plus PBS (where available)		
	Number of Stations	Average Number of Options	Proportion of Options	Number of Stations	Average Number of Options	Proportion of Options	Number of Stations	Average Number of Options	Proportion of Options
St. John's	2	1.58	.79	2	1.58	.79	-	-	-
Halifax	2	1.65	.83	4	2.48	.62	5	3.33	.67
Quebec	5	2.61	.52	7	3.10	.44	-	-	-
Montreal	4	2.65	.66	7	3.30	.47	8	3.89	.49
Ottawa-Hull	8	3.44	.43	10	3.81	.38	-	-	-
Toronto [1]	6	3.25	.54	10	3.78	.38	11	4.35	.40
Kitchener	6	2.84	.47	9	3.31	.37	-	-	-
London	4	2.42	.60	9	3.16	.35	10	3.71	.37
Windsor	2	1.70	.85	6	3.04	.51	-	-	-
Winnipeg	2	1.70	.85	6	2.70	.45	-	-	-
Regina	2	1.66	.83	2	1.66	.83	-	-	-
Edmonton	3	2.09	.70	4	2.32	.58	5	3.15	.63
Calgary	2	1.50	.75	4	2.25	.56	5	3.08	.62
Vancouver	3	1.67	.56	9[2]	3.35	.37	-	-	-

1. This excludes station CICA for which program data was not available on tape.
2. This includes the PBS station, KCTS, as this station qualifies as an audience competitor.

was derived by hand from program logs published in TV Guide or in newspapers. The results are shown in Table 11.5

An examination of the results for Canadian audience competitors reveals that the Average Number of Options does not increase proportionally with the number of stations. The more stations there are in a market, the less likely than any one of them is offering, in any half-hour period, a program type different from all the others. This is best illustrated by the fact that, in general, the more stations there are in a market, the lower the Proportion of Options. The exception is Vancouver which, with three stations, has a lower proportion than Montreal and London with four. Thus eight Canadian audience competitors in Ottawa-Hull provide only twice as many choices as two competitors in Windsor and Winnipeg. The result that stands out is the low number of choices, for a three station market, provided in Vancouver. The Average Number of Options in Vancouver is less than that for the two station markets of Windsor and Winnipeg.

The results for all audience competitors show that the inclusion of U.S. audience competitors increases the Average Number of Options, but at a decreasing rate as indicated in each case by a fall in the Proportion of Options. In Winnipeg, for example, the inclusion of four American competitors increased the Average Number of Options to 2.70 from the 1.70 provided by the two Canadian stations. In London, the addition of five U.S. competitors to the four Canadian competitors increases the Average Number of Options by only 0.74. To make it easier to see the incremental effect of American stations on viewer choice, the increase in the Average Number of Options is shown in Table 11.6.

The effect of adding the PBS station, for markets where this is applicable, on viewer choice is significantly different from the effect of adding U.S. commercial stations. As Table 11.5 indicates, in each case the addition of the PBS station actually increases the Proportion of Options. In Toronto, we see from Table 11.6 that one PBS station adds more to viewer choice than four U.S. commercial stations. Obviously, PBS does provide complementary and different programs. Its low audience ratings, however, leads one to wonder whether this is what most viewers want.

Another matter of interest is the effect of cable on viewer choice. In a number of markets the Canadian audience competitors are received over-the-air while American stations are received by cable. For such markets, the effect of cable can readily be deduced from Table 11.5. In other markets Canadian stations may be received by cable only and/or U.S. stations may be received over-the-air. CFTM and CKTM in Quebec, and CFTM, CFCF, and CKWS in Ottawa-Hull are received only by cable. In Toronto, all stations except CKVR, and in Kitchener all stations except WBEN and WKBW are received over-the-air. KCND in Winnipeg and KVOS in Vancouver are received over-the-air.[21]

Table 11.6

THE INCREMENTAL EFFECT ON VIEWER CHOICE OF U.S. STATIONS

Market	Canadian Audience Competitors		U.S. Audience Competitors		PBS	
	Number of Stations	Average Number of Options	Additional Number of Stations	Average Number of Options	Additional Number of Stations	Increase in Average Number of Options
St. John's	2	1.58	0	–	0	–
Halifax	2	1.65	2	.83	1	.85
Quebec	5	2.61	2	.49	0	–
Montreal	4	2.65	3	.65	1	.59
Ottawa-Hull	8	3.44	2	.37	0	–
Toronto [1]	6	3.25	4	.53	1	.57
Kitchener	6	2.84	3	.47	0	–
London	4	2.42	5	.74	1	.55
Windsor	2	1.70	4	1.34	0	–
Winnipeg	2	1.70	4	1.00	0	–
Regina	2	1.66	0	–	0	–
Edmonton	3	2.09	1	.23	1	.83
Calgary	2	1.50	2	.75	1	.83
Vancouver	3	1.67	6	1.68	0	–

Table 11.7

THE EFFECT OF CABLE ON VIEWER CHOICE

Market	Over-the-Air		Over-the-Air Plus Cable		
	Number of Stations	Average Number of Options	Additional Number of Stations	Average Number of Options	Increase in Average Number of Options
Halifax	2	1.65	5	3.33	1.68
Quebec	3	2.31	7	3.10	1.34
Montreal	4	2.65	8	3.89	1.46
Ottawa-Hull	5	3.10	10	3.81	0.71
Toronto	5	3.18	11	4.35	1.17
Kitchener	7	3.13	9	3.31	0.18
London	4	2.42	10	3.71	1.29
Winnipeg	3	2.26	6	2.70	0.44
Edmonton	3	2.09	5	3.15	1.06
Calgary	2	1.50	5	3.08	1.58
Vancouver	4	2.09	9	3.35	1.26

Source: Computed by the authors from data supplied by the CRTC and the CBC.

The effect of cable on the Average Number of Options is shown by market in Table 11.7. The "Over-the-Air Plus Cable" results include the PBS station, if any. The markets of St. John's, Windsor and Regina are omitted because they have no cable service. The increase in the Average Number of Options varies from 0.18 in Kitchener to 1.68 in Halifax. Not surprisingly, given some of our other findings, the markets which receive a PBS station by cable tend to gain the most, particularly if their over-the-air choice is limited. Thus Halifax and Calgary, the market with the next biggest gain, have two over-the-air stations and cable provides the programming of three more stations, one of which is a PBS station.

To test the effect of different types of stations on viewer choice an ordinary least squares regression was run with the following variables[22]:

Dependent Variable: X_0 = the number of viewer choices (6:00 P.M. to 11:30 P.M., November 3 - 9, 1974) on All Stations (including PBS) in the market.

Independent Variables:

X_2 = number of CBC-owned English stations in the market.
X_3 = number of CBC-owned French stations in the market.
X_4 = number of CBC English affiliate stations in the market.
X_5 = number of CTV affiliate stations in the market.
X_6 = number of Global stations in the market.
X_7 = number of Canadian Independent stations in the market.
X_8 = number of U.S. Commercial stations in the market.
X_9 = number of U.S. PBS stations in the market.

Two other independent variables were considered but omitted. CBC French affiliates were omitted because there is only one such station in our markets. TVA affiliates were omitted because of a very high correlation with CBC-owned French stations. The results are shown in Table 11.8.

The coefficients indicate the marginal effect on the number of viewer choices of an increase in one of this type of station when everything else is held constant.[23] With the exception of X_5, all the coefficients have the correct sign. The principal findings are the statistically significant and substantial effects of PBS and CBC-owned French stations on viewer choice. The first finding is consistent with the results of our earlier analysis of choice. CBC-owned French stations ranked well in our analysis of balance and diversity of programming. It appear these aspects are reflected in the substantial effect of these stations on viewer choice. The coefficient for U.S. commercial stations, the only other significant result (90 percent level), is low, presumably reflecting a high duplication with the programming of a number of other station types. The average number of U.S. stations in our markets is 2.65. The coefficient of 11.17 indicates the increase

Table 11.8

MULTIPLE REGRESSION ON VIEWER CHOICES IN 14 MARKETS

Constant	X_2	X_3	X_4	X_5	X_6
138.67	21.32	63.43	12.40	-16.79	34.08
(6.40)**	(.92)	(3.78)**	(.79)	(0.75)	(1.23)

	X_7	X_8	X_9	R^2
	14.62	11.17	66.95	.93
	(.79)	(1.94)*	(3.10)**	

Number of observations = 14.
Mean of dependent variable = 239.57.
Figures in parentheses are t-statistics.
*   denotes significant at 90% level of significance
    in a two-tailed test.
** denotes significant at 95% level of significance
    in a two-tailed test.

Table 11.9

PROGRAM BALANCE BY GROUP TYPE, 1974/75

Group Type	Number of Stations	Heavy Entertainment	Light Entertainment	Information
Newspaper	5	.05%	77%	23%
Broadcasting	26	4%	82%	15%
Single	8	2%	76%	22%

Note: Newspaper group includes radio stations belonging to a corporation that owns a newspaper. Broadcasting group includes radio stations belonging to a corporation that owns another radio or television station but no newspaper. Single includes radio stations not belonging to a newspaper or broadcasting group.

Table 11.10

BALANCE AND DIVERSITY OF PROGRAMMING BY AM AND FM STATIONS, 1974/75

Station Type	Number of Stations	Heavy Entertainment	Light Entertainment	Information	C.I.
AM	96	2%	77%	21%	.47
FM	7	12%	83%	5%	.32

in the number of viewer choices from adding one more U.S. station
to a market that has this average number. However, as each additional U.S. station is added, the increment to viewer choice dim-
inishes. Thus adding a U.S. commercial station to a market from a
base of zero or one would be expected to have a greater effect
than 11.17.

11.3.4 Radio Programming Performance

The radio program data supplied by the CRTC was for a sample
of 103 stations that excluded CBC stations. As a consequence it
proved impossible to undertake any analysis of programming at the
market level.

An analysis of programming by different station groupings is
possible. One aspect of interest is whether the type of ownership
of the station affects the overall balance of programming. This
is examined for three groupings of stations and the results reported in Table 11.9. All the stations included are in one of our
16 markets and the proportions shown apply to the period September
29, 1974, to September 27, 1975. The most noteworthy result is
the substantially lower Aggregate Proportion of Information offered by the stations in the broadcasting group.

As we indicated in section 11.2, the CRTC has been anxious to
prevent FM stations offering programming which is indistinguishable from AM stations. To obtain evidence on the extent of their
success by the period in question, balance and diversity were
measured for 96 AM stations and 7 FM stations. We have thus included all the AM and FM stations in the sample and a number of
the stations will not be in any of our fourteen markets. The results, which again apply to the period September 29, 1974, to
September 27, 1975, are shown in Table 11.10. They do give evidence of some degree of complementarity with FM providing more
Heavy Entertainment and a lot less Information. However, both FM
and AM have a very substantial emphasis on Light Entertainment and
low C.I. values; much lower than television.

11.4 SUMMARY AND CONCLUSIONS

The best overall balance of television programming is provided by CBC-owned French stations and CBC-owned English stations.
An interesting discovery was that CTV, Global, and the Independents all show (for prime time) a higher proportion of Canadian
Information programming than Canadian Light Entertainment programming although the All Program split is about 30 percent to 70
percent respectively. This is consistent with a strategy of using
Information programs to fill a substantial portion of Canadian
content requirements thus permitting a higher portion of foreign
programs to be of the more lucrative Light Entertainment variety.

Both measures, L.I. and C.I., of diversity indicated that
CBC-owned French stations and CBC-owned English stations, and in

that order, provide more diversity than the other Canadian networks or groupings. The L.I. and C.I. by market revealed that
diversity is lowest in those markets without a CBC-owned station.
Regression analysis to test the effect of different types of stations on L.I. diversity showed that the presence of a CBC-owned
French station has a significant positive effect on the diversity
offered in a market.

The examination of viewer choice revealed that the average
number of options provided by Canadian stations does not increase
proportionately with the number of Canadian stations serving the
market: for example, eight Canadian audience competitors in Ottawa-Hull provide only twice as many choices as two competitors in
Windsor and Winnipeg. Similarly, American commercial stations
increase the average number of options less than proportionately.
For example, in Winnipeg the average number of options provided by
the two Canadian stations is 1.00 and this figure only increases
to 2.70 when we include four U.S. commercial stations. The effect
of including a PBS station is very different, with the average
number of options increasing more than proportionately. In Toronto, one PBS stations adds more to viewer choice than four U.S.
Commercial stations. Not surprisingly, the effect of cable on the
average number of options is greatest where cable introduces a PBS
station to a market, such as Halifax or Calgary, that has a limited number of stations available over-the-air. The significant
results of a regression analysis of viewer choice were that both
the presence of a CBC-owned French station and the presence of a
PBS station have a substantial effect on the average number of
options in a market whereas the presence of an American Commercial
Station has only a small effect.

The limited analysis of radio programming indicates less diversity than for television. This is consistent with the prediction made in the model developed in Appendix 9.1. There is some
evidence of complementarity between the offerings of FM and AM
Stations.

Notes to Chapter 11

1. P.O. Steiner, "Program Patterns and Preferences, and the Workability of Competition in Radio Broadcasting," Quarterly Journal of Economics, Vol. 66, May 1952, pp. 194-223.

2. See, for example, B.M. Owen, Diversity and Television (Washington, D.C.: Office of Telecommunications Policy, August
1972).

3. Canadian Radio-television and Telecommunications Commission,
"C.R.T.C. Background Paper: The Economic Realities of Cana-

dian Television Production," Symposium on Television Violence (Ottawa: Information Canada, 1976).

4. The CRTC estimates revenue on the basis of published 30 second advertising rates, as quoted in Canadian Advertising Rates and Data (January 1975), and second the assumption that 80 percent of the maximum allowable commercial minutes per hour are sold. Costs of U.S. programs are those paid by American networks to independent production companies as published in Broadcasting, May 12, 1975, pp. 22-23. Costs of Canadian programs are identified as production costs but no source is given.

5. See Section 6A(5) of the Television Broadcast Regulations, and the Canadian Radio-Television Commission, Annual Report 1972-1973 (Ottawa: Information Canada, 1973).

6. Canadian Radio-Television Commission, Annual Report 1975-1976 (Ottawa: Minister of Supply and Services Canada), p. 8.

7. Ibid.

8. Canadian Radio-television and Telecommunications Commission, Annual Report 1976-77, (Ottawa: Minister of Supply and Services Canada, 1977), p. ix. More generally, see Robert E. Babe, Canadian Television Broadcasting Structure, Performance and Regulation (Ottawa: Economic Council of Canada, 1979).

9. Canadian Radio-television and Telecommunications Commission, Special Report on Broadcasting in Canada 1968-1978, 2 Volumes (Ottawa: CRTC, 1979, Vol. 1), p. 48.

10. See Canadian Radio-Television Commission, Annual Report 1974-75 (Ottawa: Information Canada, 1975), p. 6.

11. Canadian Radio-television and Telecommunications Commission, F.M. Radio in Canada: A Policy to Ensure a More Varied and Comprehensive Radio Service (Ottawa: Information Canada, 1975).

12. R.E. Babe, Canadian Television Broadcasting Structure, Performance and Regulation (Ottawa: Economic Council of Canada, 1979), pp. 185-209.

13. R.R. Richwood, Private Broadcasters and Broadcasting Policy in Canada, University of Toronto, unpublished Ph.D. Thesis, 1971, p. 749.

14. D.M. Blank, "The Quest for Quantity and Diversity in Television Programming," American Economic Review, Vol. 56, May 1966, pp. 448-456.

15. See Canadian Radio-Television Commission, Annual Report 1972-1973 (Ottawa: Information Canada, 1973), p. 18.

16. See CRTC, F.M. Radio in Canada..., op. cit., p. 1.

17. Ibid., p. 6.

18. Canadian Radio-television and Telecommunications Commission, Decision 72-197, March 28, 1972.

19. H. Land and Associates, Television and the Wired City (Washington, D.C.:   National Association of Broadcasters, 1968).

20. See R. Caves, Diversification, Foreign Investment, and Scale in North American Manufacturing Industries (Ottawa: Economic Council of Canada, 1975), pp. 22-23.

21. Following the usage in Chapter 4, a station is classified as over-the-air if the proportion of over-the-air viewing allocated to a station in the market is 50 percent or more of the proportion of cable viewing allocated; if the proportion is 50 percent or less the station is considered to be "cable only."

22. This regression is similar to that undertaken by H.J. Levin, "Program Duplication, Diversity, and Effective Viewer Choices: Some Empirical Findings," American Economic Review, Vol. 61, No. 2, May 1971, pp. 81-88.

23. In evaluating the additional choices provided by different types of station, it should be borne in mind that the maximum number of viewer choices a station could add is 77, a value equal to the number of half-hour time periods, 6:30 P.M. to 11:30 P.M., in a week.

Appendix 11.1

A MODEL RELATING PROGRAMMING PERFORMANCE TO INDUSTRY STRUCTURE

The assumptions of the model have been presented in Section 11.1 of the text. In brief they are that private broadcasters are profit maximizers and hence (assuming costs of different programs are identical) will choose the program mix that miximizes audience size, that programs can be categorized in such a way that viewers regard programs within a category to be closer substitutes than any program outside the category, and that if two or more programs within a category are offered at the same time each program will obtain an equal share of the audience for this category. The model is developed on the basis of these assumptions; the implications of relaxing the assumptions of identical program costs and equal audience shares for programs in the same category are examined later. The one-period model is presented immediately below and the multi-period model in the suceeding section.

A11.1 THE ONE-PERIOD MODEL

Let V represent the audience that prefers a given program type, denoted by the subscript, to all other program types and hence will watch it when all program types are offered. Let α represent the proportion of viewers who will watch another category, given the program types offered and the non-availability of their preferred category. The subscripts attached to α denote the preferred category and the other category respectively.

One station will choose the program type, from n program categories, which maximizes:

$$V_1 + \alpha_{21}V_2 + \alpha_{31}V_3 + \ldots + \alpha_{n1}V_n$$

$$V_2 + \alpha_{12}V_1 + \alpha_{32}V_3 + \ldots + \alpha_{n2}V_n$$

$$V_3 + \alpha_{13}V_1 + \alpha_{23}V_2 + \ldots + \alpha_{n3}V_n$$

$$\cdot \quad \cdot \quad \cdot \quad \cdot$$
$$\cdot \quad \cdot \quad \cdot \quad \cdot$$
$$\cdot \quad \cdot \quad \cdot \quad \cdot$$

$$V_n + \alpha_{1n}V_1 + \alpha_{2n}V_2 + \alpha_{3n}V_3 + \ldots + \alpha_{(n-1)n}V_{n-1}.$$

In general terms, one station chooses program j which maximizes $V_j + \Sigma\alpha_{ij}V_i$ where i denotes the other n-1 program types.

A second station will duplicate the program offering of the first if:

$$(V_j + \Sigma\alpha_{ij}V_i)/2 > V_k + \Sigma\alpha_{ik}V_i$$

where i on the LHS represents the other n-1 program types and on the RHS represents the other n-2 program types, and k is the program type, assuming program j is produced, that maximizes $V_k + \Sigma\alpha_{ik}V_i$. If, for purposes of illustration we assumed j is program type 1, then a second station will chose the program type that maximizes:

$$(V_1 + \alpha_{21}V_2 + \alpha_{31}V_3 + \ldots + \alpha_{n1}V_n)/2$$

$$V_2 + \alpha_{32}V_3 + \ldots + \alpha_{n2}V_n$$

$$V_3 + \alpha_{23}V_2 + \ldots + \alpha_{n3}V_n$$

$$\begin{matrix} \cdot & \cdot & \cdot & \cdot \\ \cdot & \cdot & \cdot & \cdot \\ \cdot & \cdot & \cdot & \cdot \end{matrix}$$

$$V_n + \alpha_{2n}V_2 + \alpha_{3n}V_3 + \ldots + \alpha_{(n-1)n}V_{n-1}.$$

It should be noted that the values of $\alpha_{32} \ldots \alpha_{n2}$, $\alpha_{23} \ldots \alpha_{n3}$, and $\alpha_{2n} \ldots \alpha_{(n-1)n}$ will generally differ from their value when program 1 is not already offered. This is because some of the people who prefer program n, for example, will watch program 2 if it is the only program offered but may choose to watch program 1 if both 1 and 2 are offered.

For the n station case, where x_s is the number of duplications of program s, the nth station will produce the program for which $(V_s + \Sigma\alpha_{is} V_i)/(x_s + 1)$ is at a maximum. This will be an existing program j, rather than an unproduced program k, if:

$$(V_j + \Sigma\alpha_{ij}V_i)/(x_j + 1) > V_k + \Sigma\alpha_{ik}V_i.$$

A new station will produce an existing program if its potential share of the existing audience is greater than the known audience, V_k, for the unproduced program plus the viewers who switch from existing programs plus previous non-viewers who choose to watch k.

As in the 2-station case, each time a new program is produced, the potential size of the audience for the remaining unproduced programs is affected. There is a shift in the preference function indicated by changes in various α values. If the ratios of α values for unproduced programs change in favour of those with smaller known audiences, V_k, then further duplication is more likely, whereas if it changes in favour of those with larger known audiences, further duplication is less likely. Production of a new program also affects the size of audience for existing programs. Indeed, with the addition of a new program, an existing program may even lose enough of its audience to the new program that another previously unproduced program may be able to attract a larger audience and hence replace it.

The one-period model indicates that audience maximizing behaviour by individual stations can obviously result in duplication of program types. The extent of duplication, given the number of program types and the number of stations, is obviously a function of the relative size of V_i, the proportion of people who will watch another program when their first choice is not offered, and the effect on the potential size of audiences of the shift in preference functions when a new program is produced. If the assumption of equal shares of shared audiences is relaxed then the greater the equality in the share of the audience the greater the tendency to duplication. If the assumption of equal costs is relaxed there will be less duplication if the programs which attract the larger audiences are more expensive to produce and more duplication if they are less expensive to produce.

A11.2 THE MULTI-PERIOD MODEL

If one takes as the relevant time span for television an evening of 5 hours of prime time divided into 10 half-hour periods, then with two stations there are 20 station-periods and for n stations there are 10n station-periods. The choice of this time span is an obvious one. Most people have a break from viewing between the end of prime time one evening to the beginning of prime time the next evening. It is reasonable to assume that they begin viewing the next evening with the same preferences as they had at the start of the previous evening.

If preferences do not change within an evening of prime time, that is viewers have a constant marginal utility for all program types, then the multi-period case is simply a period by period repetition of the one-period program pattern.

The implication of the other extreme assumption, namely zero marginal utility for repeats of a program type within an evening of prime time viewing, is that it would pay a station to offer a new program k in the first station period for which:

$$V_k + \Sigma \alpha_{ik} V_i > (V_j + \Sigma \alpha_{ij} V_i)/(x_j + 1)$$

where, for this multi-period case, x_j is the number of station-periods in which program j is already offered; it is assumed that the audience for j is equally shared among these x_j station-periods. Obviously there are considerable opportunities for diversity of offerings and program choice in given time periods.

A priori it would seem that the preferences of most viewers for most program types would lie between the constant marginal utility and zero marginal utility extremes. Diminishing marginal utility would occur in the ten-period time span but not to the extent that viewing any program type for more than 30 minutes provides zero utility. As a consequence, we can expect neither the period-by-period repetition of the first case, with the number of program types offered in an evening never more than the number of stations and very possibly less, nor the degree of diversity of offerings suggested by the latter. A viewer may or may not prefer a second offering of program j to a first offering of program k.

In the multi-period context radio differs significantly from television. The peak listening period tends to be the early morning when people are having breakfast and going to work. Many people listening during this period are available to the broadcaster for a relatively short time, a time span too short for diminishing marginal utility to be a factor. This leads to the expectation that radio programming would be more repetitive than television programming.

Appendix 11.2

CRTC PROGRAM CATEGORIES

SCHEDULE

(s. 5)

Item	Description of Subclass	Key figures		
		1st digit	2nd digit	3rd digit
1	Where country of origin is:			
	(1) Canada	1		
	(2) United States	2		
	(3) United Kingdom	3		
	(4) France	4		
	(5) Other	5		
2	Where broadcast origination point is:			
	(1) Local station		1	
	(2) Other station		2	
	(3) Network		3	
3	Where composition is			
	(1) Live			1
	(2) Recording of live program—first play			2
	(3) Repeat broadcast of either subitem (1) or (2)			3
	(4) Other recorded program			4
	(5) Program lip-synchronized in Canada			5

Program Categories

I. *Information and Orientation:*

1. News and news commentaries including newcasts, news reviews and road, weather and market reports.

2. Community and special events including information about community activities and celebrations.

3. Public affairs including talks, discussions, interviews, editorials, addresses and documentaries.

4. Religion.

5. Education:

(a) formal—classroom instruction in school or college;

(b) informal—adult education, occupational guidance, hobbies.

II. *Light Entertainment:*

6. Music and dance intended for background or light entertainment:

(a) hit parade (Palmarès);

(b) popular and dance music other than hit parade including folk, western, country dance and band music.

7. Drama, story and light verse, including serial and situation drama or story presentation, adventure and suspense drama, tales and readings and motion pictures intended as light entertainment.

8. Quiz and games.

9. Variety (revue) and music hall.

III. *Arts, Letters, and Sciences:*

General—Programs of recognized classics of earlier generations and contemporary achievements exceptionally distinguished in conception or performance that come within any category of programs set out in any of items 10 to 13.

10. Music and dance programs including classical, symphony, opera, choral recital and ballet programs, and interpretative dance music, experimental jazz and music hall, except programs of popular music intended primarily for background or light entertainment.

11. Drama, poem and story programs of exceptional distinction including masterpieces from various cultures and selected contemporary productions.

12. Critical evaluation in arts, literature and public affairs.

13. Science, including programs aimed at clarification of scientific principles or interpretation of scientific exploration and discovery.

IV. *Sports and Outdoors:*

14. Sports and outdoors—sportscasts, reviews and descriptions of all indoor and outdoor, land, water and air sports and exercises, including major sporting events such as hockey, football, skiing, baseball and golf and such sports as track and field, hunting, fishing, boating, climbing, camping, gliding, motor races and rallies, bowling and curling.

Chapter 12

The Cable Television Industry

Cable television is a delivery provision of signals unavailable "off-the-air" and improved reception of signals that can be
obtained "off-the-air." The industry has grown dramatically in
Canada. As of 1975 there were 388 cable systems operating ranging
in size from a few hundred subscribers to over 200,000. In 1976
this figure was 477 with 188 companies with more than 1,000 subscribers accounting for 98 percent of total subscribers.[1]

An examination of the cable television industry is an important component of a study of broadcasting in Canada. Cable television exerts a significant influence on the types of television
programming that Canadians watch as a result of its importation,
at zero cost, of American signals. In economic terms it expands
the market area of Canadian stations but fragments their audiences. This fragmentation reduces the market power and potential
profits of television broadcasters. These issues have already
been examined.

This chapter provides an overview of the structure of the
cable TV industry in Canada. The purpose is to characterize and
estimate the principal relationships: demand, price-cost, and
profit equations. These estimates can then be utilized to examine
the nature of the cost function and the profit equation will provide information of how profits vary with firm and market size.
This analysis is a first stage by which one may then evaluate regulatory policies. It also serves as a starting point to examine
the magnitude of rents associated with restrictive entry, whether
the industry has the economic characteristics for a regulated industry (e.g., is it a natural monopoly).

Section 12.1 provides an overview of the operating characteristics of cable television. Section 12.2 describes and estimates
the demand and price relationship. A cost analysis is presented
in section 12.3 together with the profit equations.[2] Analysis
and summary are contained in section 12.4.

12.1 AN OVERVIEW OF CABLE TV

The rapid growth of cable television in Canada over the last decade has not been equally distributed across the provinces. Table 12.1 shows the distribution of cable systems across provinces in 1975. An indication of the resources available to and controlled by cable television, are presented in Tables 12.2 and 12.3[3]. We observe that the largest companies (measured by number of subscribers) have significantly larger trunk and distribution systems while having a low proportion of indirect subscribers (subscribers in multiple unit buildings). We also note that those companies with a greater proportion of indirect subscribers have larger profits. This results from the ability of these firms to achieve greater economies of density.

Table 12.1

CABLE-TELEVISION SYSTEMS IN CANADA BY PROVINCE, 1975

Province	Operating Systems	Number of Subscribers
Nfld.	1	325
P.E.I.	0	0
N.S.	10	52,247
N.B.	12	33,483
Que.	146	510,540
Ont.	118	1,136,397
Man.	6	124,319
Sask.	7	11,243
Alta.	20	206,474
B.C.	68	560,909

Source: Statistics Canada, Cable Television, Cat. No. 56-205 (1975).

We can see in Tables 12.2 and 12.3 that generally the larger companies have significantly more indirect subscribers. Tables 12.4, 12.5 and 12.6 present the financial and income characteristics of cable companmies by size groups. The figures suggest that the larger companies are more profitable than smaller firms. The figures, however, do not fully reflect the exercise of market power. Cable operators are licenced for specific markets by the CRTC and their market power is in reference to the signal area and not the national market to which the figures in the tables refer. The ability of larger firms to be more profitable may result from larger markets, or more dense markets (thereby achieving density economies). One thing is clear, however, the cable firms are quite profitable with an average rate of return of 14 percent.[4]

The principal reason for the greater than normal rate of return is the licencing restrictions imposed by the CRTC. In reviewing the various proclamations made by the CRTC regarding cable operations, one can see the protectionist evolution. As Babe

Table 12.2

SUBSCRIBER AND OTHER OPERATING CHARACTERISTICS OF CANADA'S LARGEST CABLE TELEVISION COMPANIES, 1976

	Companies by Order of Size							
	1 - 5	6 - 10	11 - 15	16 - 20	21 - 25	26 - 30	31 - 188*	1 - 188
Total Subscribers (000's)	1,019	514	278	217	152	104	802	3,086
Direct Subscribers (000's)	795	331	219	185	115	86	710	2,441
Indirect Subscribers (000's)	224	183	58	33	37	17	92	664
Total Households Offered Cable Service (000's)	1,678	687	374	350	199	158	1,172	4,618
Total Households in Licensed Areas (000's)	1,715	696	386	403	202	161	1,320	4,883
Strand Miles of Distribution Cable	6,925	3,496	2,192	2,026	1,114	912	10,942	27,607
Strand Miles of Main or Trunk Cable	2,017	992	661	627	451	300	3,218	8,266
Average Size of Company No. of Subscribers per Company (000's)	204	103	56	43	30	21	5	16
Number of Employees	1,402	709	318	330	231	133	1,925	5,048

* Excludes those licensees having less than 1,000 subscribers.

Source: Department of Communications, Statistical Information Services, Ottawa.

Table 12.3

SUBSCRIBER AND OTHER OPERATING CHARACTERISTICS OF CANADA'S LARGEST CABLE TELEVISION COMPANIES, 1976

	Companies by Order of Size							
	1 - 5	6 - 10	11 - 15	16 - 20	21 - 25	26 - 30	31 - 188*	1 - 188
Indirect Subcribers Proportion (Indirect Subscribers Divided by Total Subscribers)(%)	22.0	35.7	21.0	15.0	24.3	16.8	11.5	20.8
Penetration Ratios (%) a) Subscriber Utilization of Cable (Number of Subscribers divided by number of households offered service)	60.7	74.8	74.3	62.1	76.2	65.7	68.4	66.8
b) Household Penetration (Number of subscribers offered service relative to number of households in licensed areas)	59.4	73.9	72.3	53.8	75.2	64.6	60.8	63.2
c) Cable Penetration (Number of households offered service relative to number of households in licensed areas)	97.8	98.7	96.9	86.8	98.5	98.1	88.8	94.6
Distribution Cable per Thousand Subscribers	6.8	6.8	7.9	9.3	7.3	8.8	13.6	8.9
Trunk Cable per Thousand Subscribers	2.0	1.9	2.4	2.9	3.0	2.9	4.0	2.7
Number of Employees per Thousand Subscribers	1.4	1.4	1.1	1.5	1.5	1.3	2.4	1.6

* Excludes those licensees having less than 1,000 subscribers. The latter excluded group has only two percent of total subscribers.

Source: Department of Communications, Statistical Information Services, Ottawa.

Table 12.4

INCOME CHARACTERISTICS OF CANADA'S LARGEST CABLE TELEVISION COMPANIES, 1976

	Companies by Order of Size							
	1 - 5	6 - 10	11 - 15	16 - 20	21 - 25	26 - 30	31 - 188*	1 - 188
Total Operating Revenues (000's)	62,671	31,257	18,992	13,581	9,336	6,791	52,148	194,776
Revenue from Direct Subscribers (000's)	51,781	24,604	15,891	11,880	7,518	6,023	46,053	163,750
Revenue from Indirect Subscribers (000's)	5,406	3,374	1,835	685	876	394	1,033	13,603
Installation (Including Reconnect) Revenues (000's)	2,938	1,236	1,220	940	417	248	3,933	10,932
Other Cable Operating Revenues (000's)	2,546	2,044	47	76	525	125	1,128	6,491
Total Operating Expenses (000's)	32,634	15,933	10,389	8,219	5,748	3,125	29,290	105,348
Program Origination Expenses (000's)	2,676	1,538	1,105	919	523	450	2,878	10,089
Technical Expenses (000's)	14,671	6,685	4,846	3,501	2,722	1,123	10,186	43,734
Sales and Promotion Expenses (000's)	2,962	1,870	1,058	771	467	293	1,869	9,290
Administrative and General Expenses (000's)	12,326	5,840	3,380	3,028	2,036	1,269	14,357	42,236
Net Operating Revenues (Operating Income) (000's)	30,038	15,325	8,603	5,363	3,588	3,655	22,856	89,428
Depreciation (000's)	12,773	6,823	3,273	2,582	2,165	1,448	9,959	39,023
Interest Expenses (000's)	5,190	2,611	1,250	1,753	1,058	773	4,724	17,359
Pretax Profit (000's)	14,113	6,961	5,148	1,851	929	1,554	4,813	35,369
Net Income (000's)	6,940	3,900	2,878	1,382	414	994	1,386	17,894

* Excludes those licensees having less than 1,000 subscribers. The latter excluded group has only two percent of total subscribers.

Source: Department of Communications, Statistical Information Services, Ottawa.

Table 12.5

BALANCE SHEET CHARACTERISTICS OF CANADA'S LARGEST CABLE TELEVISION COMPANIES, 1976

	Companies by Order of Size							
	1 - 5	6 - 10	11 - 15	16 - 20	21 - 25	26 - 30	31 - 188*	1 - 188
Total Assets (000's)	128,890	66,222	27,725	26,818	14,507	9,897	110,083	384,142
Land, Property and Equipment at Cost (000's)	142,046	57,303	36,342	29,825	17,342	14,524	116,806	414,188
Accumulated Depreciation (000's)	66,064	28,567	13,158	11,437	7,095	6,372	45,629	178,322
Net Fixed Cable TV Assets (000's)	75,982	28,735	23,184	18,388	10,247	8,152	71,177	235,865
Total Liabilities (000's)	88,882	45,255	18,342	23,059	13,567	8,687	79,565	277,357
Long-Term Debt (000's)	40,143	7,821	7,993	14,542	3,442	5,139	61,051	140,131
Current Liabilities (000's)	33,428	14,690	6,948	4,846	5,042	2,808	29,628	97,391
Deferred Income Taxes (000's)	13,350	4,404	3,327	731	1,033	349	3,269	26,463
Total Equity (000's)	40,008	20,967	9,383	3,759	940	1,210	30,518	106,785
Funds Used for Capital Additions - Cable TV Only (Investment Expenditures) (000's)	22,508	5,514	5,998	6,229	2,369	1,308	27,044	70,970

* Excludes those licensees having less than 1,000 subscribers. The latter group has only two percent of total subscribers.

Source: Department of Communications, Statistical Information Services, Ottawa.

Table 12.6

RATIOS OF FINANCIAL HEALTH OF CANADA'S LARGEST CABLE TELEVISION COMPANIES, 1976

	Companies by Order of Size							
	1 – 5	6 – 10	11 – 15	16 – 20	21 – 25	26 – 30	31 – 188**	1 – 188
Operating Revenues*	61.50	60.77	68.36	62.51	61.42	65.56	65.02	63.12
Operating Expenses*	32.03	30.98	37.39	37.83	37.81	30.27	36.52	34.14
Operating Income*	29.48	29.79	30.97	24.68	23.61	35.29	28.50	28.98
Depreciation*	12.54	13.27	11.77	11.90	14.24	13.92	12.42	12.65
Interest*	5.09	5.08	4.50	8.08	6.96	7.43	5.89	5.63
Pretax Profit*	13.85	13.53	18.53	8.52	6.11	15.01	6.00	11.46
Net Income*	6.81	7.58	10.36	6.36	27.2	9.59	1.73	5.80
Total Assets*	126.49	128.74	99.79	123.44	95.43	95.55	137.26	124.48
Long-Term Debt*	39.40	15.20	28.77	66.93	22.64	49.61	76.12	45.41
Current Liabilities*	32.81	28.58	24.99	22.33	33.17	27.00	36.94	31.56
Deferred Income Taxes*	13.10	8.56	11.87	3.36	6.80	3.37	4.08	8.58
Equity Divided by Total Assets (%)	31.0	31.7	33.8	14.0	6.5	12.2	27.7	27.8
Long-Term Debt Divided by Total Assets (%)	31.1	11.8	28.8	54.2	23.7	51.9	55.5	36.5
Current Liabilities Divided by Total Assets (%)	25.9	22.2	25.1	18.1	34.8	28.4	26.9	25.4
Deferred Income Taxes Divided by Total Assets (%)	10.4	6.7	12.0	2.7	7.1	3.5	3.0	6.9
Investment*	22.09	10.73	21.58	28.71	15.59	15.59	33.72	23.00

* Per subscriber.
** Excludes those licensees having less than 1,000 subscribers. The latter excluded group has only two percent of total subscribers.

Source: Department of Communications, Statistical Information Services, Ottawa.

notes, initially the CRTC had neither an awareness of, nor concern
for, the impact of cable television on broadcasting.[5] However,
once the effect of cable on Canadian content and market fragmentation became clear, the CRTC became highly protectionist, primarily on Canadian content grounds, but partially on the basis of de-
structive competition.[6] The CRTC has now softened its protectionist stance and allowed greater importation of U.S. programs.
Private broadcasters' financial position has been protected within
cable television since the CRTC requires program substitutions,
commercial deletions and direct payments from cable to broadcast
firms. Also, revenues are augmented by Canadian stations insert-
ing advertising into imported U.S. programs.[7]

Cost relationships in the cable television industry in Canada
provide a basis for evaluation of CRTC regulation of the industry.
These relationships provide the information on the viability of
systems in particular areas and the optimal number or size of system which should be licenced.

12.2 DEMAND RELATIONSHIPS

Our treatment of the demand for cable TV rests on a partial
equilibrium framework in which we attempt to establish the demand
relationship for a particular form of entertainment rather than
for entertainment generally. In this latter case general macro
economic variables such as unemployment, income distribution and
shorter work weeks would be relevant variables. We take the view,
however, that the work-leisure time allocation has been made and
that our task is to determine which variables influence the demand
for cable, i.e., how is time allocated within the leisure component. In this sense we argue that the demand for cable may be
viewed like that of any economic good, it is a function of its own
price, the price of substitutes and complements, and income. Previous work by Park[8] and Good[9] has centered on the penetration
rate (the ratio of subscribers to dwelling units passed by cable)
as the measure of demand. Park's characterization in terms of a
non-linear demand model was followed by Good.

Rather than use the penetration rate, this study used total
subscribers as the measure of demand. This characterization allows an evaluation of the effects of market size as well as the
traditional variables. One difficulty with both this measure and
the penetration rate is the failure to segment direct and indirect
subscribers. Direct subscribers are those in single family dwel-
lings while indirect subscribers live in large units such as
apartment buildings. Since the average charge per subscriber will
be influenced by the costs of servicing, and costs vary between
these two different types of units, some information is lost by
failing to segment subscribers and using the average charge per
subscriber.

The exogenous (independent) variables were the average charge
per subscriber, (X_1), the average income of the area in which the

station is located (X_2), the population of the area (X_3), the amount spent on local programming (X_4), and the age of the system (X_5). Two variables which are not included but should have been are the net addition of network and non-network stations. Since these variables are excluded our estimates will be biased.

As Good [10] points out, the model is clearly simultaneous. The number of subscribers is a function of price, price is a function of cost and cost is a function of the number of subscribers. Initial estimates were made using ordinary least squares, but the simultaneity requires the use of instrumental variables to provide consistent estimates.

The data for 1975 for both the demand and cost analysis were provided by the federal Department of Communications. Individual firm data was augmented by Statistics Canada data and data from the Ministry of State for Urban Affairs. The sample consists of 175 individual firms. These were selected by excluding all firms with less than 1,000 subscribers as complete financial data were not available for these firms, and, by excluding group-owned firms where the balance sheet was a consolidated statement for all firms.

Estimates of the demand and price equations are contained in Table 12.7. The signs of all coefficients are as expected. The variables included consist of those which economic theory would suggest as well as variables which Good[11] describes as "quasi-regulated," variables which are a function of other variables important in CRTC decision making. As an example, economic theory argues that the own price as well as the price of substitutes and complements should be included in the demand function. The CRTC regulates price and its' decisions are influenced by such things as the age of the system, the penetration rate and the amount spent on local programming. Thus these variables are included in the estimation.

Economic theory argues that a profit maximizing monopolist will never operate on the inelastic portion of his demand curve. Since cable firms are licenced and are granted a monopoly in a section of an urban area, one expects the estimated demand elasticity to be equal to or greater than one. However, given the substitutability between cable and other entertainment media, particularly over-the-air TV, cable companies do not have an entertainment monopoly despite having the cable monopoly.

The evidence from the demand equation indicates an own price elasticity of approximately 1.1. This suggests that firms have established output where marginal and average revenue are both greater than zero.

Marginal revenue (MR) per year is approximately $28.00 per subscriber per year on average, which is less than the estimated marginal costs (MC) of approximately $33.00 per year. The equi-

Table 12.7

ESTIMATES OF DEMAND AND PRICE EQUATIONS FOR CABLE-TELEVISION

	Constant	X_1	X_2	X_3	X_4	X_5	X_6	X_7	X_8	X_9	R^2
1.	17388.1	-3871.23	.459	.005	.3867					2965.6	.78
	(1.93)	(-3.62)	(2.47)	(2.51)	(8.5)					(.70)	
2.	10,482.5	-3339.4	.3927	.005	.3836	480.1					.79
	(1.02)	(-3.11)	(1.41)	(2.83)	(8.41)	(1.73)					
3.	11,695.7	-9125.7	1.789	.004	.398	157.3					.76
	(2.24)	(-3.26)	(1.47)	(1.77)	(6.89)	(1.47)					
4.	2.93		.0002		.00002	-.0268	.0211		-.0006		.21
	(4.96)		(3.05)		(1.13)	(1.48)	(5.77)		(1.03)		
5.	2.82		.0002		.00002	-.0254	.022				.27
	(4.81)		(3.07)		(1.81)	(-1.42)	(6.21)				
6.	2.74		.0002		.00002	-.0263	.022	-.095			.37
	(3.88)		(3.06)		(1.82)	(-1.41)	(6.17)	(-2.20)			
7.	4.31		.0002		.00002	-.047	.007	-.382			.34
	(5.86)		(2.61)		(.536)	(-2.38)	(2.24)	(-1.79)			
8.	3.89		.0002		.00001	-.046	-.008				.30
	(5.42)		(3.42)		(1.36)	(-2.35)	(-3.23)				

X_1 = Average charge per subscriber.
X_2 = Average income of market.
X_3 = Population.
X_4 = Amount spent on local programming.
X_5 = Age of the system.
X_6 = Average cost.
X_7 = Penetration rate.
X_8 = Miles of cable in system.
X_9 = Microwave dummy variable.

Notes: — The figures in parenthesis are t-statistics. The sample size was 175. Equations 1, 2, 3 are demand equations with total subscribers as the dependent variable. Equations 1 and 2 were estimated using ordinary least squares, equation 3 with instrumental variables. Equations 4 - 8 are price equations; 4 - 6 were estimated using ordinary squares, equations 7 and 8 with instrumental variables.

librium position of the firm is shown in Figure 12.1. In the absence of regulation, the profit maximizing cable firm would establish MR = MC at an output S_1 (Where S is the number of subscribers) and price P_1. However, the regulator has established a price less than P_1, say P_2. The demand curve now becomes P_2 aD while the Marginal revenue curve is discontinuous, P_2 abMR. The output is S_2. This result may, in part, be attributed to the action of the CRTC which regulated prices. These results are tentative however, as variables for additional signals and variety have been omitted from the equation with the result that the elasticity measure may be somewhat biased upward.

Good[12] claims firms are operating on the inelastic portion of the demand curves, but Good really hasn't estimated a demand curve since his dependent variable is the penetration rate. What he has estimated is a share equation with some peculiar properties, for example, if the firm increases its size, the penetration rate falls.

In the price equations in Table 12.7, there is evidence that subscription rates are lower for older systems and higher penetration rates. The latter variable operates through two mechanisms. First, as the penetration rate increases, fixed costs are spread over more units of ouput, and second, the penetration rate is similar to a "load factor" and as the load factor increases average costs decrease.[13]

In both the demand (total subscribers) and the price equations, the coefficient of the local programming costs variable is positive. As the amount spent on local programming increases, either the quantity or quality increases. American studies[14] have found a high positive correlation between the amount spent on a program and its quality as measured by audiences ratings. Therefore, in the demand equation one might interpret this positive sign to mean that as local programming expenses - and thus quality - increase by, for example, 10 percent, total subscribers increase by approximately 3.8 percent. The evidence here is consistent with that of Good.[15] The effect of local programming expenses on price is positive as one would expect, but its influence is negligible as shown in equations 5 and 6.

The population variable is positive and significant at the 95 percent level in equation 1 and 2. Population represents a scale variable and the results suggests that areas of greater population have greater demand. Good[16] argues that population is a proxy for alternative entertainment medium, suggesting that the availability of alternatives increases with the population. His results have a negative sign and are statistically significant. We would argue that this reasoning is wrong and the negative sign results because his dependent variable (penetration rate) is a ratio with the denominator positively correlated with the population variable.

Figure 12.1

EQUILIBRIUM PRICES AND REGULATED PRICES

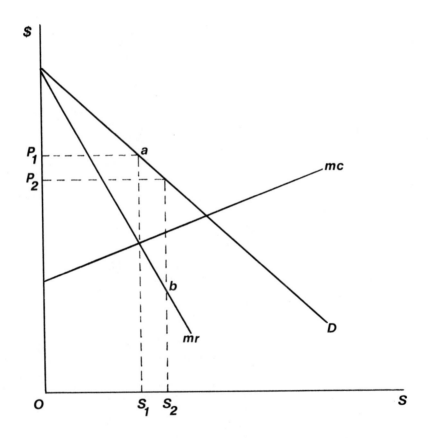

12.3   COST RELATIONSHIPS

As Babe[17] has noted, the study of cost relationships is important for at least three reasons.   First, the granting of (free) licences within urban areas on a fragmented basis makes sense on efficiency grounds only if the economies of scale are not large and there are economies of density.   Second, industries regulated via entry regulation (exclusive licences) should, on economic grounds, possess specific cost characteristics i.e., increasing returns to scale.[18]   Third, the cost relationships with respect to scale and density provide some information regarding the feasibility of extending cable service to rural areas.

The cost functions estimated below are part of the system of simultaneous of equations presented earlier.   Good[19] presented estimates of costs for cable.   He segmented the costs into operating and fixed costs and estimated two equations.   From the fixed cost equation he attempted to evaluate scale economies and from the operating cost function he purported to examine economies of density.   The difficulty is that in neither case has he held the alternative variable constant so it is not clear what the economies of density are, holding firm size constant.   An added difficulty arises in his specification of the fixed cost equation which fails to segment miles of cable into above and below ground.   This is important since the cost, in 1975, of above-ground cable was approximately \$4,000/mile while below-ground cable was approximately \$13,000 per mile.[19]

For example, Good estimates an equation of the form:

$$D = a + B_1M + B_2M^2 + B_3M^3$$

where D is depreciation and M is miles of cable.   Estimates of this equation with and without segmenting cable into above ground (M_a) and below ground (M_b) were as follows:

$$D = 7638.69 + 539.1M + 1.19M^2 - .0004M^3 \qquad R^2 = .83$$
$$\quad\ (.384) \qquad (2.89) \quad\ (3.93) \quad\ (4.03)$$

and

$$D = 10,500 + 199.9M_a + 2387.4M_b + .989M_a^2$$
$$\quad\ (.609) \qquad (0.824) \qquad (3.02) \qquad (1.99)$$

$$+ 13.71M_b^2 - .002M_a^3 - .044M_b^3 \qquad R^2 = .90$$
$$\ \ (2.46) \qquad (-1.01) \quad\ (-4.46)$$

These estimates clearly indicate that the optimal size of plant, measured in cable miles, is much smaller for a firm that employs below ground cable than one employing above ground cable.   Cable systems in urban areas utilize more below than above ground cable and their plants tend to be smaller than rural systems.   However, the optimal mix is not independent of the density of subscribers, and one must insure that economies of scale for plants are evaluated for a given density.

In this study, rather than separate the two costs and esti- mate separate regressions, we estimate a total cost function in an attempt to evaluate economies of density in terms of percent vari- able. Percent variable (PV) is simply the ratio of marginal costs to average cost. Therefore, PV < 1 implies increasing returns and PV = 1 implies constant returns to scale. It is a measure of the elasticity of cost with respect to a change in output. The per- cent variable concept is a particularly helpful summary measure, but one which must be carefully utilized. As Griliches[21] points out, percent variable is "variable" in that it does not remain the same at different levels of output. In our case, the percent var- iable must be evaluated for a given output and for a given ratio of subscribers to homes passed by cable.

In specifying the cost-output relationship, a problem of de- flation by size arises. One wishes to deflate to minimize the influence of extremely large observations. As Griliches notes, "Implicitly, it is assumed that the larger the observation the larger is the error associated with it, and that by dividing them by a size measure one gets numbers whose errors are roughly com- parable to each other, that is, deflation is performed to stabil- ize the error variance."[22] In order to take account of the size influence, one may either deflate by a size variable or utilize a variance stabilizing transformation such as logarithms.

We elected to deflate by size. The measure selected was the miles of cable in the system. This measure assumes that the cost relationship specified is homogeneous in output and size or that there are no costs which are independent of size. Again Gril- iches[23] provides a good illustration of the implications of the homogeneity assumption. Consider the following specification.

$$c = \alpha m + s \qquad (1)$$

where c are the costs, m represents the miles of cable and s, the number of subscribers, is an output measure. Dividing the above equation by m to deflate, we obtain

$$c/m = \alpha + \beta \, (s/m) \qquad (2)$$

However, the true relationship may be

$$c = \alpha m + \beta s + \delta \qquad (3)$$

and deflating by m, one obtains

$$c/m = \alpha + \beta \, (s + \delta/m) \qquad (4)$$

We estimated equation 2 and 4 to determine if m was an appro- priate size deflator. If one were to use equation 2 the implication is that δ is equal to zero or that there are costs which are independent of size as measured by m. Estimates of equation 2 and 4 are given by 2* and 4* respectively; t-statistics are given in parenthesis.

$$c/m = 506.28 + 34.42(s/m) + 25747.2(1/m) \qquad (4*)$$
$$\quad\;\; (2.62) \quad (13.14) \qquad (7.49)$$
$$R^2 = .71$$

and

$$c/m = 298.36 + 44.33(s/m) \qquad\qquad\qquad (2*)$$
$$\quad\;\; (1.35) \quad (17.06)$$
$$R^2 = .62$$

The significance of the δ coefficient in 4 and the test of the significance of the goodness of fit between 2* and 4* indicate that the assumptions underlying the size deflator are not contradicted.

A number of alternative cost functions were estimated using both ordinary least squares and the instrumental variables procedure. The latter was required since we have a simultaneous system as discussed earlier. The estimates are presented in Table 12.8.

Babe has argued that cable systems are subject to strong diseconomies of scale. The diseconomies result from two sources. First, there is a limit in the distribution systems if one wishes to maintain a signal at a given quality. That is, the total length of trunk cable from the head end is limited as the method utilized in transmitting the signal relies on amplifiers at various points along the cable and these amplifiers, amplify both extraneous noise and the signal. Babe notes, "at the very maximum, seventy-five amplifiers have been cascaded, giving 30 miles of trunk cable, but normally a maximum of seventeen trunk miles is placed on system length in order to maintain high standards."[24] The second factor, contributing to diseconomies, is the channel capacity of the trunk cable which until recently was a maximum of twelve.

The evidence presented in Table 12.8 suggests that total system costs were lower for older systems. This result can be explained by the fact that older systems have achieved higher penetration rate and there appear to be economies of density as costs fall with increasing penetration.

Evidence in both Babe and Good indicates substantial decreasing returns to scale in cable systems. Babe argues that for plants of up to 200 miles, operating costs fall, but on a total cost basis, systems of less than 100 miles and greater than 600 miles face high average costs.[25] Good on the other hand states that the average total cost per cable mile is at a minimum for systems of 70 miles.[26]

Table 12.8

ESTIMATES OF COST FUNCTIONS FOR CABLE-TELEVISION

Dependent Variable	Constant	M	S	P	$\frac{S}{M}$	$\frac{1}{M}$	lnM	lnS	lnP	AGC	R^2
1. Total Costs	32660.4 (1.34)	654.07 (3.67)	31.49 (19.14)								.95
2. Total Costs	285253 (3.02)	483.7 (2.61)	32.76 (19.52)	-324244 (-2.77)							.95
3. Total cost per mile	506.28 (2.62)				34.41 (13.14)	25747.2 (7.49)					.72
4. Total cost per mile	1113.68 (2.59)			-876.65 (-1.58)	34.88 (13.28)	26308.9 (7.65)					.73
5. Log of total costs	5.09 (23.35)						.8984 (1.76)	.807 (16.03)			.93
6. Log of total costs	4.81 (18.63)						-.894 (-10.98)	1.87 (4.58)	-.846 (-5.39)		.94
7. Total costs per mile	964.5 (3.33)				35.09 (13.42)	25356.7 (7.44)				-49.65 (-2.11)	.73

Where M = miles of cable.
      S = number of subscribers.
      P = penetration rate.
      ln = natural logarithm.

Note: - Equations 6, 7 were estimated utilizing instrumental variables.
       - t-statistics are in parenthesis.

From the estimates in Table 12.8, the percent variable measure (PV) is calculated to be approximately .98 to .91. Since this value is less than one, it implies minor increasing returns to scale where scale is measured in miles of plant and the PV figures is calculated at the average. This is opposite to the evidence of Babe and Good. One possible explanation is that we have not estimated a long run cost function which is the traditional interpretation from a cross-sectional analysis. The evidence for this is that the constant term in all regressions is significant. Another possibility is that since the sample has not been segmented into various size classes, we have counteracting phenomena working. First, the small firms are on the downward sloping portion of their short run average cost curve, while at the same time because of their predominately rural nature, they have low densities (subscribers/mile) and they are not achieving the density economies. On the other hand, large firms are achieving economies of density and have low levels of cost functions because of high penetration rates. What may be happening is that the small firm influence outweighs the large firm influence and thus the average firm exhibits increasing return.

Equations 6 and 7, the unrestricted logarithic form, suggest increasing returns with a percent variable of .89 which implies some excess capacity. To see what is going on, consider Figure 12.2. Points S_1, S_2 and S_3 represent optimum levels of output. If small firms have excess capacity, they will not be on the long run cost function but will be to the left on the short run cost function such as points X_1, X_2 and X_3 (since each short run curve corresponds to a firm of a given mileage). On the other hand the large firm will be to the right of the optimal point. Such as point Y_1, Y_2 and Y_3. The estimated regression line may then be AB, with a greater than 45 degree slope from the origin and thereby generate a percent variable measure of less than one.

A significant problem which arise in the interpretation of all of the cost function is the extent to which we are estimating points on different cost function for alternative penetration rates. The estimates show that average total costs are lower at approximately 66,000 subscribers. These results, it should be noted are in very close agreement with Good.

An examination of the average total costs per subscriber under alternative penetration rates was also made. At low penetration rates (.3) the average cost was approximately $50 per subscriber, at medium penetration rates (.3 to .6) the average cost falls to approximately $42 per subscriber and at high penetration rates (.67) the figure is approximately $39 per subscriber.

Babe found that the fixed investment per potential subscriber for low penetration systems is $25 to $28 and for highly penetrated systems, which are also large systems, the costs average $25 to $40 per potential subscriber.[27]

Figure 12.2

ACTUAL AND ESTIMATED COST FUNCTIONS OVER ALTERNATIVE
SIZES OF FIRMS

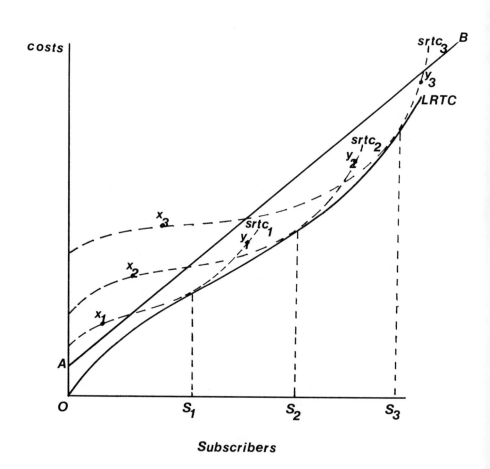

Subscribers

The movement down the average cost curve with penetration rates is nothing more than the phenomenon of capacity utilization. In airlines, the "load factor" is comparable to the penetration rate. Keeler finds that the cost function, and therefore the price per passenger, falls as the load factor increases.[28] One may therefore calculate the average cost per home and compare this cost, which assumes a penetration rate equal to 1, to costs at lower penetration rates. This gives some indication of how price changes as average cost falls. Indeed, the high profitability of cable firms may be explained by this phenomenon since the average penetration rate for the sample is .74. At a penetration rate of 1.00, the average cost per subscriber is approximately $37, therefore, a price of $3.08 per month would yield total revenue to cover total cost. At the average penetration rate of .74, the average cost per subscriber rises to $50 which requires a price of $4.16 per month to generate sufficient revenues. The existing average price for cable is justified only if the penetration rate is approximately 55 percent. Table 12.9 presents an example of costs with given numbers of subscribers and miles of cable.

Table 12.9

ESTIMATED COSTS FOR ALTERNATIVE FIRM SIZES[1]

No. of Subscribers	Miles of Cable	Total Cost per Mile	Total Annual Cost	Total Cost per Subscriber
150,000	1000	6254.8	6,254,800.	41.69
100,000	900	4892.6	4,403,406.	44.03
60,000	700	4008.0	2,805,600.	46.76
50,000	600	3931.8	2,362,987.	47.25
45,000	500	4174.2	2,087,106.	46.38
27,000	400	3397.2	1,358,876.	50.32
21,000	300	3506.0	1,051,806.	50.08
10,000	200	2846.0	569,256.	56.92
8,600	100	4236.0	432,610.	49.25

1. All numbers estimated from equation 7 of Table 12.8

A profit equation was also estimated for the sample of 175 cable operations. Two alternative definitions of profit were used. One was the rate of return on equity defined as profit before taxes plus depreciation and interest over the sum of share capital and earned surplus. The second measure was the price-cost margin. The estimates are as follows:

$$ROR = 3.28 + .0019Y + .0017M + .00002POP + 1.87PEN + .317AGE$$
$$(3.57) \quad (.423) \quad (2.73) \quad (1.15) \quad (3.03)$$
$$R^2 = .16$$

$$P\text{-}C = .2557 + .0023Y + .0002M + .0003HPM + .091PEN + .308AGE$$
$$(3.30) \quad (.889) \quad (3.44) \quad (.858) \quad (1.51)$$
$$R^2 = .12$$

242 Canadian Broadcasting

where ROR is the profit measured by rate of return, P-C is the price-cost margin, Y is income, m is miles of cable, PEN is the penetration rate, HPM is the homes per mile of cable, POP is the population of the market.

The results are clearly weak. Some of the data is inadequate (for example the inability to separate direct and indirect subscribers on a firm basis) and certain critical variables have been excluded. Despite these limitations, there still remain some interesting interpretations. First, cable firms are licenced by the CRTC and this licence represents an entry barrier which creates a monopoly in a given area. As a result, the firm is able to earn above normal profits, all or part of which is rent attributable to the artificial barrier. The constant term in the equation should be interpreted as the effect on the dependent variable of the mean of excluded explanatory variables. Therefore, one may interpret the constant term as reflecting the value or profitability attributable only to the licence. In order to obtain a true measure, one would have to estimate profit equations for cable firms and for other types of industries in Canada and take the difference between the constant terms of the two equations. This would provide an estimate of the rents attributable to the licence if the other industries were competitive having no rents to artificial barriers reflected in their constant terms. Also, one would not expect, under competitive conditions, the constant term of the non-cable regressions to be statistically significant. For example, in the ROR equation above, one might argue that 3.29 percentage points of the rate of return are represented by rents to the licence.

The second important point that arises is the high average profitability of cable firms. The unweighted average rate of return (ROR, as defined above) in the sample was 24 percent. A survey of the cost equation shows a marginal cost of approximately $35 per subscriber. However, the average revenue per subscriber is $64 per year. The price is almost twice the marginal cost, reflecting the monopoly pricing power of the cable firms. This result is not surprising since the CRTC does not regulate on the rate of return although it must approve the monthly charge per subscriber.

The size of the market and the size of the firm also have positive effects on the profit rate; larger firms in larger markets are more profitable. The variable which has the largest effect of increasing profits is the penetration rate. As we have seen, costs per subscriber decrease with increases in penetration.

12.4 POLICY CONCLUSIONS

A major policy question facing both policy makers and regulators concerns mergers and cross-ownership with their attendant effects on prices and programming.

There exist two opposing views on merger policy. One group, the traditionalists, argue that mergers lead to increased concentration which in turn leads firms to raise prices and restrict output. Restricting output results in resource misallocation and ineffeciency in the economy while higher prices generate income transfers from consumers to producers. A second group argues that mergers lead to real economic benefits. One source of benefit would be the reduced output of resources required per unit of output, as output expands due to economies of scale; this is a real gain to society if scale economies exist. Another source of benefit often identified is the increase in bargaining power which accompanies size. A larger cable firm could, for example, extract more favourable (reduced) prices for programs. This, however, is not a social benefit but represents merely a transfer of income from program suppliers to cable operators; there is no <u>real</u> resource gain to the society.

Our investigation of cable suggests there are few economies of scale and thus mergers between firms would not result in large benefits to society through cost decreases. On the other hand there is evidence of substantial economies of density. If it was felt that one wished to increase the availability of cable to non-urban areas, there may be some value in mergers of system in low and high density areas. One must realize that this form of "regulation" is implicit taxation to redistribute income between areas or groups[29] and one would have to insure that such a scheme such as mergers was the most efficient means of achieving this objective.

Cable television mergers designed to increase prices are not a likely outcome under current technology. Each system is given a licence to operate in a given area and by definition has a monopoly. Since cable operators do not compete for cable subscribers in any given area there would seem to be little chance for greater monopoly pricing if a number of licences were controlled by one firm. This line of reasoning, however, does suggest that one of the factors limiting monopoly abuses by cable operators is that they have no control over other entertainment media which are substitutes for cable-television. Therefore, mergers between cable and other media (i.e., cross-media ownership) would likely lead to monopoly pricing. The same result would occur although through a different mechanism if cable operators were allowed to merge vertically with program producers. Here the abuse lies in the potential for cable operators having a monopoly in programming or type of programs. While it is true that networks currently have advantages in this area, one cannot ignore the effects of cable television system on broadcasters' audience size (through fragmentation) and hence revenues from ad rates. The large cable system which was vertically integrated into program producrion would have the power to coerce broadcasters into buying their programs even if programs were substitutes and there was only a loose oligopoly in the program production industry.

Finally, one of the merger questions is whether mergers would allow greater "dynamic efficiency" - new cost-saving technologies. Here we can offer little information. As new technologies of reception, transmission and distribution are introduced, one would expect both the cost and demand functions to shift. Perhaps some economies of scale could be introduced.

The other important policy consideration deals with programming and the argument that larger firms with their greater resources are able to produce and obtain greater diversity and quality of programming. We found that local programming expenditures were not influenced by either the size of the firm or its profitability.

In summary, Canadian cable firms are quite profitable. The industry is also clearly characterized by a cost function which quickly exhausts all economies of scale. However, the economies of density are substantial. With the substantial economies of density, the optimal number of firms will be a function of the expected penetration rate, but the optimal size of the firm is related to both the number of miles of cable and the number of subscribers. These two dimensions both affect the average cost per subscriber. The CRTC, which establishes the boundaries of cable systems, should therefore consider these cost elements in establishing boundaries and in determining the number of licences per market.

Having characterized the demand and supply sides of cable, what remains is to utilize this information to determine the value of licences according to firm, market and ownership. Also, the compensation to either broadcasters or artists for the use of inputs must also be determined and the effects of alternative compensation schemes on the number and size distribution and firms as well as their profitability.

Notes to Chapter 12

1. Data from Statistics Canada, Cable Television, Cat. No. 56-205 (annual). See also Robert E. Babe, Canadian Television Broadcasting Structure, Performance and Regulation (Ottawa: Economic Council of Canada, 1979), Ch. 6.

2. Balance sheet data are provided by Statistics Canada for stations with one thousand subscribers or more. Data used in the statistical analysis did not include firms with less than 1000 subscribers since this data was not available, nor did it include firms who operated a number of stations and did not report separately for these operating units.

3. Tables 12.2 to 12.6 are developed from data provided by the federal Department of Communications. These data were not available in the form required for 1975 so 1976 data were used. Despite some year to year changes in the industry, these data are reflective of the macro characteristics of the industry.
4. For the basis of the figure, see Chapter 2.

5. The Commission expressed for the first time its concern of the adverse effect of CATV on broadcasters in a public announcement on December 3, 1969. R.E. Babe, Cable Television and Telecommunications in Canada (East Lansing, Mich.: Michigan State University, 1975). See also Babe, op. cit. (note 1).

6. As we have noted above, these arguments are certainly not convincing since CATV may have increased the profitability of some broadcasting operations.

7. For a discussion of this, as well as the audience fragmentation effects of cable see Babe (1975) op. cit.

8. R.E. Park, "Prospects in Cable in the 100 Largest Television Markets," Bell Journal of Economic and Management Science, Vol. 3, No. 1, 1972, pp. 130-150.

9. L. Good, An Econometric Model of the Canadian Cable Television Industry and the Effects of CRTC Regulation (paper presented at the Canadian Economics Association Meeting, June 1975). This is based on a thesis with the same title - Ph.D. thesis, University of Western Ontario, 1974.

10. Ibid., p. 4.

11. Ibid., p. 9.

12. Ibid., p. 28.

13. See Babe (1975) op. cit., p. 27.

14. See for example, Park, op. cit.

15. Good, op. cit., p. 16.

16. Ibid., p. 7.

17. Babe (1975) op. cit., p. 9.

18. Babe (1975) op. cit., Chapter III, suggests this waste can be determined from comparisons of the amount of capital invested per subscriber.

19. Good, op. cit., pp. 60-74.

20. Currently these figures, according to federal Department of Communications officials, have risen to approximately $8,000/mi. above ground and $17,000/mi. below ground.

21. Z. Griliches, "Cost Allocation in Railroad Regulation," Bell Journal of Economics and Management Science, Vol. 3, No. 1, Spring 1972, pp. 26-42.

22. Ibid., p. 32.

23. Ibid., pp. 21-22.

24. R.E. Babe (1975) op. cit., p. 13.

25. R.E. Babe (1975) op. cit., pp. 31-31.

26. L. Good, op. cit., Fig. 1.

27. R.E. Babe (1975) op. cit., p. 31.

28. T.E. Keeler, "Airline Regulation and Market Performance," Bell Journal of Economics and Management Science, Vol. 3, No. 2, 1972, pp. 399-425.

29. See Richard A. Posner, "Taxation by Regulation," Bell Journal of Economics and Management Science, Vol. 2, No. 1, Spring 1971, pp. 22-51.

Chapter 13

Summary and Conclusions

The focus of this study has been the economics of the radio, television, and cable industries in Canada. The current ownership pattern of each of these industries, both at the local market and national level, has been documented and special attention given to the effects of this ownership pattern on firm conduct, in terms of pricing and programming, and on performance, in terms of profitability and program choice and diversity.

13.1 CHAPTER 2

An overview of the television, radio, and cable-television industries is provided in Chapter 2. In September 1975 there were 64 private commercial television stations in Canada. These include parent, full-time and part-time, program originating stations and excluded rebroadcasters. Of the 64 stations, 44 percent were owned by firms which owned only a single television station while the remainder were group-owned. The proportion of stations group-owned has increased dramatically from only 38 percent in 1968. The average gross revenue in 1975 was $3.4 million for a group-owned station compared to $2.8 million for a single-owned station.

In 1975 there were 376 private, program originating AM-FM radio stations. This total excludes non-commercial stations and CBC stations. Eighty-one percent of all private radio stations were group-owned. This represents a sizable increase from the situation of 1968 when 64 percent were group-owned, with the remainder being "singles." This large percentage is partly a result of the common occurrence of AM-FM twins. The average gross revenue of a group-owned radio station was $585,000 compared to $456,000 for a single-owned station.

Canada had 350 cable-television systems in 1975. Group-owned systems constituted 53 percent of the total while 47 percent were privately owned. The group-owned systems accounted for 77 percent of total revenues and the average gross revenue of $643,000 for a group-owned system was approximately three times that of a single-owned station.

13.2 CHAPTER 3

In Chapter 3 we describe the structure of the industries at both the macro and the micro level. At the macro level of the national economy, the structure of television, radio, and cable, is examined in terms of the ownership pattern within and across media. In television the top two groups, Baton and Télé-Métropole, which own CFTO-TV in Toronto and CFTM-TV in Montreal respec- tively, accounted for 24 percent of total industry revenue. The top four groups, which include Southam-Selkirk and B.C. Television (Western Broadcasting), accounted for 40 percent of industry reve- nue, while the top 10 groups (consisting of a total of 21 televi- sion stations) accounted for 65 percent of total industry revenue in 1975.

The 10 largest radio groups accounted for 44 percent of all radio industry revenues during 1975. As in the case of televi- sion, a large proportion of this concentration of revenue resulted from the location of group-owned stations in major markets. For example, the two largest groups, Standard and CHUM, accounted for 14 percent of industry revenue. The Standard groups holdings in- cluded CFRB-AM in Toronto and CJAD-AM in Montreal. CHUM owned CHUM-AM in Toronto, CFUN-AM in Vancouver, CFRW-AM in Winnipeg and CFRA-AM in Ottawa. The four largest, and the eighth largest radio groups were owned by concerns also in the top ten television groups: Standard, CHUM, Western, Southam-Selkirk, and Baton.

In cable-television the four largest groups (Premier, Cable- systems, Nationale, and Maclean-Hunter) account for 41 percent of total revenue. The largest 10 groups account for 64 percent of all cable-television revenues.

An important factor in developing concentration measures for the television and radio industries is the definition of the market. Other studies, particularly in the United States, have treated the market as a national one. We argue that this is not correct since the programming outputs of distant stations are not substitutable on either the demand or supply side: a television station in St. John's is not in competition with a station in Vic- toria. The relevant market is the "signal shed," that area about urban areas in which consumers may substitute one signal for ano- ther. We therefore develop concentration measures of competition for 14 television markets and 16 radio markets. Similarly, where- as the cable-television industry can be analyzed on a national basis, each firm has a monopoly position in its local market and it therefore makes little sense to calculate national concentra- tion measures for the cable industry.

The measure of concentration calculated for the individual markets is the Herfindahl index. The results are reproduced in Table 13.1. Kitchener and London each have a revenue Herfindahl index for television of 1.00 reflecting the monopoly position in the television advertising market of the single station operating in each of these markets. The indices overstate the concentration in television markets, such as Toronto and Vancouver, where there are U.S. revenue competitors that are excluded. To the extent that language differences sub-divide the television advertising markets of Montreal, Ottawa-Hull, and to a lesser extent Quebec City, into sub-markets, the actual seller concentration in each sub-market is greater than indicated by the Herfindahl index in the table.

Table 13.1

REVENUE HERFINDAHL INDICES BY MARKET FOR THE TELEVISION AND
RADIO INDUSTRIES, 1975

Market CMA	Television Revenue Herfindahl Index	Radio Revenue Herfindahl Index
St. John's	.60	.52
Halifax	.62	.35
Quebec	.64	.42
Montreal	.39	.13
Ottawa-Hull	.50	.28
Toronto	.27	.27
Hamilton	[1]	.48
Kitchener	1.00	.44
London	1.00	.35
Windsor	1.00	.61
Winnipeg	.52	.25
Regina	.74	.37
Edmonton	.39	.22
Calgary	.54	.25
Vancouver	.63	.18
Victoria	[2]	.34

1. Included in Toronto CMA.
2. Included in Vancouver CMA.

For most markets we find the revenue Herfindahl index to be lower for radio than for television. This reflects the fact that in general there are more competitors in radio. The larger markets again tend to have the lower concentration.

In Chapter 3 we also identify cross-ownership within a market. We consider this important because cross-ownership reduces the number of independently owned media outlets competing for advertising revenue in a market and may reduce costs. Cross-ownership, of a variety other than the almost universal AM-FM type, is found in the St. John's, Quebec City, Ottawa-Hull, London, Winnipeg, Regina, Edmonton, Calgary, and Vancouver markets.

13.3 CHAPTER 4

In Chapter 4 we begin our examination of conduct. Both television and radio broadcasters sell audience exposures to commercial messages. Therefore, firms in both industries engage in audience and price competition. Specifically, in Chapter 4 we examine the competition for television audience and relate this element of conduct to the market structure. Estimates from reduced form models are obtained for audience demand equations. The results obtained demonstrate that ownership, or more precisely network-affiliation, is an important determinant of television audience size.

Aside from some flat, or constant, number of viewers common to all stations, CTV affiliates attract (within their CMA) 3.04 times potential number of viewers. CBC owned and affiliated stations attract 2.64 times potential. Local Canadian independents, including Global and TVA affiliates attract only 1.26 times potential. CTV network offerings thus attract the largest proportion of potential viewers. The higher Canadian content and greater public affairs/public service orientation of the CBC appear to have a discernable but not severe impact on prime-time audience size. In part this reflects the success of the CBC's strategy of including some American programming with high audience ratings in their prime time schedule. On the other hand, the inability of Canadian independent stations to spread programming costs over a larger number of network stations appears to be the cause of their weak competitive position. Their limited ability to attract viewers may also reflect the start-up problems of the Global network.

American stations available over-the-air in leading markets are revealed to be potential competitors for audience attracting 1.59 times potential audience. These stations, which are not subject to Canadian content and other regulatory constraints, clearly afford strong competition for television advertising revenue in major Canadian markets.

Canadian stations located outside major markets show little ability to attract viewers in those markets. This holds true whether they are received over-the-air or only via cable. Presumably this weak showing results from the fact that in most cases such stations were only able to provide a duplication of either CTV or CBC network services.

The small audiences attracted by American stations available only by cable contrast sharply with those of U.S. stations available over-the-air. This contrast demonstrates the magnitude of the competitive disadvantage resulting from the cable-only reception handicap. Part of this disadvantage stems from restriction to an audience of cable subscribers, a sub-set of all potential viewers; part from the ability of Canadian stations to schedule episodes of popular American series to appear prior to their appearance on competing American channels. The magnitude of the cable-only handicap has significant public policy implications. It suggests that permitting additional U.S. (and non-local Canadian) channels to be carried by cable systems may have only minor effects in terms of fragmenting the audience of existing Canadian broadcasters in those markets.

13.4 CHAPTER 5

In Chapter 5 we examine another aspect of conduct in the television industry, namely the pricing of commercial time. The estimates obtained in the preceding chapter are used in a simultaneous equation model of the determinants of advertising rates. In line with the basic structure-conduct-performance approach, the analysis of the pricing of television time is directed at identifying the links between advertising rates and elements of market structure such as those describing the competitive position of the firm, local market characteristics, and ownership structure.

We find evidence that increases in a television station's prime time audience, one of the most important indications of its competitive position, are associated with increases in the rate changed for a 30 second commercial (with an increase of 1,000 in prime time daily viewing hours leading to a $.15 rate increase). Other evidence indicates however that this result may be attributable largely to the effect of changes in audience drawn from areas outside a station's local CMA. One set of estimates also provided evidence that population, possibly acting as a proxy for potential audience, influences ad rates in the same way as audience size.

Turning to local market characteristics, the most significant finding was the identification of the important role played by market concentration in the pricing of television commercial time. An increment of .10 in the revenue Herfindahl index is associated with a $26.70 increase in 30 second ad rates (in prime time) or alternatively an increase of from $1.20 to $1.60 in the 30 second rate per 10,000 viewer hours. The magnitude of this influence can be better appreciated by recalling that revenue-based Herfindahl indexes in major Canadian markets, as shown in the table above, vary from .272 in the case of Toronto to 1.00 in a city such as London. Thus 30 second commercials in London would be priced some $175 higher and rates per 10,000 would be some $8.50 to $11.00 higher than those for Toronto on account of market concentration alone. The respective mean values are $271.50 and $9.02.

We find that a $1,000 increment in average incomes in the station's CMA (all other things being equal) is associated with an estimated increase in 30 second ad rates of $150 and an increase in rate per 10,000 of $3.80.

Ownership structure was analyzed both at the local market level and for the country as a whole. When the analysis focuses on the ownership structure of the <u>local market</u> itself, CBC ownership, television/newspaper cross-ownership, and competition against a CBC station are associated with <u>reductions</u> in the advertising rate per 10,000 of $14.11, $4.68, and $5.95 respectively.

In the case of 30 second rates, local television/radio groups are associated with increases of $78.41, whereas local television/ newspaper groups are associated with rate decreases of $83.79.

When variables are defined on the basis of <u>national</u> rather than local market ownership patterns, television/<u>radio</u> cross-ownership and competition with such stations are associated with increases in the 30 second ad rate of $260.63 and $128.38 respectively, while the converse is true for television/newspaper cross-ownership which was associated with a decrease of $209.20 in the rate. Membership in a television/television group, CBC ownership, conglomerate ownership, and competition with a conglomerate owned station are associated with decreases in advertising rates on a per 10,000 audience basis of $4.92, $10.10, $10.88, and $6.23 respectively.

13.5 CHAPTER 6

We then turn to an examination of conduct in the radio industry beginning in Chapter 6 with an analysis of competition for radio audience. As for television, a potential audience approach is adopted in the analysis of factors influencing radio station audience sizes. Since radio audiences are measured in terms of total <u>weekly</u> listening hours the multiples involved are larger. The programming of radio stations is characterized not by network affiliation but by the format description in <u>Broadcaster</u>, a trade journal.

The general audience for all stations, both AM and FM, is estimated to consist of a flat or constant 338,000 weekly hours tuned plus 2.94 times potential audience (i.e. population divided by number of stations).

Out-of-market stations suffer a substantial audience handicap (estimated at 13.99 times potential audience). It is estimated that losses of out-of-market stations are more than "recaptured" by local stations. FM stations are estimated to suffer an audience handicap of 7.79 times potential audience.

Radio station programming formats are found to have an important influence on station audience size. Also interesting differences between AM and FM stations are uncovered. For example, while AM station middle-of-the-road format is associated with an 11.41 times potential audience increment, for FM stations it is associated with a sharp decrease in audience size. Another example is provided by minority language broadcasting. If an AM station broadcasts in a minority language this is associated with a 10.93 times potential audience decrease in weekly hours tuned, but if the station broadcasts on the FM band the associated change is an increase of 6.57 times potential audience. Country and western format for AM stations is associated with audience losses of 13.21 times potential audience. Classical format for FM stations is associated with gains of 13.42 times potential. The formats which proved detrimental to FM station audience size are progressive (7.32 times potential audience) and jazz (20.01 times potential).

13.6 CHAPTER 7

In Chapter 7 we examine the pricing of radio commercial time. We find that local market audience size had an important influence on the price of a 30 second radio commercial with an increase of 100,000 hours in weekly CMA audience adding between $1.50 and $2.10 in the case of AM stations and between zero and $1.10 in the case of FM stations. The respective means are $41.43 and $18.77. On the other hand, no direct relationship is established between advertising rates and the size of a station's audience drawn from areas outside its local CMA. Together these could support the target audience hypothesis, i.e., the idea that commercial radio time is priced primarily on the basis of audience delivered in the station's CMA alone.

We find the evidence with respect to the influence of the level of market concentration on the level of radio advertising rates to unequivocally suuport the hypothesis suggested by economic theory. When market revenue is concentrated in a few hands the resultant market power is the single most important factor in driving up the price of commercial air time. When the price of 30 second spot commercials is considered, a .10 increase in the Herfindahl index of market concentration is estimated to result in rate increases ranging from $3.93 to $4.28 for AM stations (mean = $41.43) and from $4.17 to $6.66 for FM stations (mean = $18.77). On a rate per 100,000 weekly audience hours basis the corresponding increases range from $1.02 to $1.39 for AM stations (mean = $3.73) and from $1.29 to $1.83 for FM stations (mean = $2.57). Compared to their respective mean values these are very powerful effects indexed. Recall that the Herfindahl indexes for our 16 sample markets range from .128 for Montreal to .848 for Regina. This is a spread of .72 and it implies that on a conservative estimate the price of a 30 second AM radio commercial can be expected to be ($3.93 x 7.2) = $24.70 higher in Regina than in Montreal solely on account of the greater market power of Regina firms. The corresponding increase for FM advertising rates would be ($4.17 x 7.2) = $30.02.

The level of average income in the local CMA was found to be an important factor in the pricing of commercial time on AM, but not FM, radio stations. Surprisingly, the relationship is the converse of that which would be expected. Consumers in high income areas may have greater spending power, but contrary to the case of television, they are not thereby valued more highly by AM radio advertisers. The evidence seems clear that AM radio commercials are worth more in lower income areas. A $1,000 decrease in average income levels is associated with an increase of between $9.40 and $12.00 in 30 second ad rates or between $3.40 and $3.50 on a rate per 100,000 weekly audience hours basis. We surmise that radio may be the most cost-effective method of reaching lower income audiences as a result of low newspaper readership rates and the high costs of television advertising. If so, despite the lower purchasing power of the audience involved, this type of comparative advantage could put a premium on the price of radio commercial time in low income areas.

Ownership of more than one radio station in the same CMA, which in theory could be expected to increase a firm's market power, is found to be associated with a $7.02 increase in 30 second AM advertising rates. Nearly all of these radio/radio groups are AM/FM twins, but there is no evidence that the FM twin involved is able to charge higher rates on account of group ownership. Examination of radio/radio group ownership on a national basis yields weaker results. This is as expected since market power is little affected when group stations are located in different markets.

13.7 CHAPTER 8

Having examined the structure and conduct of the television and radio industries, in Chapter 8 we turn to an important element of their performance, the measurement and assessment of their profitability. The first measure of rate of return used is the total of interest expense plus profits after tax divided by the total of long-term debt plus shareholders equity, adjusted where necessary to reflect only broadcasting assets. For purposes of comparison a competitive rate of return is estimated to be approximately 13 percent.

The groupings, by television revenue size class, show highest rates of return, 40 percent, to be earned by the corporations with the largest brodcasting asset base. The smallest corporations earn 19 percent with intermediate sizes lower still. The overall average weighted rate of return in 1975 for all 59 television corporations is 32 percent. This rate of return appears to be far in excess of that required to attract investment capital to the industry under competitive conditions in capital markets.

Certain group owners, for accounting convenience or other reasons, segregate individual broadcast undertakings in separate corporations. Using group ownership information it is possible to aggregate the results of these various entities and produce profit measures on a group basis. The results reveal television-television groups to be earning an overall weighted average rate of return to total capital of 45 percent. The corresponding figure for groups with television-radio cross-holdings was 20 percent.

When we considered the profitability of radio we find that the overall rate of return in 1975 for all 216 radio corporations is 18 percent. The highest rates of return occur in the case of the smallest (32 percent) and the largest (22 percent) corporations with no discernable trend evident in between. Examination of rates of return after classification by cross-ownership holdings of groups, reveal some interesting differences from the tele-

vision case. The radio-television group rate remains constant and
equal to that of the identically defined television-radio group at
20 percent. But, whereas television-television groups achieve
rates of interest plus profits return on total capital of 45 percent, radio-radio groups, whether defined to include or exclude
AM-FM combinations, earn a rate of return identical to that of
radio-television groups. The only significant variation occurrs
in the case of radio-newspaper chains which earn returns of 28
percent in 1975.

We then turn to a consideration of risk. Risk is relevant
because it is generally accepted that investors are risk averse.
Hence, if there are two companies, one with a higher return and
greater risk than the other, investors may prefer the performance
of the lower return/less risk company. A high return, therefore,
does not necessarily indicate superior economic performance from
the viewpoint of investors. The crucial issue is whether the return of a company is higher or lower than appropriate for its level of risk. To examine this issue we consider whether unusually
high returns could be explained in terms of compensation for high
risk.

On the basis of a sample of six broadcasting companies we
find no evidence to suggest that broadcasting is of above average
risk and hence no support for such an explanation. In addition,
the results of an evaluation of the return-risk performance of
these companies exhibit, on balance, a superior performance although no test of significance is possible. The concept of risk
employed is the risk borne by an investor holding a diversified
portfolio. The idea of a market-established, return-risk trade-
off is based on a theory of asset pricing widely accepted in the
modern business finance literature.

13.8 CHAPTER 9

We find, in Chapter 8, that television broadcasting profits
(for 1975 at least) appear abnormally high. In Chapter 9, we examine the determinants of these profits. Profitability is one of
the most important aspects of economic performance to be considered when attempting to establish links between both market structure and conduct and performance. Because of difficulties in
measuring the total amount of capital invested in an individual
television station embedded in a large corporation it proved necessary to adopt the price-cost margin as an indicator of station
profitability. Examination of revenues and expenses provides information on the underlying forces affecting profitability.

Although it is true that what television stations sell is
audience exposures to commercial messages, our results indicate
that it is overly simplistic to view audience size as the driving
economic force in a station's operations. Television station
total expenses, for example, were found to be unrelated to market
audience size. It was estimated that a massive 100,000 daily

hours increase in market audience would be required to increase a station's revenue by $450,000 (mean value = $7.3 million) and its price-cost margin by .03 (mean = .18).

On the other hand, a similar increase in audience drawn from areas outside a station's local CMA, while being unrelated to revenues and price-cost margins, is associated with an increase of from $.5 million to $1.0 million in expenses (mean = 5.6 million). These findings suggest that not only is it expensive to build up audience size outside a station's CMA (presumably because of incremental programming and transmission costs), but also such audiences contribute little to station revenues and profitability. A notable lack of incentives to service fringe viewers would seem to exist.

No statistically significant relationship is found between the size of a television station's revenues and the population of the market in which it is based. There is evidence of minor expense side effects with each 100,000 population increment associated with an estimated $275,000 increase in expenses and a price-cost margin reduction of .01.

Stations in high income markets are characterized by higher revenues and lower expenses. Each $1,000 in average income is associated with an increase of from .25 to .33 in price-cost margins. Since the income levels in our sample ranged from $3,180 (St. John's) to $4,970 (Ottawa/Hull) they could account for as much as .45 difference in price-cost margin even using the more conservative estimate. Considering that the average price-cost margin of all television stations considered is only .18, average income is clearly a crucial factor in television station profitability.

One of the most significant findings of the entire study has been the identification of the important influence of market concentration on television station expenses, revenues and price-cost margins. A .10 increase in the Herfindahl index is associated with a reduction of $1.3 million in annual expenses, a revenue increase of $.6 million and a price-cost margin increase of .037. Revenue based Herfindahl indices vary from .27 in the case of Toronto to 1.00 in a city such as London. The single station in each of the latter two markets could be expected to generate a price-cost margin higher by .26 than a comparable Toronto station on account of seller concentration alone. These are powerful results and they indicate severe limitations to previous examinations of the Canadian television industry that have ignored competitive conditions at the local market level.

From an economic point of view, television appears to be basically an entertainment rather than a news medium. Each additional dollar spent on entertainment programming was associated with an increase of between $2.10 and $3.25 in revenues while a dollar spent on news programming was associated with revenue decreases of from $2.75 to $3.60. These influences are also evident in the price-cost margin analysis where a $100,000 increment in entertainment programming was associated with a .013 increase in price-cost margin while a similar increment in news programming would be linked with a price-cost margin decrease of between .049 and .055. The behavioural implications are clear. Profit-oriented owners of television stations, and presumably all except public sector owners are profit oriented, are faced with strong economic incentives to expand entertainment programming expenditures and reduce news programming expenditures. That such economic incentives may not always accord with wider public objectives seems clear.

The analysis of television station expenses reflects the influence of the harsh realities of Canadian television program production. An extra hour a day of prime time Canadian programming adds $4.4 million to $6.8 million a year to a television station's expenses. As their expenses, on average, are $5.6 million a year this represents a doubling of their expenses. In a result that may seem surprising to some, no statistical relationship was found between the volume of prime time Canadian programming and television station revenues. Nevertheless, expense side considerations were sufficiently prominent that an additional hour a day (per year) of Canadian programming was associated with a .22 reduction in price-cost margin (mean value = .18). While the economic disadvantages of increased Canadian content may show up only on the production cost side this alone offers only cold comfort to television station owners. Even if Canadian programming is able to attract advertisers, its production cost disadvantage provides an unambiguous market incentive for station owners to reduce their Canadian programming to the legally constrained minimum.

The evidence on local programming indicates that for the average station an additional hour per day of load programming would add $666,000 annually to expenses; generate additional annual revenues of $650,000; and result in an increase of between .05 and .08 in the price-cost margin (mean = .18). These results seem to constitute the only "good news" on programming competition. While economic incentives favour entertainment over news, and foreign programming over Canadian programming, at least they do point television station owners in the direction of increased local programming.

CRTC regulation has prevented television/television group ownership at the local market level. Our work provides no evidence that stations belonging to <u>national</u> television/television groups enjoy price-cost margins any higher than other stations.

Television/radio cross-ownership, on the other hand, is associated with revenue increases of between zero and $5.6 million and expense reductions of between $2.6 million and $3.1 million in 1975. These forces combine to make television/radio cross-ownership the most important element of ownership structure insofar as television station price-cost margins are concerned. Where the owners of a television station also own a radio station in the same market this alone accounts for a .60 increase in the station's price-cost margin. Ownership of a radio station located elsewhere in Canada is associated with a .46 increase in pricecost margins. The magnitude of these effects can be best appreciated by comparison to the average price-cost margin for all sample stations of .18. Moreover, television/radio cross-owned stations appear to be such strong competitors that their presence in the market reduces the revenues and profits of all stations forced to compete against them. Revenue losses of each competing station are estimated at $2.2 million with price-cost margin reductions estimated at between .15 and .16.

No evidence is found that owners of television/newspaper cross-holdings are able to increase the price-cost margins of their television stations on this account. In fact, in line with the ad rate results, revenues of such stations were estimated to be $2.6 million lower (local ownership specification) than other stations. On the other hand, stations which find themselves fortunate enough to compete against a firm owning both a television station and a local newspaper can expect to find their price-cost margin enhanced by .32 on this account alone. Those stations which compete against CBC stations can be expected to experience a .32 reduction in price-cost margin.

Ownership structures contributing to excessive profit levels are not in the public interest. The evidence of this study points to television/radio cross-ownership whether at the local market or national level as a major offender on this score. These findings call into question the regulatory stance which has permitted the existence of widespread television/radio cross-holdings. The role of CBC stations in holding down the profits of their competitors points to a previously unexpected economic effect of the operations of the public corporation.

13.9 CHAPTER 10

In Chapter 10 we examine the determinants of radio station profitability, revenues, and expenses. Because a number of corporations in the radio industry own only one station it was possible to calculate rates of return (interest plus profits before tax divided by the total of long-term debt plus equity) for these stations and examine the determinants of rates of return directly. Unfortunately, analysis of such a sample provided little information on the influence of ownership structure. For this purpose price-cost margin data again provided the best approach. Results of the analysis of economic performance in the radio industry were less informative than those for the television industry possibly because of the wide dispersion in the price-cost margins of the sample stations resulting from the presence of some stations with large negative price-cost margins.

The profit rate for the average radio single is .21. Our analysis indicates that increases in revenue share are associated with higher radio profit rates (profit rate increasing by .24 for each .10 increment in share). On the other hand, increases in audience size alone are associated with reductions in both price-cost margins and single station profit rates (decreases of .20 and .06 respectively for each 100,000 increment in local market audience). This audience result appears to be traceable to the large expense outlays required to achieve and maintain large audience sizes.

No statistical relationship is established betwen the local market characteristics - seller concentration, population, and income levels - and the price-cost margin of radio stations. In the analysis of the profit rates of single station corporations, stations in large cities are found to have lower profits with a 100,000 increment in CMA population associated with a decrease of between .39 and .44 in rate of return. This profit reduction appears to result from the higher expenses of stations in larger cities.

The results of the analysis of programming competition contrast with those for television. Expenditures in the radio industry on news programming are just as important as, if not more important than, expenditures on entertainment programming in terms of their influence on profitability. Increases of $100,000 in news programming expenditure (mean = $125,000) resulted in estimated price-cost margin increases of between .84 and .95 percentage points while the corresponding increases for entertainment programming expenditures (mean = 1.5 million) are between .58 and .96.

The price-cost margin analysis, covering both AM and FM stations, provides no evidence of a link between local market radio/radio group ownership and price-cost margins. Since nearly all local market radio/radio groups are AM/FM twins it seems that the influence of group ownership on profitability has been obscured by the grouping of the results for the strong AM stations and the weak FM stations.

Contrary to our expectations, we find that both radio/television and (significant at only the 90% level) radio/newspaper cross-ownership at the local market level are associated with decreases in price-cost margins. None of the nationally-defined groups and cross-ownership arrangements are found to have any statistically significant influence on radio station price-cost margins. This finding is of some importance since it means that national ownership structure, which has long been the focus of concern at the policy level, may be of little economic significance to the operation of the radio industry.

13.10   CHAPTER 11

In Chapter 11 we turn to another aspect of television and radio conduct and performance, that relating to programming. Again
we attempt to explain conduct and performance in terms of structure and in particular in terms of the number of stations in the
market and whether they are privately or publicly owned. A spatial competition model is developed that predicts that an industry
comprised of private broadcasters, financed by advertising revenue, will provide inadequate balance, diversity, and choice. The
applicability of this model to the Canadian television and radio
industries was examined and we consider how the predictions of the
model are affected by the economics of Canadian program production
versus purchase, and by the presence of the CRTC and the CBC.
Finally, an empirical investigation into programming performance
is undertaken.

CRTC research shows that, during the 1974-75 season, American
television programs could be purchased for far less than Canadian
programs could be produced while U.S. programs attracted larger
audiences than Canadian stations and permitted the charging of
higher ad rates. As a consequence, it was estimated that, for the
prime time schedule of January 1975, CTV was obtaining an average
margin (revenue-cost) per half hour of $21,000 for foreign pro-
grams and only $55 for Canadian programs. Our results in Chapter
9 also bear on this question. We find that an extra hour per day
of prime time Canadian programming reduces a station's price-cost
margin by .219, a very substantial reduction when we recall that
the average price-cost margin is only .18. The economics are
obviously such that private broadcasters, if left to their own
devices, would purchase the overwhelming majority of their programs from abroad. The primary influence of the CRTC has been to
prevent this by the use of Canadian content regulations. Profit
maximizing broadcasters would be expected to react to such regulations in a number of ways. These include evasion and attempts
to obtain exemptions, production of low cost Canadian programs in
order to minimize possible losses, co-production with foreign producers in order to spread the cost of production and provide an
expectation of selling abroad and by, as far as possible, satisfying the Canadian content requirement in prime time by scheduling
Canadian programs at the less popular times when the opportunity
cost is smallest (for example, early and late in the evening or in
the summer off-season). We found evidence of all of these types
of behaviour.

We hypothesize that the presence of the CBC, a Crown corporation, should also affect program offerings. The CBC only obtains
20 percent of its television revenues from advertising. In addition, its legislative mandate is to contribute to national goals
and provide balanced programming.

The results of an empirical investigation, using 1974-75
data, into programming performance generally support our expec-

tations and the predictions of the model. Highlights of the empirical analysis of television programming performance are:

- The best overall balance of programming is provided by CBC-owned French stations and CBC-owned English stations.

- The most diversity of program offerings is provided by the CBC French Network. The CBC English Network also offered more diversity than the other Canadian networks or groupings.

- The average number of program options provided by Canadian stations in a market does not increase proportionately with the number of Canadian stations serving the market. For example, eight Canadian audience competitors in Ottawa-Hull provided only twice as many choices as two competitors in Windsor and Winnipeg. Similarly, U.S. commercial stations increase the average number of options less than proportionately: for example, in Winnipeg the average number of options provided by the two Canadian stations is 1.00 and this figure only increases to 2.70 when we included four U.S. commercial stations.

- The effect of including a PBS station is very different, with the average number of options increasing more than proportionately. In Toronto one PBS station adds more to viewer choice than four U.S. commercial stations.

- The effect of cable TV on the average number of options is greatest where cable introduces a PBS station to a market, such as Halifax or Calgary, that has a limited number of stations available over-the-air.

- The statistically significant results of a regression on viewer choice are that both the presence of a CBC-owned French station and the presence of a PBS station has a substantial effect on the average number of options available in a market whereas the presence of a U.S. commercial station has only a small effect.

These results have obvious policy implications. In recent years the very concept of a Crown corporation in broadcasting has been under attack. Critics have charged that the CBC has used taxpayers' money by showing television programming virtually indistinguishable from that of the private broadcasters. Our results, while they can indicate nothing about the quality of CBC programming, certainly refute the suggestion of very similar programming. CBC does, in line with its mandate, provide a better overall balance of programming and more diversity than the Canadian private networks or groupings. In addition the presence of a CBC-owned French station in a market has a substantial effect on viewer choice.

There are also policy implications for licensing. It is obvious that licensing of an additional private broadcaster adds a relatively small amount to viewer choice in a market. On the

tations and the predictions of the model. Highlights of the empirical analysis of television programming performance are:

● The best overall balance of programming is provided by CBC-owned
French stations and CBC-owned English stations.

● The most diversity of program offerings is provided by the CBC
French Network. The CBC English Network also offered more diversity than the other Canadian networks or groupings.

● The average number of program options provided by Canadian stations in a market does not increase proportionately with the
number of Canadian stations serving the market. For example,
eight Canadian audience competitors in Ottawa-Hull provided only
twice as many choices as two competitors in Windsor and Winnipeg. Similarly, U.S. commercial stations increase the average
number of options less than proportionately: for example, in
Winnipeg the average number of options provided by the two Canadian stations is 1.00 and this figure only increases to 2.70
when we included four U.S. commercial stations.

● The effect of including a PBS station is very different, with
the average number of options increasing more than proportionately. In Toronto one PBS station adds more to viewer choice
than four U.S. commercial stations.

● The effect of cable TV on the average number of options is
greatest where cable introduces a PBS station to a market, such
as Halifax or Calgary, that has a limited number of stations
available over-the-air.

● The statistically significant results of a regression on viewer
choice are that both the presence of a CBC-owned French station
and the presence of a PBS station has a substantial effect on
the average number of options available in a market whereas the
presence of a U.S. commercial station has only a small effect.

These results have obvious policy implications. In recent
years the very concept of a Crown corporation in broadcasting has
been under attack. Critics have charged that the CBC has used taxpayers' money by showing television programming virtually indistinguishable from that of the private broadcasters. Our results,
while they can indicate nothing about the quality of CBC programming, certainly refute the suggestion of very similar programming.
CBC does, in line with its mandate, provide a better overall balance of programming and more diversity than the Canadian private
networks or groupings. In addition the presence of a CBC-owned
French station in a market has a substantial effect on viewer
choice.

There are also policy implications for licensing. It is obvious that licensing of an additional private broadcaster adds a
relatively small amount to viewer choice in a market. On the

other hand, the addition of a CBC-owned station to a market has a substantial effect. Similarly, if cable is permitted to import programming from a Canadian private station little is added to viewer choice, whereas importation of a CBC-owned station has a substantial effect. Cable importation of the programming of an American commercial station adds little to viewer choice whereas importation of the programming of a PBS station has a substantial effect.

The examination of radio programming performance is more limited. We find that stations affiliated to a broadcasting group offer less programming of an "Information" variety than those affliated to a newspaper group or those singly owned. Overall radio exhibits an even greater emphasis than television on "Light Entertainment" programming. Evidence is found of some degree of complementarity between the programming of FM and AM stations. This is consistent with CRTC policy and presumably is indicative of some success in this respect.

13.11 CHAPTER 12

We examine the conduct and performance of cable television in Chapter 12. The product sold by cable is very different from that sold by television and radio broadcasters. Cable provides an alternative method of transmitting television programming to the home and charges the home-owner a monthly price (after the initial hook-up charge) for this service. Home-owners demand this service because cable provides the programming of television stations unavailable over-the-air and/or improves the reception from stations that can be received over-the-air.

Cable TV affects the market power and hence profits of television broadcasters. It expands the geographical area of the market for many Canadian stations but, at the same time, by importing programming from stations unavailable over-the-air, it fragments the local audience.

Cable assets are significantly larger than either radio or television. The net profits after tax are lower than television but greater than radio. Also larger firms are more profitable than medium size or small size cable firms. Cable firms receive an average 14 percent rate of return on cable fixed assets (in 1975). This is a weighted aggregate measure and does not reflect the very large profit differences among cable firms. The measure above also does not include profit measures for the large "groups" since these companies do not report for each undertaking. This would bias downward the above "average" reported.

A simultaneous equations model of demand, price, and cost relationships revealed the following:

• The price elasticity of demand for cable TV is approximately 1.1. This measure is biased upward because data on net addi-

tional signals due to cable could not be included in the estimates.

- The CRTC seems to have some impact on the pricing of cable
  firms. The marginal revenue in 1975 is estimated to be approximately $28 per year on average while the marginal cost is esti-
  mated to be approximately $33 per year.

- Subscriptions rates for cable tend to decrease with both the age
  of the system and the penetration rate but they do not do so
  monotonically.

- The cost estimates indicate minor economies of scale. This would
  suggest that few resources would be saved through the merger of
  two or more cable firms.

- There is evidence of substantial economies of density - the decrease in average cost holding firm size constant - as the firm
  obtains more subscribers per mile of cable. Costs in 1975 per
  subscriber (average cost) fall from $50 to approximately $39 as
  penetration increases from .3 to greater than .67 respectively.
  This would suggest that although some room for competition between cable firms in some dense urban areas does exist, care
  must be taken not to overwire and generate substantial excess
  capacity; that is at the expense of losing these density economies.

- Our cost equations suggest a marginal cost of $33 to $35 per
  subscriber per year for the sample in 1975. This value reflects
  movements along the short run average cost curve which is appropriate for pricing and investment decisions.

- An important policy consideration deals with local programming
  and the argument that larger firms with their greater resource
  pools are able to produce and obtain greater diversity and quality of programming. We found that local programming expenditures
  are not statistically significantly influenced by either the
  size of the firm or its profitability.

    In summary, cable firms are quite profitable. The industry
is clearly characterized by a cost function which quickly exhausts
all economies of scale. However, the economies of density are
substantial. With the substantial economies of density, the optimal number of firms will be a function of the expected penetration
rate, but the optimal size of the firm is related to both the
total number of miles of cable and number of subscribers to a
given system.

Bibliography

Anderson, J.A., R.L. Coe, J.G. Saunders, "Economic Issues Relating to the FCC's Proposed One-to-a-Customer Rule," Journal of Broadcasting, Vol. 13, No. 3, Summer 1969, pp. 241-252.

Babe, Robert E., "The Impact of Cable Television on Viewing Time of Canadian Television Stations" (Ottawa: Carleton Economic Papers, Carleton University, 1973).

-----, "Public and Private Regulation of Cable Television: A Case Study of Technological Change and Relative Power," Canadian Public Administration, Vol. 17, No. 2, Summer 1974, pp. 187-225.

-----, Cable Television and Telecommunications in Canada (East Lansing, Michigan: Michigan State University, 1975).

-----, Regulation of Private Television by the Canadian Television Commission: A Critique of Ends and Means," Canadian Public Administration, Vol. 19, No. 4, Winter 1976, pp. 552-586.

-----, Canadian Television Broadcasting Structure, Performance and Regulation (Ottawa: Economic Council of Canada, 1979).

Baer, Walter S., Henry Geller, Joseph A. Grundfest and Karen B. Passner, Concentration and Mass Media Ownership: Assessing the State of Current Knowledge (Santa Monica, Cal.: RAND, 1974).

Barnet, Harold and Edward Greenberg, "On the Economics of Wired City Television," American Economic Review, Vol. 58, June 1968, pp. 503-508.

Baxter, W.F., "Regulation and Diversity in Communications Media," American Economic Review, Vol. 64, No. 2, May 1974, pp. 392-399.

Beebe, J.H., "Institutional Structure and Program Choices in Television Markets," Quarterly Journal of Economics, Vol. 91, No. 1, February 1977, pp. 15-37.

Besen, Stanley M., "The Economics of the Cable Television 'Consensus'," Journal of Law and Economics, Vol. 17, No. 1, April 1974, pp. 39-51.

-----, The Value of Television Time and the Prospect for New Stations (Santa Monica, Cal.: RAND, 1973).

----- and Paul J. Hanley, "Market Size, VHF Allocations, and the Viability of Television Stations," Journal of Industrial Economics, Vol. 24, September 1975, pp. 41-54.

----- and Bridger M. Mitchell, "Noll, Peck, and McGowan's Economic Aspects of Television Regulation," Bell Journal of Economics and Management Science, Vol. 5, No. 1, Spring 1974, pp. 301-319.

----- and Bridger M. Mitchell, "Watergate and Television - An Economic Analysis," Communication Research, Vol. 3, No. 3, July 1976, pp. 243-261.

----- and Ronald Soligo, "The Economics of the Network Affiliate Relationship in the Television Broadcasting Industry," American Economic Review, Vol. 63, No. 3, June 1973, pp. 259-268.

Blake, Harlan M. and Jack A. Blum, "Network Television Rate Practices: A Case Study in the Failure of Social Control of Price Discrimination," The Yale Law Journal, Vol. 74, No. 8, July 1965, pp. 1339-1401.

Blank, David M., "The Quest for Quantity and Diversity in Television Programming," American Economic Review, Vol. 56, May 1966, pp. 448-456.

-----, "Television Advertising: The Great Discount Illusion or Tonypandy Revisited," Journal of Business, Vol. 41, No. 1, January 1968, pp. 10-38.

Bowman, Gary W. and John U. Farley, "TV Viewing: Application of a Formal Choice Model," Applied Economics, Vol. 4, No. 4, December 1972, pp. 245-259.

-----, "Demand and Supply of Network Television Advertising, Bell Journal of Economics, Vol. 7., No. 1., Spring 1976, pp. 258-267.

Boyle, Gerald J., "Financing the Corporation for Public Television," National Tax Journal, Vol. 26, No. 2, June 1973, pp. 199-208.

Breton, Albert, "A Framework for the Economic Analysis of the Quality of Radio and Television Output," unpublished paper, University of Toronto, March 1971.

Broadcaster, "Fall '74 Directory: Radio Stations," November 1974.

Bunce, Richard, Television in the Corporate Interest (New York: Praeger Publishers, 1976).

CTV, License Renewal Application to the Canadian Radio Television Commission on Behalf of the CTV Televison Network Limited (Ottawa: CTV, 1975).

Canadian Advertising Rates and Data (Toronto: Maclean-Hunter, April 1975).

Canadian Broadcasting Corporation, A Measure of the Impact of Cable TV in Canada as of November 1976 (Ottawa: CBC Research Department, 1968).

-----, Cable T.V. and Audience Fragmentation: At Year End 1971 (Ottawa: CBC Research Department, 1972).

-----, Annual Report (Ottawa: CBC, Annual).

-----, Patterns of Television Viewing in Canada (Ottawa: CBC Research Department, 1973).

Canadian Radio-Television Commission, "A Single System," Policy Statement on Cable Television (Ottawa: CRTC, 1971).

-----, Cable Television in Canada (Ottawa: Information Canada, 1971).

-----, Cable Television Systems in Canada (Ottawa: Information Canada, 1975).

-----, FM Radio in Canada: A Policy to Ensure a Varied and Comprehensive Radio Service (Ottawa: CRTC, 1975).

-----, List of Broadcasting Stations in Canada (Ottawa: Information Canada 1975).

-----, Policies Respecting Broadcast Receiving Undertakings (Cable Television) (Ottawa: CRTC, 1975).

-----, "CRTC Background Paper: The Economic Realities of Canadian Television Production," Symposium on Television Violence (Ottawa: Ministry of Supply and Service Canada, 1976).

-----, Committee of Inquiry into the National Broadcasting Service Report (Ottawa: CRTC, 1977).

-----, The Contemporary Status of Ownership and the Level of Concentration in the Candadian Broadcasting Industry (Ottawa: CRTC, Vol. II, 1977).

-----, Report on Pay Television (Ottawa: CRTC, March 1978).

Canadian Radio-television and Telecommunications Commission, The Contemporary Status of Ownership and the Level of Concentration in the Canadian Broadcasting Industry, Background Study II to the Report of the Ownership Study Group (Ottawa: CRTC, 1978).

-----, Ownership of Private Broadcasting: An Economic Analysis of Structure, Performance and Behaviour, Report of the Ownership Study Group (Ottawa: CRTC, October, 1978).

-----, Ownership of Private Broadcasting: An Economic Analysis of Structure, Performance and Behaviour, Report of the Ownership Stud Group (Ottawa: CRTC, October, 1978).

-----, Special Report on Broadcasting in Canada 1968-1978, 2 volumes (Ottawa: CRTC, 1979).

-----, Annual Report (Ottawa: Minister of Supply and Services Canada, Annual).

-----, Special Report on Broadcasting in Canada, 1968-1978, 2 volumes (Ottawa: CRTC, 1979).

-----, Annual Report (Ottawa: Minister of Supply and Services Canada, annual).

Cherington, Paul W., Leon V. Hirsch and Robert Brandwein (eds.) Television Station Ownership, A Case Study of Federal Agency Regulation (New York: Hastings House, 1971).

Coase, R.H., "The Economics of Broadcasting and Government Policy," American Economic Review, Vol. 56, No. 2, May 1966, pp. 440-447.

Cohen, Stanley E., "The Advertiser's Influence in T.V. Programming," Osgoode Hall Law Journal, Vol. 8, No. 1, August 1970, pp. 91-117.

Comanor, William S. and Bridger M. Mitchell, "Cable Television and the Impact of Regulation," Bell Journal of Economics and Management Science, Vol. 2, No. 1, Spring 1971, pp. 154-212.

Committee for Economic Development, Research and Policy Committee, Broadcasting and Cable Television: Policies for Diversity and Change (New York: Committee for Economic Development, 1975).

Committee on Broadcasting, Report (Ottawa: Queen's Printer, 1965).

Crandall, Robert W., "The Economic Effect of Television-Network Program 'Ownership'," Journal of Law and Economics, Vol. 14, No. 2, 1971, pp. 385-412.

-----, "FCC Regulation, Monopsony and Network Television Program Costs," Bell Journal of Economics and Management Science, Vol. 3, 1972, pp. 483-508.

-----, "The Economic Case for a Fourth Commercial Television Network," <u>Public Policy</u>, Vol. 22, No 4, Fall 1974, pp. 513-536

-----, and Lionel L. Fray, "A Re-Examination of the Prophecy of Doom for Cable Television," <u>Bell Journal of Economics and Management Science</u>, Vol. 5, No 1, Spring 1974, pp. 264-289.

Dawson, Donald A., "The Canadian Radio-Television Commission and The Consumer Interest" (Ottawa: Canadian Consumer Council, 1972).

Department of Communications, <u>Annual Reports</u> (Ottawa: annual).

-----, <u>Proposals for a Communications Policy for Canada: A Position Paper of the Government of Canada</u> (Ottawa: Information Canada, March, 1973).

-----, <u>Communications: Some Federal Proposals</u> (Ottawa: Information Canada, 1975).

-----, <u>Bill C-43: An Act Respecting Telecommunications in Canada</u> (Ottawa: 1977).

Drummond, I., "The CBC, Private Broadcasters, and the Economic Logic of Broadcasting," in <u>Canadian Perspectives in Economics</u>, edited by J. Chant et al., Carleton University, 1972.

Economic Council of Canada, <u>Responsible Regulation</u> (Ottawa: Minister of Supply and Services Canada, 1979).

<u>Financial Post</u>, "Special Report on the Media," annual.

Fisher, F.M. and V.E. Ferral Jr., "Community Antenna Television Systems and Local Television Station Audience," <u>Quarterly Journal of Economics</u>, Vol. 80, No. 2 1966,pp. 227-251.

Flynn, P.H., "Countervailing Power in Network Television," <u>Journal of Broadcasting</u>, Vol. 14, No. 3, Summer 1970, pp. 297-305.

Foundation '70, "A Cable is a Very Big Wire," <u>Yale Review of Law and Social Action</u>, Vol. 2, No. 3, Spring 1972, pp. 199-297.

Garnham, Nicholas, <u>Structures of Television</u> (London: British Film Institute, 1973).

Goldberg, Victor, "Marginal Cost Pricing, Investment Theory and CATV: Comment," <u>Journal of Law and Economics</u>, Vol. 14, No. 2, October 1971, pp. 513-519.

Goldin, Hyman H., "Financing Public Broadcasting," <u>Law and Contemporary Problems: Communications, Part II</u>, School of Law, Duke University, Vol. 34, No. 3, Summer 1969, pp. 650-670.

Good, L.M., An Econometric Model of the Canadian Cable Television Industry and the Effects of CRTC Regulation (Ph.D. thesis, University of Western Ontario, 1974).

Goodfriend, H.E. and F.T. Pratt, "Community Antenna Television," Financial Analysts Journal, March 1970, pp. 48-57.

Goodhardt, G.J., A.S.C. Ehrenberg and M.A. Collins, The Television Audience: Patterns of Viewing (London: Saxon House, 1975).

Grant, Peter S., "The Regulation of Program Content in Canadian Television: An Introduction," Canadian Public Administration, Vol. 11, No. 3, Fall 1968, pp. 322-394.

-----, Broadcasting and Cable Television Regulatory Handbook, Vols. 1 and 2 (Toronto: Law Society of Upper Canada, Department of Continuing Education, May 1973).

Greenberg, Edward, "Television Station Profitability and FCC Regulatory Policy", Journal of Industrial Economics, Vol. 17, No. 3, July 1969, pp. 210-221.

-----, and Harold Barnett, "TV Program Diversity: New Evidence and Old Theories," American Economic Review, Vol. 61, No. 2, May 1971, pp. 89-100.

Groombridge, Brian, Television and the People (Harmondsworth: Penguin Books, 1972).

Hall, W. Clayton Jr. and Robert B.D. Batlivala, "Market Structure and Duplication in TV Broadcasting," Land Economics, Vol. 47, No. 4, November 1971, pp. 405-410.

Hallman, Eugene S. and H. Hindley, Broadcasting in Canada (London: Routledge and Kegan Paul, 1977).

Howard, Herbert H., "The Contemporary Status of Television Group Ownership," Journalism Quarterly, Vol. 53, No. 3, Autumn 1976, pp. 399-405.

Irving, Hohn A. (ed.) Mass Media in Canada (Toronto: The Ryerson Press, 1962).

Johnson, Leland L., The Future of Cable Televison: Some Problems of Federal Regulation (Santa Monica, Cal.: RAND Corporation, January 1970).

Johnson, Nicholas, "Freedom to Create: The Implications of Antitrust Policy for Television Programming Content," Osgoode Hall Law Journal, Vol. 8, No. 1, August 1970, pp. 11-63.

Johnson, P.W., "The CRTC and Canadian Contract Regulation," Journal of Broadcasting, Vol. 17, No. 4, Fall 1973, pp. 465-474.

Johnson, R.C. and R.T. Blau, "Single Versus Multiple-System Cable Television," Journal of Broadcasting, Vol. 18, No. 3, Summer 1974, pp. 323-346.

Jowett, Garth S., James Linton and Hugh Edmuńds, Effects of Broadcast Content in English Canada (Windsor, Ontario: The Centre for Communication Studies, University of Windsor, October 1976).

Kestenbaum, Lionel, Common Carrier Access to Cable Communications: Regulatory and Economic Issues (Washington, D.C.: U.S. Department of Health, Education, and Welfare, 1971).

-----, "Competition in Communications, Antitrust Bulletin, Vol. 16, 1971, pp. 769-787.

Kiefl, John Barrett, A Study of Mass Communication: Cable Television in Canada (Masters Thesis, Boston University, 1973).

Kubin, Karen J., "The Antitrust Implications of Network Television Programming," Hastings Law Journal, Vol. 21, May 1976, pp. 1207-1229.

La Pierre, D. Bruce, "Cable Television Programming and the Promise of Programming Diversity," Fordham Law Review, Vol. 42, 1973-74, pp. 25-124.

Lago, Armando M., "The Price Effects of Joint Mass Communication Media Ownership," Antitrust Bulletin, Vol. 16, 1971, pp. 789-183.

H. Land and Associates, Television and the Wired City (Washington, D.C.: National Association of Broadcasters, 1968).

Law Society of Upper Canada, Department of Continuing Education Communications Law Workshop Materials, Broadcasting and Cable Television: Law and Administrative Practice (Toronto: The Law Society of Upper Canada, May 1973).

Lees, F.A. and C.Y. Yang, "The Redistributional Effect of Television Advertising," Economic Journal, Vol. 76, June 1966, pp. 328-336.

Lehmann, D.R., "Television Show Preference: Application of a Choice Model," Journal of Marketing Research, Vol. 8, February 1971, pp. 47-55.

Levin, Harvey J., Broadcast Regulation and Joint Ownership of Media (New York: New York University Press, 1960.)

-----, "Competition, Diversity, and the Television Group Ownership Rule," Columbia Law Review, Vol. 70, No. 5, May 1970, pp. 791-834.

-----, "Spectrum Allocation Without Market," American Economic Review, Vol. 60, No. 2, May 1970, pp. 209-224.

-----, "Program Duplication, Diversity, and Effective Viewer Choices: Some Empirical Findings," American Economic Review, Vol. 61, No. 2, May 1971, pp. 81-88.

-----, "Television's Second Chance: A Retrospective Look at the Sloan Cable Commission," Bell Journal of Economics and Management Science, Vol. 4, No. 1, Spring 1973, pp. 343-365.

Lewis, J.D., "Programmer's Choice: Eight Factors in Program Decision-Making," Journal of Broacasting, Vol. 14, No. 1, Winter 1969-70, pp. 71-82.

Linton, James and Hugh Edmunds, Canadian Television Viewing Habits: Present Patterns and Future Prospects (Windsor, Ontario: The Centre for Canadian Communication Studies, University of Windsor, October 1976).

Litwin, George H., The Effects of Common Ownership on Media Content and Influence (Washington, D.C.: National Association of Broadcasters, July 1969).

Maclean-Hunter Research Bureau, A Report on Advertising Revenues in Canada (Toronto Maclean-Hunter Research Bureau, November 1974).

Mallock, Kati, Broadcasting in Canada (Montreal: McGill University, 1974).

Manitoba, Minister of Consumer, Corporate and Internal Services, Broadcasting and Cable Television: A Manitoba Perspective (Winnipeg: Queens Printers, 1974).

Mathewson, G.F., "A Consumer Theory of Demand for the Media," Journal of Business, Vol. 45, No. 2, April 1972, pp. 212-223.

McKay, Bruce, The CBC and the Public (Stanford: Institute for Communication Research, Stanford University, 1976).

McNulty, Jean, "Pay Television and the Cable T.V. Industry," in The Crisis in Canadian Broadcasting (Halifax: Canadian Broadcasting League, 1976).

Miller, R.E., "The CRTC Guardian of the Canadian Identity," Journal of Broadcasting, Vol. 17, No. 2, Spring 1973, pp. 189-199.

Minasian, Jora R., "Television Pricing and the Theory of Public Goods," Journal of Law and Economics, Vol. 12, October 1964, pp. 71-80.

Mitchell, Bridger M., in association with Robert H. Smiley, "Cable, Cities, and Copyrights," Bell Journal of Economics and Management Science, Vol. 5, No. 1, Spring 1974, pp. 235-263.

Neilson, R.P., "International Marketing Public Policy: U.S. Penetration of Canadian Television Program Market," Columbia Journal of World Business, Vol. 11, No. 1, Spring 1976, pp. 130-139.

Noll, Roger G., Merton J. Peck and John J. McGowan, Economic Aspects of Television Regulation (Washington, D.C.: The Brookings Institution, 1973).

Ohls, James C., "Marginal Cost Pricing, Investment Theory and CATV," Journal of Law and Economics, Vol. 13, No. 2, October 1970, pp. 439-461.

Ontario Royal Commission on Violence in the Communications Industry, The Media Industries: From Here to Where?, Vol. 7 (Toronto: Ontario Queen's Printer, 1977).

Owen, Bruce, "Public Policy and Emerging Technology in the Media," Public Policy, Vol. 18, Summer 1970, pp. 539-552.

-----, Diversity and Television (Washington, D.C.: Office of Telecommunications Policy, August 1972).

-----, "Newspaper and Television Station Joint Ownership," Antitrust Bulletin, Vol. 18, Winter 1973.

-----, Economics and Freedom of Expression (Cambridge, Mass.: Gallinger Publishing Company, 1975)

-----, Jack H. Beebe and Willard G. Manning Jr., Television Economics (Lexington, Mass.: Lexington Books, D.C. Heath and Company, 1974).

Park, Rolla Edward, Potential Impact of Cable Growth on Television Broadcasting (Santa Monica, Cal.: RAND Corporation, October 1970).

-----, "The Growth of Cable TV and its Probable Impact on Over-the-Air Broadcasting," American Economic Review, Vol. 61, No. 2, May 1971, pp. 69-73.

-----, "Television Station Performance and Revenues," Educational Broadcasting Review, Vol. 5, No. 3, June 1971, pp. 43-49.

-----, "Prospects in Cable in the 100 Largest Television Markets," Bell Journal of Ecomomics and Management Science, Vol. 3, No. 1, 1972, pp. 130-150.

-----,"Cable Television, UHF Broadcasting, and FCC Regulatory Policy," Journal of Law and Economics, Vol. 15, No. 1, 1972, pp. 207-231.

Peers, Frank W., "The Canadian Radio-Television Commission on the State of Canadian Broadcasting and its Prospects," Canadian Public Administration, Vol. 17, 1974, pp. 654-658.

Pepin, Rene, "Introduction à l'Étude du Phénomène de la Propriété des Mass Média Électroniques au Canada," Revue de Droit, No. 7, 1976, pp. 49-148.

Peterman, J.L., "The Structure of National Time Rates in the Television Broadcasting Industry," Journal of Law and Economics, Vol. 8, 1965, pp. 77-131.

-----, "Concentration of Control and Price of Television Time", American Economic Review, Vol. 61, No. 2, May 1971, pp. 74-80.

Posner, Richard J., Cable Television: The Problem of Local Monopoly (Santa Monica, Cal.: RAND Corporation, May 1970).

-----, "Taxation by Regulation," Bell Journal of Economics and Management Science; Vol. 2, Spring 1971, pp. 22-49.

-----, "The Appropriate Scope of Regulation in the Cable Television Industry," Bell Journal of Economics and Management Science, Vol. 3, No. 1, Spring 1972, pp. 98-150.

-----, "The Probable Effects of Pay Cable Television on Culture and the Arts," in Richard Adler and Walter S. Baer, The Electronic Box Office (New York: Praeger Publishers, 1974).

Preshing, William Anthony, The Canadian Broadcasting Corporation's Commercial Activities and Their Interrelationship to the Corporation's Objectives and Development (Ph.D. thesis, University of Illinois, 1965).

Rao, Vithala, R., "Taxonomy of Television Programs Based on Viewing Behavior," Journal of Marketing Research, Vol. 12, No. 3, August 1975, pp. 355-358.

Richwood, Roger R., Private Broadcasters and Broadcasting Policy in Canada (Ph.D. thesis, University of Toronto, 1971).

Rosse, J.N., B. Owen, and D. Grey, "Economic Issues in the Joint Ownership of Newspaper and Television Media," Memorandum 97, Research Centre in Economic Growth, Standard University, May 1970.

Romanow, Walter Ivan, The Canadian Content Regulations in Canadian Broadcasting: An Historical and Critical Study (Ph.D. thesis, Wayne State University, 1974.)

Rotlenberg, Jerome, "Consumer Sovereignty and the Economics of TV Programming," Studies in Public Communications, No.4, Fall 1962, pp. 45-55.

Royal Commission on Broadcasting, Report (Ottawa: Queens Printer, 1957).

Royal Commission on Corporate Concentration, Report (Ottawa: Minister of Supply and Services Canada, 1978).

Secretary of State, The Film Industry in Canada (Ottawa: Secretary of State, 1977).

Seiden, Martin H., Who Controls the Mass Media? (New York: Basic Books, 1974).

Senate Special Committee on Mass Media, Report (Ottawa: Queens Printer, 1970).

Shea, Albert A., Broadcasting The Canadian Way (Montreal: Harvest House, 1963).

Singer, Benjamin D. (ed.) Communications in Canadian Society (Toronto: Copp Clark, 1972).

Skornia, H.J., Television and Society: An Inquest and Agenda for Improvement (New York: McGraw-Hill, 1965).

Sloan Commission, Report of the Sloan Commission on Cable Communications, On the Cable: The Television of Abundance (New York: McGraw-Hill, 1971).

Smith, Ralph Lee, "Ownership Policy and the Cable Industry," Yale Review of Law and Social Action, Spring 1972, pp. 263-274.

Special Senate Committee on Mass Media, Mass Media, 3 volumes (Ottawa: Information Canada, 1970).

Spence, Michael and Bruce Owen, "Television Programming, Monopolistic Competition, and Welfare," Quarterly Journal of Economics, Vol. 91, No. 1, February 1977, pp. 103-126.

Spry, G., "The Decline and Fall of Canadian Broadcasting," Queen's Quarterly, Vol. 68, Summer 1961, pp. 213-225.

-----, "The Costs of Canadian Broadcasting," Queen's Quarterly, Vol. 68, Winter 1961, pp. 503-513.

Statistical Research Inc., The Potential Impact of CATV on Television Stations (Report for the National Association of Broadcasters, 1970).

Statistics Canada, Radio and Television Broadcasting (Ottawa: Minister of Supply and Services Canada, annual).

-----, Cable Television (Ottawa: Minister of Supply and Services Canada, annual).

Steiner, Peter O., "Program Patterns and Preferences and the Workability of Competition in Radio Broadcasting," Quarterly Journal of Economics, Vol. 66, May 1952, pp. 194-223.

Sterling, C.H., "Trends in Daily Newspaper and Broadcast Ownership, 1922-1970," Journalism Quarterly, Vol. 52, No. 2, Summer 1975, pp. 247-256 and 320.

Stewart, W. Brian, "The CBC: Canadian? Regional? Popular? An Examination of Program Objectives for English Television," Canadian Public Administration, Vol. 18, No. 3, Fall 1975, pp. 337-365.

Toogood, A.F., Broadcasting in Canada: Aspects of Regulation and Control (Ph.D. thesis, Ohio State University, 1969).

Treynor, Jack L., "How to Rate Management of Investment Funds," Harvard Business Review, January-February 1965, pp. 63-75.

Tuchman, Gaye (ed.) The TV Establishment: Programming for Power and Profit (Englewood Cliffs, N.J.: Prentice-Hall, 1974).

Turetsky, Howard B., Broadcasters: Canada Versus the United States, Report prepared by Faulliner, Hawkins and Sullivan for the Department of Communications (April 17, 1975).

Varis, Tapio, "Global Traffic in Television," Journal of Communication, Vol. 24, No. 1, Winter 1974, pp. 102-109.

Webbink, Douglas W., "Regulation, Profits and Entry in the Television Broadcasting Industry," Journal of Industrial Economics, Vol. 21, No. 2, April 1973, pp. 167-176.

Weir, E. Austin, The Struggle for National Broadcasting in Canada (Toronto: McClelland and Stewart Ltd., 1965).

Weiss, Elaine F., U.S. Television and Canadian Identity (Columbia: Miss: Freedom of Information Centre Report No. 324, University of Missouri, 1974).

Wiles, P., "Pilkington and the Theory of Value," Economic Journal, Vol. 73, June 1963, pp. 183-200.

Williamson, Oliver E., "Franchise Bidding for Natural Monoplies -
In General and with Respect to CATV," Bell Journal of Economics and Management Science, Vol. 7, No. 1, Spring 1976, pp.
73-104.

Wirth, Michael O. and James A. Wollert, "Public Interest Program
Performance of Multimedia-owned TV Stations," Journalism
Quarterly, Vol. 53, No. 2, Summer 1976, pp. 223-230.

Wolf, Frank, Television Programming for News and Public Affairs
(New York: Praeger Publishers, 1972).

Woodside, C.M., Systems Analysis of the T.V. Production Industry
in Canada (Ottawa: Second Progress Report, Carleton University, June 1973).

The Institute for Research on Public Policy
PUBLICATIONS AVAILABLE*
September, 1980

BOOKS

Leroy O. Stone & Claude Marceau	*Canadian Population Trends and Public Policy Through the 1980s*. 1977 $4.00
Raymond Breton	*The Canadian Condition: A Guide to Research in Public Policy*. 1977 $2.95
Raymond Breton	*Une orientation de la recherche politique dans le contexte canadien*. 1978 $2.95
J.W. Rowley & W.T. Stanbury, eds.	*Competition Policy in Canada: Stage II, Bill C-13*. 1978 $12.95
C.F. Smart & W.T. Stanbury, eds.	*Studies on Crisis Management*. 1978 $9.95
W.T. Stanbury, ed.	*Studies on Regulation in Canada*. 1978 $9.95
Michael Hudson	*Canada in the New Monetary Order—Borrow? Devalue? Restructure!* 1978 $6.95
W.A.W. Neilson & J.C. MacPherson, eds.	*The Legislative Process in Canada: The Need for Reform*. 1978 $12.95
David K. Foot, ed.	*Public Employment and Compensation in Canada: Myths and Realities*. 1978 $10.95
W.E. Cundiff & Mado Reid, eds.	*Issues in Canada/U.S. Transborder Computer Data Flows*. 1979 $6.50
G.B. Reschenthaler & B. Roberts, eds.	*Perspectives on Canadian Airline Regulation*. 1979 $13.50
P.K. Gorecki & W.T. Stanbury, eds.	*Perspectives on the Royal Commission on Corporate Concentration*. 1979 $15.95
David K. Foot	*Public Employment in Canada: Statistical Series*. 1979 $15.00

---

* Order Address: The Institute for Research on Public Policy
P.O. Box 9300, Station ''A''
TORONTO, Ontario
M5W 2C7

Meyer W. Bucovetsky, ed. *Studies on Public Employment and Compensation in Canada.* 1979 $14.95

Richard French & André Béliveau *The RCMP and the Management of National Security.* 1979 $6.95

Richard French & André Béliveau *La GRC et la gestion de la sécurité nationale.* 1979 $7.95

Leroy O. Stone & Michael J. MacLean *Future Income Prospects for Canada's Senior Citizens.* 1979 $7.95

Douglas G. Hartle *Public Policy Decision Making and Regulation.* 1979 $12.95

Richard Bird (in collaboration with Bucovetsky & Foot) *The Growth of Public Employment in Canada.* 1979 $12.95

G. Bruce Doern & Allan M. Maslove, eds. *The Public Evaluation of Government Spending.* 1979 $10.95

Richard Price, ed. *The Spirit of the Alberta Indian Treaties.* 1979 $8.95

Peter N. Nemetz, ed. *Energy Policy: The Global Challenge.* 1979 $16.95

Richard J. Schultz *Federalism and the Regulatory Process.* 1979 $1.50

Richard J. Schultz *Le fédéralisme et le processus de réglementation.* 1979 $1.50

Lionel D. Feldman & Katherine A. Graham *Bargaining for Cities. Municipalities and Intergovernmental Relations: An Assessment.* 1979 $10.95

Elliot J. Feldman & Neil Nevitte, eds. *The Future of North America: Canada, the United States, and Quebec Nationalism.* 1979 $7.95

Maximo Halty-Carrere *Technological Development Strategies for Developing Countries.* 1979 $12.95

G.B. Reschenthaler *Occupational Health and Safety in Canada: The Economics and Three Case Studies.* 1979 $5.00

David R. Protheroe *Imports and Politics: Trade Decision-Making in Canada, 1968-1979.* 1980 $8.95

G. Bruce Doern	*Government Intervention in the Canadian Nuclear Industry*. 1980 $8.95
G. Bruce Doern & R.W. Morrison, eds.	*Canadian Nuclear Policies*. 1980 $14.95
W.T. Stanbury, ed.	*Government Regulation: Scope, Growth, Process*. 1980 $10.95
Yoshi Tsurumi with Rebecca R. Tsurumi	*Sogoshosha: Engines of Export-Based Growth*. 1980 $8.95
Allan M. Maslove & Gene Swimmer	*Wage Controls in Canada, 1975-78: A Study in Public Decision Making*. 1980 $11.95
T. Gregory Kane	*Consumers and the Regulators: Intervention in the Federal Regulatory Process*. 1980 $10.95
Albert Breton & Anthony Scott	*The Design of Federations*. 1980 $6.95
A.R. Bailey & D.G. Hull	*The Way Out: A More Revenue-Dependent Public Sector and How It Might Revitalize the Process of Governing*. 1980 $6.95
Réjean Lachapelle & Jacques Henripin	*La situation démolinguistique au Canada: évolution passée et prospective*. 1980 $24.95
Raymond Breton, Jeffrey G. Reitz & Victor F. Valentine	*Cultural Boundaries and the Cohesion of Canada*. 1980 $18.95
David R. Harvey	*Christmas Turkey or Prairie Vulture? An Economic Analysis of the Crow's Nest Pass Grain Rates*. 1980 $10.95
Stuart McFadyen, Colin Hoskins & David Gillen	*Canadian Broadcasting: Market Structure and Economic Performance*. 1980 $15.95
Richard M. Bird	*Taxing Corporations*. 1980 $6.95

OCCASIONAL PAPERS

W.E. Cundiff (No. 1)	*Nodule Shock? Seabed Mining and the Future of the Canadian Nickel Industry*. 1978 $3.00
IRPP/Brookings (No. 2)	*Conference on Canadian-U.S. Economic Relations*. 1978 $3.00

Robert A. Russel (No. 3)	*The Electronic Briefcase: The Office of the Future.* 1978 $3.00
C.C. Gotlieb (No. 4)	*Computers in the Home: What They Can Do for Us—And to Us.* 1978 $3.00
Raymond Breton & Gail Grant Akian (No. 5)	*Urban Institutions and People of Indian Ancestry.* 1978 $3.00
K.A. Hay (No. 6)	*Friends or Acquaintances? Canada as a Resource Supplier to the Japanese Economy.* 1978 $3.00
T. Atkinson (No. 7)	*Trends in Life Satisfaction.* 1979 $3.00
M. McLean (No. 8)	*The Impact of the Micro-electronics Industry on the Structure of the Canadian Economy.* 1979 $3.00
Fred Thompson & W.T. Stanbury (No. 9)	*The Political Economy of Interest Groups in the Legislative Process in Canada.* 1979 $3.00
Gordon B. Thompson (No. 10)	*Memo from Mercury: Information Technology* **Is** *Different.* 1979 $3.00
Pierre Sormany (No. 11)	*Les micro-esclaves: vers une bio-industrie canadienne.* 1979 $3.00
K. Hartley, P.N. Nemetz, S. Schwartz, D. Uyeno, I. Vertinsky & J. Young (No. 12)	*Energy R & D Decision Making for Canada.* 1979 $3.00
David Hoffman & Zavis P. Zeman, eds. (No. 13)	*The Dynamics of the Technological Leadership of the World.* 1980 $3.00
Russell Wilkins (No. 13a)	*Health Status in Canada, 1926-1976.* 1980 $3.00
Russell Wilkins (No. 13b)	*L'état de santé au Canada, 1926-1976.* 1980 $3.00
P. Pergler (No. 14)	*The Automated Citizen: Social and Political Impact of Interactive Broadcasting.* 1980 $4.95
Zavis P. Zeman (No. 15)	*Men With The Yen.* 1980 $5.95

WORKING PAPERS (No Charge)**

W.E. Cundiff   *Issues in Canada/U.S. Transborder Computer Data*
(No. 1)   *Flows*. 1978 (Out of print; in IRPP book of same
                      title.)

John Cornwall   *Industrial Investment and Canadian Economic*
(No. 2)   *Growth: Some Scenarios for the Eighties*. 1978

Russell Wilkins   *L'espérance de vie par quartier à Montréal, 1976:*
(No. 3)   *un indicateur social pour la planification*. 1979

F.J. Fletcher &   *Canadian Attitude Trends, 1960−1978*. 1979
R.J. Drummond
(No. 4)

** Order Working Papers from
The Institute for Research on Public Policy
P.O. Box 3670
Halifax South
Halifax, Nova Scotia
B3J 3K6

45894

McFadyen, Stuart
    Canadian broadcasting

DATE DUE | BORROWER'S NAME